L 2a

D0780191

## DATE DUE

| | | | |
|---|---|---|---|
| | | | |
| | | | |
| | | | |
| | | | |
| | | | |
| | | | |
| | | | |
| | | | |
| | | | |
| | | | |
| | | | |
| | | | |
| | | | |
| | | | |

Structure and Theme

# Structure and Theme
## Don Quixote to James Joyce

Margaret Church

Ohio State University Press : Columbus

The portion of the Introduction devoted to the structure of *Don Quixote*
has been condensed and reprinted by permission of the
New York University Press from *Don Quixote—The Knight of La Mancha*,
by Margaret Church. Copyright © 1971 by New York University.

Chapter 3 has been revised from an article entitled "A Triad of Images:
Nature in *Madame Bovary*" that originally appeared in *Mosaic: A Journal
for the Comparative Study of Literature and Ideas*, published by The
University of Manitoba, vol. 5, no. 3 (spring 1972), pp. 203–13, to
which acknowledgment is herewith made.

Chapter 5 has been revised from an article of the same title published
originally in the fall 1969 issue of *Literature and Psychology*.
Used by permission.

Portions of chapters 6 and 7 have been revised from a paper entitled
"Fiction: The Language of Time, Thomas Mann and James Joyce"
published originally in 1978 by Springer Verlag in *Study of Time III*.
Used by permission.

The portion of chapter 7 devoted to James Joyce's *A Portrait of the
Artist as a Young Man* has been revised from a paper that originally
appeared as "*A Portrait* and Giambattista Vico: A Source Study" in
*Approaches to Joyce's "Portrait": Ten Essays*, edited by
Thomas F. Staley and Bernard Benstock, published in 1976 by the
University of Pittsburgh Press. Used by permission.

The portion of chapter 7 devoted to James Joyce's *Dubliners* has been
revised from an article entitled "*Dubliners* and Vico" published
originally in the winter 1968 issue of the *James Joyce Quarterly*.
Used by permission.

Chapter 8 has been revised from an article of the same title published
originally in the July 1977 issue of the *International Fiction Review*.
Used by permission.

Quotations from: Virginia Woolf. [Mrs. Dalloway]. Holograph notes,
unsigned, dated 9 November 1922–2 August 1923. The Henry W. and
Albert A. Berg Collection, The New York Public Library,
Astor, Lenox, and Tilden Foundations. Used by permission of the
New York Public Library and Professor Quentin Bell.

Quotations from personal letters to Margaret Church from
Marina Bergelson Raskin, of the Department of English at Purdue
University, and Richard Pearce, of the Department of English at
Wheaton College, are used by permission.

*Library of Congress Cataloging in Publication Data*

Church, Margaret, 1920–
   Structure and theme—Don Quixote to James Joyce.
   Bibliography: p.
   Includes index.
   1. Fiction—Technique. 2. Fiction—History and criticism.
I. Title.
PN3365.C49   1983          809.3          83-2292
ISBN 0-8142-0348-5

# Contents

Foreword by Thomas P. Adler · vii

Preface · ix

Introduction. *Don Quixote* as Prototype · 3

Chapter One. The Art of Life: The Comic Epic
Poem in Prose · 11

Chapter Two. *The Sorrows of Young Werther:* The
Structure of *Sturm und Drang* · 39

Chapter Three. A Triad of Images: Nature as
Structure in *Madame Bovary* · 61

Chapter Four. Spatial Patterns in *The Brothers
Karamazov* · 81

Chapter Five. Dostoevsky's *Crime and Punishment*
and Kafka's *The Trial* · 103

Chapter Six. The Interplay of Circular and Spiral
Form in Mann's *The Magic Mountain* · 121

Chapter Seven. How the Vicociclometer Works:
The Fiction of James Joyce · 135

Chapter Eight. Joycean Structure in *Jacob's Room*
and *Mrs. Dalloway* · 169

Conclusion. The More or Less Inward Turn of Post-
Renaissance Fiction · 185

Bibliography · 193

Index · 201

# Foreword

Margaret Church died unexpectedly on 30 August 1982. At the time of her death, work on *Structure and Theme* was substantially complete. The manuscript, including the bibliography, had been copy edited. All that remained for me when I undertook seeing the book through press was to read the galleys and page proofs and prepare the index. Everything in these pages about the thirteen novels Margaret Church has chosen to discuss appears exactly as she wrote it, and all of the very substantial credit for this work belongs to her. Each author prepares an index differently, and I can only guess what form this one might have taken had the author herself completed it. In deciding which terms and titles to index here, I have gone back to Margaret Church's first book and adopted it as my model. Naturally, I take full responsibility for whatever deficiencies the resultant index may have.

For almost thirty years, Margaret Church was a member of the Purdue University English Department. Born at Boston in 1920, she received her A.B. from Radcliffe (1941) and her M.A. from Columbia (1942) before returning to Radcliffe for the Ph.D. (1944). After teaching at Temple (1944–46) and Duke (1946–53), she came to Purdue, where she became a full professor in 1965—the same year she assumed the chairmanship of the then newly established program in comparative literature. She helped found *Modern Fiction Studies*, of which she became coeditor in 1971. An internationally eminent scholar, widely known for her work with the James Joyce Foundation, she had published, before her death, more than a dozen articles and two books: *Time and Reality: Studies in Contemporary Fiction* (1963) and *Don Quixote: The Knight of La Mancha* (1971).

Just as Margaret Church applied diligence, thoroughness, and energy to all her endeavors both inside the classroom and without, she bore her many accomplishments with modesty and grace. This present book, ranging widely over works she loved—and many of which she taught in her seminars on Joyce and Virginia Woolf and in her courses in literature and psychology and the Continental novel—reveals the mind of the continually inquiring scholar while capturing the voice of the discerning teacher. In the dozen years since I arrived at Purdue, I came to know Margaret Church as a warm and witty colleague, and I feel fortunate to be able to repay her friendship and support.

I appreciate the unquestioning confidence of Margaret Church's family, as well as the unfailing assistance of her editor at Ohio State University Press, Robert Demorest, for doing everything possible to ease my task. I acknowledge once again the helpful advice and support of my colleagues—especially of Margaret Moan Rowe—and, as always, of my dear wife Winnie during the completion of this work. But most of all, I am thankful for this opportunity to reaffirm something to which Margaret Church devoted her professional life: the existence of a community of scholars and teachers. The sadness of loss is tempered by this book, through which she continues to teach us all.

Thomas P. Adler
West Lafayette, Indiana
30 October 1982

# Preface

The structures of the novels that I discuss in the following pages provide a means of perspective on the development of the genre since *Don Quixote* and an ongoing thesis for this book. I trust that they will also provide a sense of wholeness, despite what may at first glance be mere heterogeneity. Although individual chapters may appear to be discrete, closer scrutiny will show a common concern, summed up in the final chapter where I point out that although in none of the novels discussed is structure entirely dissociated from content, character, and action, in each of them structure is more closely related to one of these elements than to the others. Form becomes then a cohort of meaning in different ways in different literary periods, fluctuating from the Renaissance, to neoclassicism, to romanticism, to realism, and to impressionism and expressionism. Moreover, it is arguable that a degree of heterogeneity is a strength, preventing a book from becoming simply a mechanical recitation of the same issue over and again. My aim, in any event, has been to provide both continuity and variety, a diversity partly justified by the interest that I hope will be generated by specific chapters.

Nor is the selection of novels to be discussed merely an arbitrary one. The thirteen books under examination here illustrate typical examples of structuring in each period mentioned above. Other novels could have been selected, but it is clear that whatever else was added, these thirteen could not have been surpassed for the purpose for which they were intended. Furthermore, they are all tied together, as the title of the book suggests, by the quixotic nature of characters in each one from Parson Adams, to Werther, to Emma Bovary, to Dmitri and Ivan Karamazov, to Raskolnikov and K., to Settembrini, and to Leopold Bloom, and by themes and techniques that also relate to the *Quixote*.

Because I have found the structural patterns discussed in this book helpful in teaching various courses and seminars (English 574, English 584, English 579) at Purdue University over the last fifteen years or so, I believe this work will be of use and interest, not only to the researcher in the field, but to students and teachers working with fiction in the classroom. Several sections of the book have already appeared in somewhat different form in *Mosaic, Literature and Psychology,* the *James Joyce Quarterly, International Fiction Review, Approaches to Joyce's "Portrait"* (University of Pittsburgh Press, 1976), and *Study of Time III* (Springer Verlag, 1978).

I am indebted to the National Endowment for the Humanities for a summer grant in 1975 that enabled me to prepare the chapters on *Joseph Andrews* and Goethe's *Werther.*

In addition, a word of gratitude should go to the James Joyce Foundation and to its founders Thomas F. Staley and Bernard Benstock, who have sponsored symposia in various European cities since 1967. Much of the chapter on Joyce, which is a focal one in the book, has roots in these meetings; and colleagues I have met there—among others Richard F. Kain, Marvin Magalaner, Zack Bowen, Richard Pierce, Morris Beja, as well, of course, as Professors Staley and Benstock—deserve mention for the perspectives they have provided on Joyce, for their dedication to scholarship on Joyce, and for good conversation over Irish coffee at Davy Byrne's.

Nor should I forget to mention the generosity of the Purdue Research Foundation (its past director, Dean Frederick N. Andrews) and the support of my own dean, Dean Robert L. Ringel, in providing me with summer travel grants that enabled me to attend James Joyce symposia in Dublin, London, Trieste, Paris, and Zurich. Dean Ringel's strong encouragement of scholarly activity in the School of Humanities, Social Science, and Education at Purdue cannot have helped but influence the outcome of my entire project.

West Lafayette, Indiana
March 1982

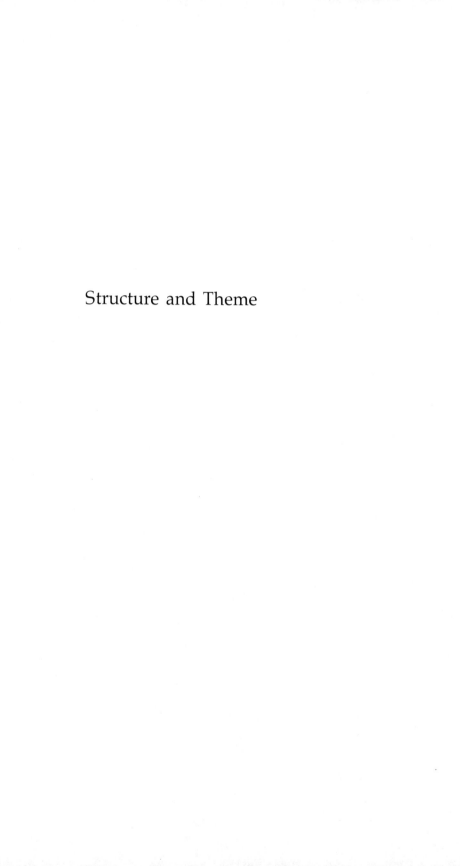

Structure and Theme

Introduction

# Don Quixote as Prototype

"The Intrinsic Sociology in Fiction," by Brent Harold, is an effort to reconcile adherents of two divisive elements in literary criticism, intrinsic and extrinsic modes. Harold makes the point that there is no real conflict between the experience of reading outlined in Wellek and Warren's *Theory of Literature* and the view of literature as social or political in intent. Harold writes: "The structure and structuring elements in the work are words, the very quality of which is to evoke life outside the work."[1]

If this be true of social and political matters, it can be proved true also of psychological or philosophical bases that undergird many works of fiction. It is one purpose of this book to indicate, in some detail, that the experience of the work of art must involve both matters intrinsic to the work itself and matters extrinsic, references and allusions to other phenomena. The insistence of certain formalist criticism on literature as a "closed system" (an art for the sake of art) is partly responsible, in the view of this author, for the current enrollment figures of courses in literature in our universities. The student is too often asked to spend time developing skills aimed at a complicated sort of gamesmanship. The self-referential nature of some formalist criticism can lead to a Nietzschean "ewige Wiederkehr." As Nietzsche himself remarked, "Who can bear the thought?" "Literary art is not the whole of poetry," writes Ortega y Gasset,* "but only a secondary activity."[2]

My plan is to examine the structural elements underlying thirteen various novels from various eras. I hope to

*Because of the many languages involved in this book, I have quoted from translations when they were available. When they were not, translations are my own.

3

show thereby how each work results not only in an art form but also in a closely connected statement—sociological, psychological, philosophical, or sometimes political in nature. It will be noted that in different novels form relates to its subject matter in different ways, sometimes complementing it, sometimes contrasting with it, or sometimes imitating it. The structures of *Joseph Andrews, Madame Bovary,* and *The Magic Mountian* relate to matters exterior to the consciousness of the protagonists whereas structures of the other books discussed relate closely to the inner worlds of their leading figures. A stress on inner or a stress on outer reality may be a characteristic of an era. On the other hand, common factors in novels of different eras often abrogate time altogether so that Leopold Bloom or Settembrini or Emma Bovary may be seen to precede or to "influence" *Don Quixote,* which we would do well, perhaps, to attribute to Flaubert (see Chapter Seven, Part One, below). A neat metaphysical, perhaps even psychological, point is thereby established.

In *Don Quixote,* the ancestor, so to speak, of all fictions and of all metafictions, we find close and complex correlations between the structure of the book, the psychological development of the hero, and consequently, psychological theory, both Renaissance and modern. In fact, it is impossible to separate in *Don Quixote* intrinsic matters from extrinsic. On the one hand, *Don Quixote* is a statement about human behavior, psychology if you will, about the relationship of the individual to his society and to himself. On the other, it is a novel fully responsive to literary history, and it may be experienced simply as fiction. Yet as Brent Harold writes, "To experience the structure of a non-literary product such as a table is to experience its implied relationship to the social system in which it was made"[3] (p. 594). With this point in mind, I intend to explore the literary structures of *Don Quixote* and of twelve other novels, showing how structure and theme are interpenetrative and how awareness of literary structure leads inevitably to a statement about the environment which produced that structure.

The naturalness of Cervantes' art has been noted again and again by critics; in following chapters in this book, statements to this effect by Flaubert, Thomas Mann, and Virginia Woolf are cited. Cervantes' craftsmanship is perhaps more intuitive than consciously designed, and it is surely not the intention of this study to impose a Procrustean bed of form upon his work or upon that of any other author. Although it seems to be clear in general that he uses the digressions in the 1605 *Quixote* as complements to the main action in developing the psychological patterns of his hero and that they are rather regularly spaced, providing a contrapuntal effect with the main plot, there is no proof that Cervantes himself was consciously aware of such a structure. The fact is that it is a structure that is inherent in the subject matter, designating, as Erich Kahler points out, *Don Quixote* as "the first modern novel."[4] By this he means that *Don Quixote* was the first novel to employ a symbolism that rises "from a purely human natural world."[5] "The whole symbolic structure," says Kahler, "is built up by the artist; it is entirely integrated."[6] Don Quixote is guided not by the planets but by himself, and he, as he himself makes clear, is author of his own book and has no hesitation in pointing out errors made by various pseudo-authors who could not possibly have been present to witness the action. It is this so-called complete fiction that *Don Quixote* introduced, and the various structures discussed for *Don Quixote* and for novels in other chapters of this book should be seen in this light. They are not imposed from outside, like the divine cosmos of Dante, but spring naturally from the subject matter and characters presented. That literary art has become more self-conscious since the time of Cervantes is due to causes outside the pale of this book, but, although more self-conscious, all the structures following that of *Don Quixote* remain closely related to their contexts, as subsequent chapters of this book will bear out. This study, in a sense, then, begins where Erich Kahler left off and explores various turns the "inward turn of narrative" took after Cervantes.

In the 1605 *Quixote*, each part of the book describes a

phase of the central theme—Don Quixote's relation to other people and to his society—and each part concludes with a digressive tale that highlights the particular psychological state of the hero at that point in the narrative. The first unit of the 1605 book (chapters 1–14) describes episodes in which Don Quixote is attempting to impose his vision of reality on all those he meets. Thus he insists that the innkeeper knight him, that the farmer free the worthless Andrew, that the merchants declare Dulcinea the most beauteous sight unseen, and even after the destruction of his library that Sancho accept the windmills as thirty monstrous giants. It is at the end of this section that we meet Marcela and listen to the tale of her life with its curious parallels to Don Quixote's own. Both feel they were "born free"; neither recognizes the unrelenting nature of the social contract or a constructive and realistic means for carrying out idealisms within the social frame. And yet Marcela also acts as a foil for Don Quixote; her retirement springs from fear and negation whereas Don Quixote's retirement at this point, among the goatherds, contains a positive note of peace, is a return to nature in order to gather strength for the next sally into combat with the world of material values.

The second part of the 1605 *Quixote* (chapters 15–27) deepens the psychological tension between Don Quixote and others whom he meets; no longer does he merely demand blind faith in his own inner world from other people. He often resorts to force, as in the slaying of the sheep; in the attack on the Master of Arts, whose leg he fractures; in the adventure with the corpse; in the assault on the barber to steal his basin; or in the freeing of the galley slaves. Instead of insisting on his beliefs, he now enforces them, thus becoming separated even more severely from the social structure than he had been in part one. He becomes, in fact, a fugitive from justice and is forced to flee into the Sierra Morena.

Here he meets Cardenio, and the tale of Cardenio is a digression, like that of Marcela, paralleling Don Quixote's current state of mind. Cardenio, also unable to cope with reality, has withdrawn from society. As Don Quixote in his penance has now substituted a bookish role, the role of Amadis of Gaul, for action in the real world, so Cardenio's penance for his lost love is wasteful and meaningless as he weeps futilely in the Sierra Morena. Both situations require rescue initiated from without. Yet Don Quixote does penance not for a Lucinda but for the human race, which mocks and cheats him. Cardenio's grief, on the other hand, does not reach beyond himself and Lucinda. The whole world has jilted Don Quixote, yet it is this world he wishes to save. The digressions thus serve as foils and parallels to the main plot and highlight the multiangularity of the novel's hero, the nobility of his inner world in contrast to the futility of his acts.

The pattern of sallying into the world and withdrawing from it is continued in the third part of the 1605 *Quixote* (chapters 28–52). Here, however, a new element appears. Don Quixote instead of acting is acted upon, becoming the passive victim of others' aggressions at the inn. First, he is rescued by Dorothea in parody of the conventional knight bent upon rescuing maidens in distress. Now it is the maiden who rescues a knight in distress. When he fights in this part, he fights wineskins in his bedroom, not people. Later his arm or his power is shackled by two prostitutes, or, as Cervantes calls them, "demi-virgins." All of these calamities culminate in his imprisonment in a cage and his return to his village drawn on a cart. This third part is punctuated by five digressions, illustrating the central polarity of the book: involvement with others and withdrawal from others. The final digression describing two jilted lovers in wasteful retirement from life parallels Don Quixote's final retirement to his home. In the melee in the inn over Mambrino's helmet, where ironically Don Quixote establishes peace in a fray he has been the cause of, or in the attack on the rainmakers, Don Quixote's activity creates only chaos. He is now manipulated by the very fantasies that have inspired his active quest to reestablish the world of chivalry. The participation-withdrawal pattern outlines the progression of Don Quixote's madness as well as the structure of the book. From one who would save the world through the idealisms of the chivalric code, who would manipulate others, he has become in the final part one who because of his chivalric fantasy becomes the responsibility of others as well as the butt of their jokes. The scenes in the inn represent his gradual withdrawal from the active role, leading to his total withdrawal in the final chapters. Thus it may be seen that the three parts of the 1605 book are closely tied in with the pattern of Don Quixote's psychological syndrome, each part representing one distinct stage in the progress of his dementia.

The 1615 *Quixote* can be outlined in a similar fashion. Briefly, instead of a participant-withdrawal pattern in his relation to society, the latter book stresses Don Quixote's search for himself, effected by a series of episodes and images using a mirror technique. Many of the characters act as mirrors reflecting the hero from different angles, such as the Knight of the Mirrors, who actually has pieces of reflecting glass sewed to his costume. Furthermore, the episodes in this book are often paired to reflect one another (replacing the function served by the digressions in the 1605 *Quixote*). Thus the episodes dealing with the Knight of the Mirrors and the wagon of players are set side by side to contrast two kinds of actors and to comment on Don Quixote's own sense of role. Or Camacho's wedding and the vision in Montesinos's cave involve two love affairs that parallel and contrast with one another as well as with Don Quixote's relation to Dulcinea. In fact, the play of mirrors becomes so complicated, the confusion between reality and illusion, between life and books, so complete, that the reader, like Don Quixote, tends to lose himself. The confusion is compounded by the fact that not only do the episodes comment on each other but the 1615 book comments on the 1605 book. Also, a third *Quixote*, that of the imposter Avellaneda, is introduced to mirror the other two. It is through this losing of self in a complicated series of self-images that Don Quixote is to find himself. The progression of the 1615 *Quixote* is thus a descent into the darkness of the earth (symbolized by descents into caves, by tramplings by hogs and by bulls). In the same way Thomas Mann's Joseph descends into the pit only to be reborn, or Hans Castorp ascends so that he may descend or vice versa, meeting Satana (Settembrini) in the Hades of Haus Berghof at the summit of the magic mountain. The mechanical structure of *Don Quixote* and the psychological development of its hero are thus interdependent. The reflexive imagery of the 1615 *Quixote* stands at the core of this book just as the wavelike fluctuation of participation and withdrawal had established the pattern of its predecessor.

This brief outline of the two central structures of *Don Quixote* may be followed in more detail by consulting the introduction to my volume *Don Quixote: The Knight of La Mancha* (pp. xviii–xxxvi). What should, however, emerge clearly is that such matters as the arranging of episodes and of digressions, the use of symbols and metaphors, or the art of foiling are not simply self-reflexive devices throwing light on the art of fiction. In *Don Quixote*, Cervantes uses these devices to produce psychological context so that, for instance, the mirror image developed in the 1615 *Quixote* makes a direct statement about narcissicism (a modern term, in this instance, relating to the Knight of the Mirrors, Sampson Carrasco) or about discovering and knowing oneself (relating here to Quixote, who sees himself in these mirrors and finds himself, the characteristic quest of Renaissance man). The imagery of withdrawal in the 1605 *Quixote* may be seen as a symbolic statement of that *atra bilis*, or melancholy, that plagued seventeenth-century man from Hamlet to John Donne. Nor is it reaching outside the novel to use the term *schizophrenic* to describe Quixote's early adjustments to society in the 1605 volume.

To relate to something verbally is to relate not only to that object as such but to the many allusions it may contain for any particular listener or reader. To a twentieth-century reader of *Don Quixote*, schizophrenia is an unavoidable association, springing from the hero's clear loss of contact with his environment and the disintegration of his personality as Alonso Quixano. It is the dialectical unity of the structure of the novel (itself "schizophrenic" in setting passages dealing with the hero's misguided participation against passages dealing with his hermetic withdrawals) and of its theme, the hero's loss of contact with reality, that forms the full experience of reading the book. Other novels examined in the same way will further exemplify the point.

Ortega y Gasset writes: "There is need of a book showing in detail that every novel bears *Quixote* within it like an inner filigree, in the same way as every epic poem contains the *Iliad* within it like the fruit its core."[7] Another purpose of my book, then, is just this, at least to the extent that Cervantes' general concepts of structure and of order can be shown to persist in the great novels that have followed *Don Quixote* in Western culture.[8]

1. Brent Harold, "The Intrinsic Sociology in Fiction," *Modern Fiction Studies* 23 (Winter 1977–78): 594.

2. José Ortega y Gasset, *Meditations on Quixote*, p. 127.

3. Harold, p. 594.

4. Erich Kahler, *The Inward Turn of Narrative*, p. 57.

5. Ibid.

6. Ibid., pp. 57–58.

7. Ortega y Gasset, p. 162.

8. The translation of *Don Quixote* referred to throughout this study will be: Miguel de Cervantes Saavedra, *The Adventures of Don Quixote*, trans. J. M. Cohen (Harmondsworth, Middlesex, England: Penguin Books, 1950).

Chapter One

# The Art of Life: The Comic Epic Poem in Prose

Fielding's mildly critical allusion in the *Covent Garden Journal* (1752) to *Don Quixote* as a series of "loose unconnected Adventures . . . of which you may transverse the Order as you please, without any Injury to the whole"[1] implies that his own works, at least ideally, have possessed a closer structural unity. Yet, in Fielding's own words, *Joseph Andrews* was "Written in Imitation of the *Manner* of Cervantes, Author of *Don Quixote*"; and so it is ironical but, at the same time, understandable that some of the devices Fielding used in *Joseph Andrews* to achieve this unity are like devices found in Cervantes' work. Likewise, Fielding's praise in *Joseph Andrews* of Cardenio's madness and the perfidy of Ferdinand (seeing them as examples of fidelity to nature) is ten years later in 1752 belied by his criticism of the stories of Cardenio and Dorothea as "extravagant and incredible" tales in which Cervantes "approaches very near to the Romances which he ridicules."[2] Despite these two contradictions—quite understandable as changes of attitude over a period of ten years—the fact remains that at the time Fielding published *Joseph Andrews* in 1742 his subtitle suggests his intent to imitate *Don Quixote*, and his text[3] indicates his admiration of the tales of Cardenio and Ferdinand as true to nature. It should be noted here in addition that Fielding had written in the late 1720s a farcical play called *Don Quixote in England*, attesting to the early and significant influence of Cervantes on Fielding's imagination. A large number of discussions of the structure of *Joseph Andrews* already exist, but I believe fresh light may be thrown on the novel by examining the structure of the book in several new ways, one of them being as a direct descendant of the structured *Don Quixote*.[4]

Two very sound studies of form in *Joseph Andrews* are those of Maynard Mack and Andrew Wright, and my intention in this chapter is to supplement rather than to question or attempt to supplant the work of these two critics. Mack discusses in his introduction to the Rinehart edition of *Joseph Andrews*[5] the way (as in a play) structure articulates theme. He shows how the action alternates between country and city and at the same time how the two poles of value (honesty and hypocrisy) are defined by life in the country and in the city; and he notes the tripartite system—country, road, city—that is used to provide setting for Fielding's characters. These are useful ways of defining thematic issues in the book, although it should be noted that honesty is not entirely confined to country life nor is hypocrisy to the city. Fielding was too fine an artist to clothe thematic issues in black and white, or to encircle them with city walls.

Andrew Wright develops his theories of the four-part division in *Joseph Andrews* in some detail, making telling points in favor of Fielding's consciousness of structural unity, such as the prefiguration of Parson Adams in book one and the opening and ending of book one, both on the subject of chastity—the theme at the cohesive center of this book. The remaining three books are described by Wright as centering on Parson Adams, education, and marriage, respectively.[6] More will be said later on alternate themes and about the way in which the inner movements of the books parallel the themes, for Wright's analysis of chapter lengths and number of chapters leaves the matter of mechanical structure simply at the point of departure.

And finally, Maurice Johnson's chapter on "The Art of Comic Romance"[7] must be mentioned. Johnson suggests that Fielding's subtitle is a clue to the general structure of *Joseph Andrews*. As in *Don Quixote*, which opens with a *"burlesca* movement" to introduce themes that become good comic prose, so Fielding's preface, which burlesques "commercial romance," sets the stage for the "good" romance to follow.[8] Johnson develops this thesis at some length in each of the four books, concluding that "the tradition established by *Don Quixote* continued in a type of novel which looks at a romantic situation from its own point of view so that the conventions of the two forms make up an ironic compound instead of a sentimental mixture."[9] What is particularly valuable about Johnson's discussion, both here and in his following chapter on poet and player, is his recognition of the part played by juxtaposition of opposites in Fielding's work and of Fielding's complex use of counterparts, ironic and otherwise, generally ignored by his critics. It is the purpose of this chapter to explore in *Joseph Andrews* these counterparts and tensions (of which *Don Quixote* is full) at somewhat greater length than Johnson does.

II

Both the 1605 and 1615 editions of *Don Quixote* were originally published in four parts, and it is of interest to observe the ways in which the four parts of these two novels compare with the four parts of *Joseph Andrews*, also originally divided into two volumes. To begin with, the sally-withdrawal pattern that punctuates *Don Quixote* (1605) and shapes each section is the essence of *Joseph Andrews* as a whole, which describes the abortive sallies of both Adams and Joseph and their return to the parish from which they started. As Leon Gottfried writes, "'Literary motif' is interwoven with the common three-part structure of home-road-home" in *Don Quixote* as it is in Fielding's *Joseph Andrews*.[10] Although the number of chapters in each book and the length of parts are far more uneven in *Don Quixote* than in *Joseph Andrews*, both works contain at least one book in which travels cease and the picaresque mode is abandoned. Thus book four of the 1605 *Quixote* is largely set at an inn where resolutions and reconciliations of the kind that take place in book four of *Joseph Andrews* occur, and book three of the 1615 *Quixote* is set at the castle of the Duke and Duchess (alternating with the ironic and counterironic counterpart of the "isle" on which Sancho is fulfilling his governorship) as book three of *Joseph Andrews* is partly set at the home of the Squire who, like Duke and Duchess, delights in playing practical jokes. Thus neither *Don Quixote* nor *Joseph Andrews* is picaresque in the strictest sense of the term, nor is Adams or Don Quixote a picaro— defined by one critic as "an offender against moral and civil laws" and as a person "low, vicious, deceitful, dishonourable and shameless."[11]

The differences in the quadripartite structures of Cervantes' books and *Joseph Andrews* lie in other considerations. As I have noted, the structure of Fielding's book is neater, sections being roughly of the same lengths, whereas Cervantes varies the lengths of his sections, one consisting of six chapters, another of twenty-four, a third of twenty-seven. Furthermore, Cervantes' numerous digressions in the 1605 *Quixote* are replaced in *Joseph Andrews* by three main digressions set in relatively similar positions in each of the last three books. The sally and withdrawal pattern, which is used by Cervantes to depict the alternating mania and depression of his hero's temper, is used by Fielding in a much different way. For example, Adams sets forth from his parish in order to sell his sermons so that he can better support his family, and Joseph (somewhat like Sancho) goes forth merely in servant capacity in the retinue of Lady Booby. Their withdrawal to their parish is not in the nature of a retreat or defeat in purpose: Adams returns because he finds he has left his sermons at home (as Don Quixote has left at home his purse, some clean shirts, and a box of ointments in his first sally in the 1605 *Quixote*, a sally that does not mark an inner turning point for the don), and Joseph returns to see his beloved Fanny. All of this emphasizes Fielding's adherence to outward symmetry, polish, and consistency in comparison with Cervantes' structure, which is almost always closely tied in with the inner and often chaotic motivations of his characters; for Don Quixote's sallies are spurred by an inner sense of wrongs that must be righted, of moral responsibil ity, of "deliberate choices made by the wills of individual human beings" and of "influences that men exercise upon one another,"[12] and such motivations become for Cervantes the basis of his artistic unity. As A. A. Parker has pointed out, what happened to Fielding between *Joseph Andrews* and *Tom Jones* was that "he came to apply the rules of epic structure to the novel so that no incident could be introduced not connected with the main action, all incidents must be bound together, and no action should be complete in itself."[13] Even in 1742 in *Joseph Andrews*, however, one sees Fielding's tendency and talent for "the perfectly coherent story" beginning to emerge. For example, the madness that informs Sancho's unerring devotion to his master is nowhere found in Joseph, whose actions are described in strict adherence to the code of behavior found in the typical hero of the romance and whose love for Adams falls short of enabling him to follow Adams to the city to sell the sermons; rather, he is concerned with returning to his Fanny (p. 64). In other words, the sallies and withdrawals of Adams and Joseph are motivated by logical consideration in the tangible world of possessions and friends whereas those of Don Quixote and Sancho are motivated by an illogical ideality, based on an inner reality and its form.

Finally, in connection with the four-part structure, it is significant to note that Fielding opens three of his four books with discourses on various aspects of the art of writing. Each of these prefatory chapters sets the tone for its book and becomes the unifying statement behind it. Cervantes, on the other hand, uses different means to obtain unity in each of his books, arranging incidents by type in polar opposition or in climactic order as they parallel the growing intensities of his hero. Fielding's disquisition on "lives" as communicating valuable patterns for readers leads naturally into the discussion of Joseph's chastity, the subject that dominates, begins, and ends book one of *Joseph Andrews*. The subject of Marcela's chastity, which concludes part two of the 1605 *Quixote*,[14] provides both contrast and parallelism, the ambiguous play of similarities and opposites provided by the knight's own "chastity" on a quite different plane. By developing two figures who illustrate "chastity" in different ways, from different motives, and in different situations, Cervantes is able to give depth and complexity to the fabric of his novel, perhaps more than Fielding creates with his brief introductory chapter on male chastity and his adherence to the formula of the comic romance, of which chastity (or its reverse) is a traditional component in building dramatic tension.

All of this leads us to Fielding's second book, which opens with a discussion of chapter divisions as resting places or inns where the traveler may stop and take a glass and which prefaces very neatly and logically a book that describes a long series of stops at a multitude of inns. In the matter of chapter divisions, Fielding and Cervantes are in agreement, for Fielding's chapters, like Cervantes', sometimes do not end at logical stopping places. Some of his chapter divisions are no endings at all, but made simply to lure the reader on into the next chapter. Thus chapter seventeen in book one ends with the sudden discovery of Betty and Mr. Tow-wouse in bed together, a subject that continues into chapter eighteen and is expanded on therein. Likewise, chapter nine in book two leaves matters *in medias res* with Adams meditating in the dark on what he fears is his murder of his opponent. Numbers of similar examples may be cited. Thus Fielding's opening remarks in book two on chapter divisions as resting places are partially ironic, for, in practice, he is quite aware of other functions of the chapter. Like Cervantes, he may recognize that the sense of the flow of time is strengthened by mechanical chapter divisions that do not coincide with the normal divisions of the narrative and serve thus to stress the existence of another time sequence, the real time, that of the mind. Later, in *Tom Jones*, Fielding is explicit on this matter, seeing himself as "the founder of a new province of writing" and "at liberty to make what laws I please therein,"[15] and stating that he does not feel obliged "to keep even pace with time."[16] Cervantes felt even less obliged "to keep even pace with time," but accompanied his practice of this point with no critical comments.

The structure of book three of *Joseph Andrews* is similar in principle to the structures of books one and two. In book three we discover an opening chapter on biography wherein Fielding mentions *Don Quixote*, renowned because it is "the history of the world in general." The chapter discusses patterns and prototypes in biography, setting up the scaffolding for the story of Mr. Wilson, which follows, the prototype of all young men who sow wild oats, reform, and live to a productive and peaceful old age. In contrast, the country squire is the prototype of the thoughtless and irresponsible idle rich, given to practical jokes and cruel folly. The peripatetic and stacatto movement of book two fitted its subject matter (human diversity) as the more static form of book three fits its subject, two types of landed gentry in their homes. Furthermore, the Squire in Mr. Wilson's story logically complements the Squire who appears just afterward and whose dogs attack Adams. The conclusion of the book, in which Peter Pounce, steward to a squire, appears, fills out the whole subject of squires and rounds off the book. (In the same way, book one on Chastity was rounded out by the actions of Betty and Mr. Tow-wouse in the bedroom of the inn.) A fine dialogue is thus established in book three between two prototypes, the good and the evil country gentleman, for Fielding is aware that vice is not the sole property of city folk. What must be noted is the thematic unity of each book, a unity undergirded and defined by each of the three opening disquisitions. Cervantes' unity, as it derives from the participation-withdrawal pattern in the 1605 *Quixote* and from the mirror images in the 1615 *Quixote*, as noted in the Introduction, seems to me more integral to the inner world of his main character. Fielding's unity, on the contrary, derives from unifying exterior elements and subjects— exterior, that is, to the character of Joseph. These subjects—the rules of society (chastity) and of literature (chapter divisions and literary types)—form the scaffolding of *Joseph Andrews*. Fielding's fourth book is, of course, the denouement for all the preceding entanglements and needs no preface, having already been prefaced three times.

III

The frequent interruptions to the plot found in *Joseph Andrews* are another means the author takes of shaping time to his own uses and demonstrating its subjective quality. They are means often discovered in *Don Quixote*. Many of them can be found in book two, the peripatetic and spasmodic character of which has already been noted. An interruption we are familiar with in *Don Quixote* is that of the uproar, found first in *Joseph Andrews* in book one, when in chapter seventeen Mrs. Tow-wouse (her very name connoting uproar) discovers Mr. Tow-wouse and Betty together in bed. Adams, Mr. Barnabas, and the bookseller (in the tradition of Don Quixote and the Canon)[17] are in the midst of an argument on whether a book should be judged good because of its popularity or because of the virtue and good instruction it conveys. Adams, who takes the latter opinion, violently offends Mr. Barnabas, who now believes he is in the company of the devil. His belief is reinforced when at that moment a "hideous uproar" is heard. Mrs. Tow-wouse's voice booms forth "like a bass viol in concert" (p. 69). Although the discussion among the three men has been broken off, it is obvious that on another level the chapter maintains its unity, an inner unity, since the movement progresses from the dissension among the polemicists to the domestic dissension at the inn. The larger subject of the entire scene, the inconstancy of human nature, is thus amply illustrated by both the fickleness of Mr. Barnabas and the faithlessness of Mr. Tow-wouse. In the same way, Don Quixote interrupts the reading of "The Tale of Foolish Curiosity" with his violent slashing of the wineskins belonging to the innkeeper,[18] and Cervantes thereby illustrates two different means of appropriating the property of one's neighbor, one idle, the other foolish. So, in one sense, the so-called interruptions are not interruptions at all but a method of sharpening a point and of adding variety to the plot.

Other violent interruptions in *Joseph Andrews* are the mock epic melee in book two, chapter five, among Adams, the innkeeper, and his wife, and later between Mrs. Slip-slop and the wife, that interrupts the history of Leonora; the fight between Joseph and Didapper that brings the reading of the tale of Paul and Leonard to an end; or the stamping and bewailing of Adams, when he hears of the drowning of his son, that interrupt his sermon on patience in the face of adversity. All of these interruptions possess a thematic thread in common with, or in contrast to, the scene that they interrupt; and the very violence of their nature makes us take note of their purpose: to act either as mirror or foil.

Another interruptive device employed by both Fielding and Cervantes is the abrupt change of subject, particularly useful when the main characters are involved in an apparently insoluble dilemma. Thus in the midst of chapter eight (book one), Don Quixote and the Basque, swords aloft, are about to demolish one another when it is discovered that the author can find no more records at this point in the story. Six long paragraphs are spent in describing the search by the second author for the missing sequel. Similarly, in book three, chapter ten, of *Joseph Andrews*, Joseph and Adams are left tied to the bedposts while Fielding interposes an ironical argument between the poet and the player. To begin with, such a device maintains the interest of the reader by heightening the suspense. It also establishes a kind of friendly but teasing complicity between author and reader, the latter agreeing, so to speak, to being tricked. Fielding himself mocks such mockery when he writes in book three, chapter nine, that such interruptions are like dances, done by persons whose heads lie in their heels, to break in upon the action of a stage tragedy. Perhaps he is only half right, for they are interruptions only in a mechanical sense, and serve at the same time to establish the collaboration of the reader and the author.

A device closely akin to the preceding one is used by Fielding in book two, chapter two, when Joseph is stranded at the inn and unable to pay for his horse's board. Fielding simply changes the subject and turns to Adams farther ahead on the road. Again in book two, chapter seven, when the people in the coach attempt to catch up with Adams to tell him he has forgotten his horse, Fielding shifts the scene to Adams, who, unaware of his followers, has taken the wrong turn and sat down to read his Aeschylus. Characters may get themselves into such predicaments that even their creators must abandon them temporarily. Characters thus come to possess lives of their own, apart from the narrator, and are capable of involving the author in fictional cul-de-sacs, at which point the author can only glance toward the reader with a helpless shrug. As a result, reader and author together become involved in extricating characters from entangling situations, and a three-way relationship (among author, character, and reader) is established. It should be noted also that such interruptions as they are used by Fielding often juxtapose parallel predicaments. For example, the argument between poet and player (book three, chapter ten) may be compared to the discussion between Adams and Joseph in the next chapter. Tied to the bedposts, back to back—that is, in polar opposition—their utterances symbolize the theory and the practice represented by the poet and the player.

A third use of interruption as a unifying method involves characters who interrupt one another. Don Quixote is continually interrupting the stories of others and sometimes, as at the puppet show, disrupting an entire performance. Likewise, Parson Adams, in the three main digressions, is perpetually inserting his own comments, opinions, and suggestions. This device, however, serves to unite the intruding tale with the main plot and helps remind the reader of the situation in which the digression has developed. It also provides a kind of counterpoint effect, for, in the tale of "the unfortunate Leonora," Adams, Slipslop, and Mrs. Graveairs (with their asides) combine to create a kind of play-within-a-play; and, in the tale of Mr. Wilson, Wilson's interpolation on vanity, encouraged by Adams's interruption begging him to proceed, is concluded by another interruption by Adams, who is searching fruitlessly for his own sermon on vanity, which he is confident that Wilson will admire (p. 206). Thus Adams through his interruptions unwittingly provides the illustration for Wilson's theory. And finally Adams's corrections of his son's pronunciation and reading in the digression on Paul and "Lennard" provides the illustration of the moral of that story, that is, to mind one's own affairs.

In *Don Quixote* the same kind of counterpoint is created. The puppet show itself is a play-within-a-play, a melodrama mirroring the melodrama of Don Quixote's own behavior. Don Quixote's identification with its leading character, Sir Gaiferous, enables us to contrast the relatively productive actions of Sir Gaiferous with the unproductive ventures of Don Quixote, who succeeds, in this instance, in demolishing only some cloth and wooden figures, despite his glowing idealisms about helping those in distress.

Critics have called the three main digressions in *Joseph Andrews* "analogues" and "negative analogues"[19] and "exempla."[20] In my introduction to *Don Quixote: The Knight of La Mancha*, I point out how the various digressions in the 1605 *Quixote* provide parallel and contrasting situations, offer commentary, establish counterparts, subplots, counsel, and conclusions, thereby creating more complexity and profounder meaning as a result of their juxtaposition with the main plot.

It is also clear that the digressions in books two, three, and four of *Joseph Andrews* are tightly integrated with the main plot. Thus the story of the unfortunate Leonora in book two acts as a foil for the faithfulness of both Joseph and Fanny. At the same time, Lenora's shifting affections parallel the rapidly shifting scenes described in the book as

Joseph and Adams travel from inn to inn, shifts in scene that foil Joseph's inner steadfeastness. If the subject of the book as a whole is human folly, amply illustrated at every stopping place and inn, then Leonora's folly only adds to the multiple examples. The tale of Leonora is, furthermore, told in transit, by a lady within a moving coach, thus reinforcing the sense of the transciency of human affections. The sense of change, of process, that characterizes the entire book is only strengthened by the story of Leonora's fickleness.

On the other hand, the tale of Mr. Wilson reinforces the sense of stability and of status quo to be found in book three, centering upon the landed gentry. In a sense Wilson's story takes up where Leonora's left off and provides us with an alternative to the solitary confinement chosen by Leonora after her jilt. After his early escapades, Wilson meets and marries Harriet Hearty, and together they "live happily ever after" with attention only for their garden, their children, and each other. The country squires who also populate the area are polar opposites to Wilson. In a book that opens with a chapter on "Lives" in order to provide "valuable patterns," Wilson's reformation, as well as the possibility of reformation itself, is instructive. Instead of action set in an endless succession of inns, as in book two, the actions of this book are divided among Wilson's home, the Squire's home, and one inn. Furthermore, the tale of Mr. Wilson may be seen to be no digression at all since Fielding links it with the main plot, through Wilson's lost son, with a strawberry mark on his left breast, later, of course, to be identified as Joseph. This so-called digression becomes then an integrated counterpart of the book as a whole.

Of further interest is the scarcity of paragraphing in the chapter on Wilson; in other words, there are few inns at which the reader may stop to rest, unlike book two. It is clear that Fielding manipulates his chapter endings and paragraphing to suit his subject matter. Lack of paragraphing suggests the rapt attention of the audience (except, of course, for Adams's exclamations of distaste at the beginning and his mention of his own sermon on vanity, making him seem all the more vain, since no one else sees fit to interrupt). Wilson's earnestness is also communicated by the sparse paragraphing, for the run-on character of the prose lends speed and intensity to the digression. The interruption provided by poet and player in book two lacks paragraphing with the same effects.

In book four the fact that the story of Leonard and Paul is not completed is a clue to its role. To begin with, the unresolved story of Leonard and Paul acts as a foil in a book full of conclusions and resolutions. But a close look at the chapter that succeeds this tale shows that Didapper and Joseph take up the roles of Paul and Leonard exactly where they were left off, and Joseph gives a sound reminder to Didapper of what happens to those who interfere in the love affairs and the marriages of others. In other words, the story does not need to be concluded, although one sees at once that Leonard is no more lion than Leonora had been lioness and that Joseph (the Joseph who refused the wife of Potiphar, that is) would never have become involved in folly to begin with to the extent that these two "lions" of the human world have allowed themselves to become involved.

In conclusion the essayistic interruption in *Joseph Andrews* and in *Don Quixote* must be mentioned briefly. In comparing Thomas Mann with Fielding and Sterne, Herman Meyer has said: "Like them, he integrates the essayistic digression on the narrative process into the entire narrative sequence by means of a sublimely complicated system of interlocking."[21] We have already noted ways in which the introductory chapters on literary matters are tightly locked into the structures of books one, two, and three. But there are also essayistic interruptions dealing with nonliterary subjects within the books themselves. Thus in chapter thirteen of book two, Fielding digresses to discuss the social ladder, on which fashionable and unfashionable people are ranked, in order to "vindi-

24

cate" Slipslop's distaste for Fanny. Only at church and in the playhouse are social groups segregated (in church, people of fashion sit in the balconies; in the playhouses, in the pit). Furthermore, sometimes people of fashion in one place become boors in another. The irrational and fluctuating character of the social ladder is, of course, one of the main topics of the entire book, for at the end, Fielding shifts his characters about on the ladder almost at will. But, more important, Fielding is commenting on the whole matter of rank in any human situation or endeavor—that it is often illusory and that distance between rungs varies according to perspective. In matters of literary structuring likewise, Fielding is aware that structure may be manipulated to one's own purposes and that an ideal structure is illusory, as we have already seen. In discussing the classics with Mr. Wilson in book three, chapter two, Adams suggests that although the *Iliad* possesses unity, that unity must be perfected by "greatness"; and he defines "greatness" as "Harmotton" or "the agreement of his action to his subject" (p. 189). At the same time, the story of Mr. Wilson, which follows this discussion, acts digressively at this point in the novel and thus mocks Aristotelian unity or any formula or hard-and-fast rule one may conceive. As we have noted, Fielding wrote in *Tom Jones*, book two, chapter one: "for as I am, in reality, the founder of a new province of writing, so I am at liberty to make what laws I please therein."[22] The whole matter of structure is, however, of crucial importance both to the action and to the meaning of his book, so Fielding's digression on the social ladder is no digression at all; for like the social ladder, the structure of the book, the author has shown, is largely a matter of point of view.

In the same way, it has been demonstrated how the discourse on arms and letters in *Don Quixote* (1605; chap. 38) undergirds the structure and meaning of the book in ironic and inverse ways. Thus Don Quixote, one whose triumphs are in the realm of the spirit and of good intentions and whose failures are in the world of arms, defends arms against letters, thereby establishing a paradox that is borne out again and again in the complex contrasts continually provided by the digressive materials in the book. On the other hand, defense of arms in the Renaissance tradition can be associated with a "humanism of arms," that is, with the belief in their worthwhile purpose. And so we can conclude that the discourse on arms and letters is no digression at all, for it both denies and affirms Quixote's idealisms in the same way that his adventures do, showing the interpretation of his character as largely a matter of point of view, like the interpretation of Fielding's social ladder.

IV

Another structural consideration significant in both *Don Quixote* and *Joseph Andrews* is the dialectic created between life and books. As Mia Gerhardt has pointed out, Don Quixote is the hero of his own novel, already published.[23] We cannot say the same, however, of Parson Adams, even though the skirt of his cassock, dangling from beneath his coat, may remind us mockingly of the tunic of classical times, in which he is well-versed. In fact, it is in the area of the tension between the inner and the outer man, spirit and body, that the widest divergence between the two books occurs. Furthermore, it is this difference that separates the centuries that produced these two novels. We have already noted in Part Two of this chapter the neater and less ambiguous structure of *Joseph Andrews* as compared with *Don Quixote;* at the same time, we have noted in Part Three Fielding's ability to manipulate and to experiment with his structure for artistic ends, and to make his own laws. In this connection we find him setting up tensions and establishing commentary "by juxtaposing the literary and the living as counterparts."[24] Maurice Johnson's "The Poet and the Player" explains the juxtaposition of two chapters in book three (ten and eleven) as illustrating this tension between the literary and the living.

As the quotation by Epictetus, used by Johnson as an epigraph, notes, "the World is a Theatre, and . . . your Part in this Play of Life is determined by the Poet." Your part is God's business, but the playing of the part "depends upon yourself."[25]

The *theatrum mundi* theme is one that permeated Renaissance writing ("All the world's a stage, / And all the men and women merely players");[26] one can trace the use of this theme back to Plato's *Laws*.[27] Various kinds of actors in life are denoted in the 1615 *Quixote*; for example, in chapter eleven when the wagon of players is followed by the appearance, shortly afterward, of Sampson Carrasco, dressed like a knight. Contrasting with them is Don Quixote himself, an actor of still another stripe. We act out our plays, Cervantes says, for different reasons and from different motives, first as a means of livelihood, next as a game, and third because we may be "holy madmen."[28] In the first instance the poet writes the play, but in the second and third instances, the actor composes his own part. Here the quotation from Epictetus is relevant to *Don Quixote*, for the failure to recognize that "your part is God's business" suggests a hubris that leads to Don Quixote's downfall.

The tension betwen poet and player (that is, between Adams and Joseph), between books and life, is somewhat different in *Joseph Andrews*. Adams writes no script, does not assume the place of God, and, unlike Quixote, does not compose his own part. His reading in the classics, particularly in the works of Aeschylus, has not turned his wits but simply given him a rather bookish set of values, and he does not identify with any figure in classical epic or drama. Poet and player in *Joseph Andrews* are contraries, tied to opposite bedposts, and, in keeping with Epictetus' statement, they perform separate functions. For Don Quixote, however, who has identified with heroes of the chivalric romances, poet and player are one. (The same is true of Sampson Carrasco, his ludicrous mirror image.) Only the actors on the wagon are not also poets, and Don Quixote calls them "phantoms." But Cervantes himself does not agree with his hero that poet and player merge into one, for he calls himself only the stepfather of his book, suggesting the divine origin of genius. Furthermore, the elaborate schemata of narrators in *Don Quixote*—Cide Hamete, the translator, and Cervantes himself—establish wide gaps between poet and player. On the other hand, Cervantes is also quite willing to acknowledge that sometimes poet and player do combine forces. As Thomas Mann has said, the only real life is "the lived life," meaning that the only reality is a living recognition of one's own historical role. Don Quixote is involved in the community of man, and his historical role defines his everyday life. Thus, according to W. H. Auden, he is "holy." Cervantes asks us a simple question: Is this madness of caring better than Sampson Carrasco's frivolity or the players' professional motives?

The confidence of the Renaissance in the ability of man to bring Christ to earth had been translated in the eighteenth century into a less ambitious and more cautious project. Adams, for all his idealisms, does not live them out in the same way that Don Quixote does. When Joseph and Beau Didapper fight, Adams picks up a pot lid for protection and steps between them; but he is under no illusion that this pot lid is a knight's shield. In other words, his life of Christian idealism is simile and not metaphor. It is of interest to note that Hamlet, like Don Quixote, wrote his own play, both at Elsinore and in the play-within-a-play. But the eighteenth-century rage for order and for logical chains of being made such a merging inconceivable. God, having been brought to earth, could not be returned to heaven, but at least He could be elevated to the top rung of the ladder, whence, as gentleman deity, He could mete out justice and genius. Mia Gerhardt discusses in detail the different kinds of readers in *Don Quixote*.[29] In *Joseph Andrews* only one kind of reader exists; although Joseph and Adams have different tastes and read different books, both remain at a distance from the subject matter. It is Fielding, not Joseph himself, who clothes Joseph in the garb of romance hero. In the Renaissance reality and illusion serve one another; in the eighteenth century they tend to act as opposites. Don Quixote's illusions are in the service of the realities he hopes to establish; Adams's ghosts and apparition are simply the vagaries of a sometimes credulous parson and are seen as polar opposites to Mr. Wilson's good sense in confronting the shepherds and their prisoners, the sheep-stealers (book three, chapter two). All of this illuminates one of the important and basic structural differences between these two books, and it comments tellingly on the two centuries from which they spring.

V

Another central structural issue is the dialectic established between Don Quixote and Sancho. Fielding may have attempted to create a similar spirit-nature pair in Adams and Joseph, but the results differed for a number of reasons, all inherent in the century in which he lived. To begin with, if Adams is an eighteenth-century Don Quixote, we find him, in Fielding, relegated to second place, appropriate in a century in which reason reigned and in which the common man was to emerge by means of two political revolutions in the Western world. The title of the eighteenth-century work is that of Joseph, that is, Sancho, a rustic and a man of the soil, the son of Gaffer and Gammer Andrews. Furthermore, Don Quixote is now a parson, in the service, more or less, of a structured religious establishment, rather than a hidalgo, an impoverished Spanish nobleman, at leisure to pursue his own religious leanings. Don Quixote is a parody of the ideal hero of myth and legend, whereas Adams is a parody of the ordinary, rather than of the extraordinary, parson. Yet neither fulfills his ideals. Adams finally succeeds in the world whereas Don Quixote eventually fails in the world, but succeeds in inspiring the love of the reader, partly because of his failures. Adams is fatuous; Don Quixote is mad. One is the product of an eighteenth-century "comic epic poem in prose," the other of a Renaissance mock chivalric tragedy. Thus Adams's success, the living given him by Mr. Booby, is largely part of the machinery of the comedy whereas Don Quixote's failure springs from his tragic inner delusions. The differences between Joseph and Adams are likewise part of the comic pattern whereas the differences between Don Quixote and Sancho spring from deeper psychological sources.

Furthermore, although the hero of the eighteenth-century novel, Joseph, is invested with a literary garment, that of the hero of a romance (rather than the chivalric romance), he wears it at the insistence of Fielding, not as a result of his own reading of romances, a genre that he avoids. Instead, he reads the Bible, *The Whole Duty of Man*, Thomas à Kempis, and the *Chronicle of the Kings of England*. And Adams, who is described like Joseph as "entirely ignorant in the ways of this world as an infant" (p. 6) (we note in this connection his "unworldly" namesakes Abraham and Adam), reads the Bible, but principally the classics, that is, Aeschylus. The differences between Adams and Joseph are not established, then, in as sharp and dramatic a way as they are between Don Quixote and Sancho. In fact, although we have discussed Adams as the descendant of Don Quixote and Joseph as the descendant of Sancho, we could also say that the chivalric knight is the forebear of the romantic lover or that the gullible Sancho is the forebear of the credulous parson. Fielding's characters are, therefore, less prototypical than Cervantes'.

Adams's classical background is, of course, appropriate to the "neoclassical" period as well as being his own distinguishing mark. It is this background that differentiates him from Quixote, who is grounded in the chivalric romance. Used by the ancients to describe the pitfalls of pride and lust, the classical drama and epic in which Adams is versed were replaced in the medieval period by the matter of the metrical romance, fantasies far removed from feudal reality. As in the medieval church, body and soul, earth and heaven, are separated in the romance by immeasurable distances to be dispelled only on Judgment Day. This is the point of medieval theology that Cervantes is parodying in creating Don Quixote and Sancho. Don Quixote is a knight who attempts to put his idealisms to practice on the highroads and byways and in the inns of sixteenth-century Spain. Don Quixote's armies are herds of sheep, his giants are fulling mills, and his knightly opponent a poor bachelor of arts from Salamanca.

The classical mode, on the other hand, from which the eighteenth century took its cue, was involved more in form than in formula. By this I mean that the dramatic and epic art of ancient Greece was employed in putting the passions and lusts and ambitions of real life into a framework, wherein they could be viewed to advantage. But in the neoclassical period, form became often an end in itself so that, in point of fact, the eighteenth century like the medieval period divided the ideal from the real and heaven from earth.

Looked at in another way, Don Quixote and Sancho are a parody of the polar opposition found in the metrical romance, for sometimes they serve the same ends and means and even exchange roles on occasion. In fact, often they are not in opposition at all, and the difference between them simply part of the illusion. It is quite clear, for example, that at mealtimes, despite his insistence on talking about a diet of herbs, Don Quixote is no more averse than Sancho to a good fat chicken. In this way Cervantes is able to imitate and at the same time to parody the chivalric formula, the recipe for the way knights should behave, but it is parody that involves two levels. Inwardly Don Quixote and Sancho are often at one; yet outwardly, as madman and realist, they stand in polar opposition.

Classical form, which Adams explains in his disquisition on the *Iliad*, takes little or no account of polarity as an artistic device. The classical world was one peopled by gods as well as by men, and it was not uncommon for a god or goddess to appear in the guise of a friend or to knock at one's door. In the plays of Aeschylus, there are no

early examples of spirit-nature pairs. Thus Fielding, in attempting perhaps to follow classical form and at the same
time to create an eighteenth-century Don Quixote and his
Sancho, finds that "knight and squire," spirit and body,
are basically one. It is not opposition but "Harmotton" (in
which action and subject combine) that Fielding strives for
in his novel; thus Joseph and Adams differ less dramatically than Don Quixote and Sancho on one level whereas,
on another, they are poles apart. Raymond Willis has suggested that at Don Quixote's death Sancho will become "a
stranger to himself and an exile in his own land."[30] But at
Adams's death, the reader can predict no such fate for
Joseph. We see him rather as the devoted husband of
Fanny and father of their brood, no stranger in any way,
and surely no exile. It is clear, therefore, that the whole
subject of polarity in the two novels is fraught with com-
.plexity, a complexity that Cervantes exploited to the fullest
and one that Fielding may have approached only to give
up in despair as his novel burgeoned.

It is interesting to conjecture that the attitude of a period
toward its gods determines in some way the literary
stances of that time. In the classical epic, peopled by both
gods and men, there is little use of spirit-nature structures—body and soul, inner and outer man. It was not
until James Joyce wrote *Ulysses* that Homer's Odysseus
possessed both soul and psychology. In the pre-Christian
*Odyssey*, however, the battles are between man and nature
(Poseidon) or between man and man. And even Oedipus
is plagued by fate more than by his own tragic flaw. But
medieval theology, which divided soul and body, this
world and the next, resulted in fiction based on sharp polarities between the ideal and the real. And the Renaissance and Reformation, by bringing Christ to earth, encouraged interaction in *this* world of the ideal and the real,
of Don Quixote and his counterparts. The conflicts of
heroes in classical and medieval times, therefore, were
waged with forces outside themselves in the world of
nature or of hell. But in post-Reformation literature, the

arena changes, and Milton writes: "Within him *hell*." Thus Don Quixote wages battle with his own illusions and Parson Adams with his own comical flaws. Furthermore, such flaws and illusions are the result of the hero's behavior and not the will of fate as in the classical mode. Thus man is perfectible, or capable of improvement, not doomed like Oedipus, and dramatic tension shifts from the problem itself to the solution of the problem. Man wins the power to control fate.

## VI

Finally, we must turn to the role of the narrator in the structure of *Joseph Andrews*. Fielding's narrator is not always on the scene, for Fielding sometimes tells us that "he" has not been able to discover a detail or a point of fact from anyone present or from anyone in the village at that time. On the other hand, Cide Hamete, though filtered through a mythical translator, is omniscient and has apparently been present, though invisible, through Don Quixote's and Sancho's wanderings. But Cervantes at one point is unable to discover Cide's manuscript. It is clear, however, that Cervantes establishes more distance between himself and Cide than Fielding does between himself and his narrator. Both authors, nevertheless, establish a narrator not to be identified with the author, since this narrator is "himself an element of the narrative fiction."[31] Mia Gerhardt suggests that Cide represents "la vie écrite" and Don Quixote "la vie vécue," but at the end of the book Cide writes, "For me alone Don Quixote was born and I for him"; and, at another point,[32] Don Quixote asserts that Cide must have put into Sancho's thoughts the title Knight of the Sad Countenance. This interaction and merging of narrator and character at once establishes and yet abolishes the narrator. Cide serves Cervantes in creating the illusion that Don Quixote is the author of the novel of which he is hero.[33]

No such suggestion is made by Fielding in *Joseph Andrews*, although the relation established between reader and narrator is close. Fielding's narrator is an element of the fiction in the sense that he takes the reader into his confidence, discusses matters of composition with him, delivers homilies to him (such as his advice to young girls to choose husbands with "lusty arms") (p. 185). Still he remains narrator, and Fielding's retention of that role as separate from that of the characters once more underlines the eighteenth-century insistence on form. For Fielding, the narrator is clearly an observer, someone outside the action; for Cervantes, Cide's omniscient presence and participation in the events of the novel marks him as a character in it. Moreover, other characters in the story, as Leon Gottfried puts it, "know about themselves as characters."[34] They are precursors of the heroes of contemporary metafiction, in which characters rise in revolt and assume roles of their own, despite their authors. This is the ultimate parody of man's power to control his fate. Not only may the author control the outcome of his own novel, but characters, created from his imagination, come alive and demand the same control. Does metafiction thus point to the logical absurdity of human "freedom"?

Herman Meyer discusses all this from another angle by suggesting that the narrator establishes himself through "the juxtaposition of contrasting textual quotations"[35] and that Cervantes, Fielding, Sterne (also Rabelais) all used this device. In Cervantes the tension between "the lofty and the lowly" and "the constant play between the stylistic elements proper to these levels"[36] is expressed through quotation in part. Quotation thus acts contrapuntally to establish unity between style and subject matter. In the same way in *Joseph Andrews*, Latin phrases misquoted by the doctor at the Tow-wouse inn underline the doctor's hypocrisy whereas Adams's frequent classical quotations accompany his high-minded but futile and ludicrous behavior. Tied to a bedpost, Adams quotes several passages from Seneca and from Boethius's *Consolation of Philosophy*. Meanwhile Joseph reinforces his own groans and sighs by quoting Macduff after he has learned from Ross that his wife and children have been slaughtered. Various purposes, both parodic and serious, are served by such a series of quotations, and through them the narrator makes himself known. Fielding's own attitude toward his narrator is one of amused indulgence; Cervantes, on the other hand, views Cide as a paragon of creativity, without whom he could not compose another word of his narrative. The whole question of who is the author of the Quixote has been explored still further by Jorge Luis Borges, who sets forth Pierre Menard as candidate. "Historical truth," writes Borges, ". . . is not what has happened; it is what we judge to have happened."[37]

VII

In conclusion, then, it is clear that for Fielding in *Joseph Andrews* Don Quixote is a kind of prototype. Homer Goldberg has shown how various works of fiction (those mentioned, in fact, by Fielding himself in book three, chapter one), such as *Don Quixote, Le Roman comique, Gil Blas,* and *La Vie de Marianne,* may have contributed to Fielding's art.[38] If we are to stress one of these, surely it must be *Don Quixote;* for innumerable parallels, not only of structure but of plot, incident, and character, abound. Just for examples we could cite: Adams's inappropriate dress and Don Quixote's armor; Adams covered with hogs' blood, Don Quixote with curds; Adams's stumbling horse and Rocinante; Adams's rescue of Fanny and Don Quixote's rescue of various damsels in distress; the bird batters and the group netting small birds in *Don Quixote* (1615; chap. 58); Adams's devotion to Aeschylus and Don Quixote's to *Amadis of Gaul;* the mock epic melee in the Tow-wouse inn and the mock epic melee in *Don Quixote* (1605; chap. 45); the battle between the squire's dogs, Adams, and Joseph, and that between Don Quixote and the sheep; the bedroom scene at Booby Hall and the attic scene in *Don Quixote* (1605; chap. 16); Slipslop and Maritornes; Mr. Wilson and the Gentlemen in Green; Adams's witchcraft and Don

Quixote's enchanters; Adams's "roasting" by the Squire and Don Quixote's "roasting" by the Duke and Duchess; Joseph's love song to Fanny and Don Louis's love song to Doña Clara; the story of Paul and Leonard and "The Tale of Foolish Curiosity." In addition, mock epic stylistic devices are common to both books: the mock invocation to the Muse; the mock epic catalogue; the mock epic chapter openings addressed to Aurora, Hesperus, and such; long mock epic similes; various mock epic personifications (for example, Fame blowing her brazen trumpet). And if these likenesses are not sufficient proof of influence, *Don Quixote* is mentioned directly a number of times in the text of *Joseph Andrews*. We find it mentioned first in the subtitle; then in book two, chapter sixteen ("the travellers had more reason to have mistaken [this inn] for a castle than Don Quixote") (p. 162); next in book three, chapter one, in praise of Cervantes' universal characters—Chrysostom, Marcela, "the mad Cardenio," "the perfidious Ferdinand," "the curious Anselmo," "the weak Camilla," "the irresolute Lothario"—and of *Don Quixote* itself, of which Fielding maintains there "is not such a book as that which records the achievements of the renowned Don Quixote, more worthy the name of a history than even Mariana's" (p. 179); and finally in book three, chapter nine, in which Adams is overcome by the Squire's henchmen, looking so black "that Don Quixote would certainly have taken him for an enchanted Moor" (pp. 252–53).

The differences between the two novels, as they have been indicated in this chapter, are, however, perhaps more significant than the similarities, numerous as they are, for the chief difference lies in the ways the two authors have handled the matter of polarization: life and books, real and ideal, Don Quixote and Sancho. We find Fielding in the eighteenth century to be more literal, more logical, and less metaphoric. His structures are more even, the motivation of his characters more reasonable. Adams is not mad, even though he sometimes may be foolish. The spirit-nature pair, who spring from Renaissance humanistic doctrine, are nowhere to be found in Fielding. Instead we have a series of characters, a progression of inns, a number of corrupt gentry, a bevy of corrupt servants. Joseph and Adams, Wilson and the Squire, Lady Booby and Mrs. Slipslop are not polar opposites but individuals in their own right. None of them is artistically dependent on his opposite. The Renaissance tension between ideal and real, between mind and body, between inner man and outer man has changed form in the eighteenth century, a century that proclaims, deistically, with Fielding, that "by observing minutely the several Incidents which tend to the Catastrophe or completion of the whole, and the minute Causes whence those Incidents are produced, we shall best be instructed in this most useful of all Arts, which I call the Art of Life."[39]

1. *Covent Garden Journal*, ed. G. E. Jensen, 1:281.

2. Ibid.

3. Henry Fielding, *The History and Adventures of Joseph Andrews and of His Friend Mr. Abraham Adams*, Introduced by Maynard C. Mack (New York: Rinehart and Co., 1948), p. 178. Subsequent references to this volume will be cited in the text.

4. Hamilton Macallister writes that the influence of *Don Quixote* on *Joseph Andrews* is "very much on the surface" (*Fielding*, p. 53), and that Fielding took the framework of Cervantes' novel "and filled [it] with his own moral purposes and comic imagination" (ibid.). Homer Goldberg's much more extended study of *Don Quixote* as prototype for *Joseph Andrews* views *Don Quixote* as mere "episodic narrative" (*The Art of "Joseph Andrews,"* p. 32), views the second sally as made up of "meandering actions . . . where one discrete episode succeeds another without consequence" (p. 34), and states at the end of his chapter on prototypes that "Fielding might understandably have concluded that a conspicuous lack of form or structure was an essential characteristic of the 'kind of writing' he was undertaking" (p. 71). Martin Battestin in his introduction to his edition of *Joseph Andrews* likewise dismisses picaresque fiction that preceded *Joseph Andrews* as "aimlessly constructed" (*Joseph Andrews and "Shamela,"* p. xxix) and sees the principle of unity, derived by Fielding from "epic regularity," as far more formative than *Don Quixote*. Parson Adams, as Battestin notes, cites the chief perfection of the *Iliad* as its adherence to "Harmotton, the correlation of structure and meaning" (ibid.). M. Digeon proposes an even more general prototype for *Joseph Andrews*, the French classical drama, as background for Fielding's struc-

ture (Aurélien Digeon, *Les Romans de Fielding,* p. 19). And Irvin Ehren-preis in an article on form in *Joseph Andrews* writes that "when Fielding is not advancing by retreats, he is generally continuing by interruptions. One scene commonly breaks in upon its predecessor rather than develops it" ("Fielding's Use of Fiction: The Autonomy of Joseph Andrews," in Charles Shapiro, ed., *Twelve Original Essays on Great English Novels,* pp. 26–27). Frederick Karl's recent discussion of *Don Quixote* and Fielding in *The Adversary Literature* should also be mentioned. Although Karl does not address himself by and large to the matter of structure, he writes that Fielding's techniques look back to old modes (epic, heroic, satiric, etc.) whereas his content presages the romantic and "sentimental" age (*The Adversary Literature,* p. 160).

5. See note 3, above.

6. Andrew Wright, *Henry Fielding: Mask and Feast.*

7. Maurice Johnson, *Fielding's Art of Fiction,* pp. 47–60.

8. Ibid., p. 49.

9. Ibid., p. 60.

10. "The Odysseyan Form: An Exploratory Essay" in *Essays on European Literature,* p. 24.

11. Alexander A. Parker, *Literature and the Delinquent,* p. 4.

12. Alexander A. Parker, "Fielding and the Structure of *Don Quixote,*" p. 16.

13. Ibid., p. 2.

14. Parts 1 and 2 are a single unit in my view. See Margaret Church, *Don Quixote: The Knight of La Mancha,* p. xix.

15. Henry Fielding, *The History of Tom Jones* (New York: Modern Library, n.d.), p. 41.

16. Ibid., p. 40.

17. Cervantes, *The Adventures of Don Quixote,* p. 440.

18. Ibid., p. 316.

19. Macallister, p. 84.

20. I. B. Cauthen, Jr., "Fielding's Digressions in *Joseph Andrews,*" p. 379.

21. Herman Meyer, *The Poetics of Quotation in the European Novel,* pp. 233–34.

22. Fielding, *Tom Jones,* p. 41.

23. Mia Gerhardt, *Don Quixote, la vie et les livres,* p. 47.

24. Johnson, p. 61.

25. Ibid.

26. *As You Like It,* 2, 7, 139–40.

27. See my *Don Quixote: The Knight of La Mancha,* pp. xvii, xxx–xxxi, 88–89. Here I discuss the *theatrum mundi* tradition in more detail.

28. W. H. Auden, *The Dyer's Hand,* p. 136.

29. Gerhardt, pp. 17–24.

30. Raymond S. Willis, Jr., "Sancho Panza: Prototype for the Modern Novel," p. 227.

38

31. Meyer, p. 11.

32. Cervantes, *The Adventures of Don Quixote*, p. 147.

33. Gerhardt, pp. 33–39.

34. Gottfried, p. 25.

35. Meyer, p. 11.

36. Ibid., p. 60.

37. Jorge Luis Borges, *Labyrinths: Selected Stories and Other Writings*, p. 43.

38. Goldberg, chapter 2.

39. Henry Fielding, *Amelia* (New York: Barnes and Noble, 1967), p. 14.

## Chapter Two

## The Sorrows of Young Werther:
## The Structure of *Sturm und Drang*

Written in four weeks (although Goethe makes plain in *Dichtung und Wahrheit* that the mental preparation for *Werther* extended for long periods before the actual writing began), "without a plan of the whole work, or the treatment of any portion of it having previously been put to paper,"[1] *The Sorrows of Young Werther* gives evidence of extraordinary symmetry of form. A product of the Bastille era, an era of revolt, and dealing with "die Einschränkung,"[2] that is, social restrictions as they conflicted with Werther's instinctive sense of individual freedom, the book's tightly woven symmetry, in contrast to its emotional context, illustrates the thematic issue.

Robert T. Clark, Jr., has shown that Goethe probably received orally from Herder, in 1770–71 or in later meetings, the tenets of Herder's psychology and that "Einschränkung" was a basic factor in his "psychology of sensation with specific reference to the arts."[3] "Die Einschränkung," in Herder's view, foredoomed the individual "to perceive always only part of the whole,"[4] to see the world only from his own perspective and never to obtain a total vision. Werther himself complains of this restriction, but at the same time tries to ignore it. As Erich Trunz[5] points out, the word *Einschränkung* is a significant one within the text of *Werther*, and Hans Reiss[6] makes note of various ways that it is used: sometimes as a source of delight for Werther when he rejoices in his restricted way of life; at other times signifying distress, when his restrictions seem unbearable; or at others, as a condemnation of his "cocoon of narrow, intense vision."[7] "Werther's conflict," writes Georg Lukács, in a different context, "Werther's tragedy, is already the tragedy of the bourgeois man, indicating even now the unsolvable conflict between the free and complete development of individuality and bourgeois society itself."[8]

It is clear that the structure of *Werther* is far more complex than is commonly recognized. Notable among treatments of the subject is Victor Lange's discussion of speech as the formative element in the novel. Lange states: "Scene, episode, action, imagery—all these structural elements must be brought together at a single emotional level which can be produced and made intelligible only through the fixed medium of speech,"[9] and "As goes the first part of the novel, so also the second, with a succession so to speak of experiments in language—to experiments in forms of expression."[10] He further shows how the novel is structured by means of patterns such as: speaking and not being able to speak; dialogue, monologue, and silence; and how these patterns generate feeling that is as much a part of the experience of reading the novel as descriptions of a simple and familiar scene.[11] My own treatment of structure in this chapter will be different, stemming from the basic psychological conflict inherent in *Sturm und Drang*, but other valid conceptions of structure in *Werther* are surely not precluded by it. One may speculate that romantic authors, in the face of the exuberance and emotionalism of *Sturm und Drang*, sought for strong frameworks and for foils for their material. In fact, the romantic preference for poetry and poetic drama over the more loosely structured novel and prose play may spring from this need for form.

We find in the romantic period a new polarity undergirding literary expression, a polarity consisting of idea as opposed to reality and differing radically from the eighteenth-century conflict between reason and feeling and from the Renaissance conflict between the ideal and the real. We have only to contrast Dulcinea, Fanny, and Lotte to understand the differences. Dulcinea, having no existence apart from Don Quixote's perception of her in the ideal world of his high-minded quest, is the opposite of the farm girl, Aldonza Lorenza. Fanny is a woman of feeling and is contrasted semicomically with Joseph's other mentor, Parson Adams, who sees himself as a man of reason, although Fanny herself is often far more reasonable than the foolish parson. Charlotte, however, like Don Quixote's love, exists in two guises. First, she is for Werther almost a principle rather than a person, a correlative figure representing the possiblity for individual freedom in a hypocritical and restrictive social setting. On the other hand, she is a simple country girl who cares for her younger brothers and sisters and tends her father's home. It is again the difference between "la vie écrite" and "la vie vécue." And yet unlike Dulcinea in the mind of Don Quixote, Lotte does not become for Werther a disembodied ideal. Lotte fulfills Werther's *idea* of the "beloved"; Dulcinea becomes Don Quixote's *ideal*. In a review of a translation of Spanish romances, Goethe had interpreted the Spanish character as one that transposed idea directly into concrete reality.[12] Werther himself in *The Sorrows of Young Werther* seems to depend on somewhat the same process.

Goethe's critical remarks on *Don Quixote* are few, and most of them were written after the sentimental crisis that *Werther* describes. Well before the revision of *Werther* in 1787, Goethe had outgrown the period of "Schwärmerei," and we find him ridiculing his romantic novel in *Der Triumph der Empfindsamkeit* (1777–78), a play incorporating a number of Quixotic features. For example, a doll stuffed with fashionable books, among them *Werther*, has caused Prince Oronaro's disease of sentimentality. The prince behaves toward this doll as Don Quixote behaved toward Dulcinea, pouring forth his devotion "in long and ardent monologues."[13] The Quixotic tension between the play and life, the role and our true nature, may be found also in Goethe's farce; at the end Goethe's moral reads: "Only then is a fool really deceived when he imagines in his folly to heed the voice of reason or to obey the Gods."[14] Very few Quixotic influences are apparent in *Werther*, however, even though Werther's irrational behavior is surely abetted by *Ossian* and even though Werther does, in his folly, believe that he heeds "the voice of reason." Nevertheless, basic polarities underlie both books, and both heroes create their own women, embodiments of their own inner faiths; in fact, Don Quixote and Werther, in different ways, author their own books, one by identifying himself as a fictional character, the other through his letters to Wilhelm. That Charlotte has an existence outside Werther's perception of her must be patently clear; likewise, Aldonza Lorenzo led a life outside Don Quixote's pale. Neither Aldonza nor Lotte is idealized by Cervantes or by Goethe: we see Aldonza winnowing wheat and Lotte's vanity and coquetry are evident in her "innocent" encouragements of Werther's passion. Werther, on the contrary, interprets her action always in the light most flattering to him. Thus he commits suicide in the firm belief that one of the three of them must die (p.108), a notion that surely never enters Lotte's mind. The conflict between idea and reality within Werther is then quite different from that between the ideal and the real as seen in Don Quixote. Charlotte is Werther's friend, a living woman with an identity apart from that bestowed on her by Werther. Dulcinea, on the other hand, is totally the creation of Don Quixote's mind, and her counterpart, Aldonza, is never a real participant in Don Quixote's life. The metaphysical emphasis of the Renaissance and humanism is thus contrasted with the more sociocentric philosophy of the late eighteenth and early nineteenth centuries.

II

The various structures of *Werther* serve to underlie the romantic conflict between individual freedom and social restriction. The strong technical unity in the book makes the wanderings and emotional outbreaks of Werther stand out in relief; the contrast thus obtained reinforces the central theme—that of *die Einschränkung*. The social norm *is* often hypocritical, insensitive, and meaningless; but

Goethe, like Cervantes, wanted to show that not Werther's ideas but his means of putting them into practice were at fault. Thus the letters of Werther must be "edited," and *Don Quixote* must be "authored" by Cide Hamete Benengeli. For different reasons, neither Werther nor Quixote was capable of accomplishing by himself the reform of the real world.

In order to reinforce the complex relations between structure and theme in *Werther*, it will be useful to examine in more detail some of the literary techniques Goethe employed. To begin with, *Werther* is divided into two books, each one consisting of three distinct parts. Book one, part one, concerns the period before Werther meets Lotte, covers 43 days and 14 pages; part two deals with Werther's meeting with Charlotte and his growing love for her, covers 44 days and 24 pages; and part three treats the period after Albert arrives in Wahlheim, covers 42 days and 19 pages. These three parts are roughly even in terms of elapsed time, each one covering approximately 43 days. However, the central section, describing Werther's happy early days with Charlotte, contains more pages than either part one or part three, suggesting the greater importance of this phase in his life by comparison with the other two phases.

In book two we find an entirely different sort of three-part structure. Part one, describing Werther's stay at the embassy, covers six and a half months and 13 pages; part two, relating Werther's visit to his first home, covers two and a half months and four pages; part three, concerning Werther's return to Wahlheim and to Lotte, five months and 53 pages. Like Werther's state of mind, the patterns here are far more chaotic than in book one, both of times elapsed and pages covered. Furthermore, the total elapsed time is longer in book two than in book one, both in each of the three parts and in the book as a whole, perhaps to parallel the tragic ennui that seizes Werther and the apparently futile and lonely road that he follows, longest of all at the embassy. However, the greatest difference between the books is seen in the variation in the lengths of the three parts in book two. Only 17 pages are spent on Werther's life apart from Lotte, whereas 53 are given to his tragic return to Wahlheim, emphasizing, even more critically than in book one, the point that reality for Werther exists primarily in his relation to Charlotte. Thus the divisions of the book are deployed in order that its structure may parallel and reinforce the sensibilities of its hero.

In the same vein, we find certain structural devices, such as parallel situations, digressions, and poetic motifs, used to reinforce the theme of the book. Although book one and book two are closely meshed, each, at the same time, remains a discrete unit. Thus a triangle situation, but one different from that which drove Werther to leave Wahlheim at the end of book one, occurs almost at once at the embassy in book two, where the relations among the Ambassador, the Count, and Werther threaten to explode. The Ambassador appears to Werther to be annoyed by Werther's liking for the Count and, according to the letter of 24 December 1771, takes every opportunity to discourage the friendship. Werther's personality, of course, encourages such situations, for his egotism leads him to believe, as with Lotte and Albert, that both Ambassador and Count crave his friendship to the exclusion of the other.

Another triangle situation had arisen in book one during Werther's brief visit to St. with Lotte on 1 July. Here Herr Schmidt had objected to Werther's conversation with Friederike, a relationship that was so innocent and so short-lived and Herr Schmidt's jealousy so exaggerated in proportion to the importance of the incident, that this triangle quickly becomes a parody of triangles in general, including the central one in the novel. In book two, on Werther's return to St., a different antagonist faces him, in the form this time of a woman, the new vicar's wife, who has had Werther's favorite walnut trees cut down. Like Herr Schmidt, the vicar's wife is a petty person and has had the trees cut for foolish reasons, as foolish as Herr Schmidt's jealousy. Thus by means of implied compari-

sons between situations that have both similar and dis-
similar elements, Goethe builds up the paradoxes and the
ambiguities of his novel, throwing different shadings and
colorings on corresponding incidents.

Furthermore, Goethe uses digressive material in the
same way. There are three main digressions in *Werther*: the
story of the woman whose husband is in Switzerland; the
story of the peasant lad who falls in love with his mistress;
and the story of the madman looking for flowers in November. The first two stories begin in book one and continue into book two, and each ends, like Werther's own
story, in tragedy. In the third digression, we learn that the
madman, like Werther, had been in love with Lotte herself. The first two digressions reinforce and contrast with
Werther's plight. One tells of a husband who returns from
his travels, empty-handed and sick with fever; the other of
a peasant lad who murders his rival and is apprehended by
the authorities. The digression about the peasant lad was
added by Goethe to the 1787 revision of the novel in order
to help exonerate Lotte and Albert and to place more firmly
the blame for the tragic events of the main plot on
Werther's shoulders. Goethe has Werther identify himself
with the unfortunate peasant lad, who had aggressively
pursued his mistress and murdered his rival. The tale also
was supposed to exonerate Lotte by implying a contrast
between her behavior and that of the widow, who is far
more seductive. In other words, Goethe uses the digression to establish meaning through both contrast and comparison with the main plot (as well as, in 1787, with the
real life situation). As in *Don Quixote* and *Joseph Andrews*,
the digressions are part of an intricate counterpoint technique. Like *Ossian*, first mentioned in book one (10 July)
shortly after Werther meets Charlotte, they are symbolic
renderings of Werther's experiences in different terms,
and they establish continuity of theme at the same time as
they establish a discontinuity, an increasingly chaotic
structure that marks Werther's downward course.

We find also numerous poetic motifs such as the seasons, trees, Lotte's pink bow, the thunderstorm, and the flood that reinforce, or serve as counterpoint to, Werther's moods. Thus the beauty of nature, which is a powerful stimulus at the beginning of the book, weighs on Werther's spirits at the end when it contrasts with his inner anguish. His meeting with Charlotte and their early pleasure in each other's company occurs at the height of summer; in fact, it is on 21 June, near Midsummer Night, when Werther declares that his days "are as happy as those God gives to his saints" (p. 23). A year and a half later, at the winter solstice, a point at which the sun is farthest removed from the northern hemisphere, Werther commits suicide. The conclusion of Werther's life just before Christmastime is particularly appropriate symbolically. Primitive festivals before the Christian era celebrated at this date the first indications of the return of the sun northward. Werther tragically takes his own life on the eve of the return of light and warmth, at the nadir of the seasons, and at twelve midnight, the moment of the beginning of a new day. With the events of renewal, rebirth, and return all about him, the suicide of Werther gains in tragic significance. [15]

The first two sections of book one, happy and serene, take place during the spring and early summer of 1771; the third section, after Albert's arrival, is set during the late summer and early fall, a period when Werther's anxieties are beginning to grow. Werther's separation from Lotte in book two occurs during the fall of 1771 and the winter of 1771–72. His return to Wahlheim does not take place until 29 July, almost exactly a year after Albert's arrival on the scene on 30 July in book one, a late summer setting foreboding the end of the growing season. The conclusion of Werther's life is traced from then until the winter solstice. The seasons as such may be seen to be tightly woven into the thematic fabric of the whole book, even though Werther's reactions to any given season vary with his circumstances. Thus the first spring (1771) near Wahlheim has been a glorious period in which he falls into raptures,

declaims, and perishes under the splendor of his visions
(p. 3) whereas the second spring (1772) in which he returns
briefly to his native home is full of memories of unfulfilled
plans, uncongenial companions, boredom, and loneliness.
Liselotte Dieckmann's article in 1962 terms such devices
"mirroring" techniques, indicating the self-reflexive nature of structure in *Werther*.[16] However, I believe, in the
case of the seasons, that Goethe uses them both as a means
of contrast and as a means of comparison, thereby effect-
ing a skillful artistic variation and augmenting Werther's
sense of "die Einschränkung."

Trees also play an important role as leitmotifs in the
book. To begin with, they represent stability and longev-
ity, neither of which Werther is destined to achieve. Like
the trees at St., he will be cut down in his prime as a misfit
in society. Yet they also provide shade from the heat of the
sun. Werther reads his Homer under the linden trees in
Wahlheim; he admires the vicar's walnut trees at St.; and,
on his return to his early home in book two, he notes in
particular that the great linden tree is still standing, even
though the school he had attended has been converted
into a shop. In his instructions to Albert and Charlotte
concerning his burial, he asks that he may lie in one corner
of the churchyard under two linden trees. "Fear no more
the heat o' the sun, / Nor the furious winter's rages."[17]
But the protective role that Werther assigns to trees stands
in contrast to the opinion of the Vicar's wife at St., who
decides the walnut trees make her courtyard dark and
gloomy. Werther's interpretation of the role of the tree
symbolizes his need for protection from the social environment. Shaded from the heat of the sun as he reads his
Homer, he is at the same time, like the suitors of Penelope,
destined to be consumed by his own fires, against which
he has no shield.

Another poetic motif, that of Lotte's pink bow, supplies
further interesting counterpoint. The color pink suggests
innocence, frivolity, pleasure, and party clothes. Yet at the
end, the pink bow adorns Werther in his coffin. Further-

more, the pink bow is sent by Albert to Werther on Werther's birthday (28 August 1771). Coming from both Albert and Lotte, such a gift must have caused Werther pain. It was a gesture that contained intimations of both condescension and of pity and was clear indication of the end of any lurking claims Werther may have felt he had to Lotte. A bow, besides being an ornament, is a tie; so the gift of this bow from both friends suggests that Werther's "tie" is to them both, not to her alone. Thus the bow, which is employed in a conventional manner in the early part of the novel, becomes in the later pages a source of pain and a macabre decoration for a coffin.

Storms and floods also provide thematic enrichment throughout the novel. The first storm that takes place during the dance (16 June 1771), when Werther meets Lotte, presages the inner turmoil that will later submerge Werther. At the same time, it is Charlotte who manages to keep matters under control, ignoring the storm, much as she later ignores Werther's passion, and turning the attention of the guests from it to a parlor game (a kind of ploy she is less successful in accomplishing with Werther in book two). The storm of 16 June contrasts with the gaiety of the dance and with Werther's high spirts during his first encounter with Lotte, as he kisses her hand "in a stream of ecstatic tears" (p. 22). It is a storm of ecstasy rather than one of pain and destruction, but ecstasy accompanied by rain. Later scenes involving storms in book two are more lugubrious. We listen as Werther reads in *Ossian* of the winds of autumn arising, of tempests in groves of oaks, of driving snow, sweet as the breathing gale, and of broken clouds (p. 116). These storms, together with the flood that occurs the night that Werther reads *Ossian* to Charlotte, accompany Werther's final torments. Likewise, the day he meets the madman in the shabby coat, a counterpart of himself, a madman looking for flowers in November, "a cold and damp west wind blew from the mountains, and heavy grey clouds spread over the plain" (p. 91). The storm imagery is used, then, both to parallel and to con-

trast with Werther's moods, and like other poetic motifs—
the seasons, the trees, and the pink bow—it serves to enrich the novel, to increase its tensions, and to balance its
parts. The parallel situations, the digressions, the various
poetic motifs are devices that in various ways strengthen
the conflict between convention on the one hand and freedom from convention on the other, the central issues of
Werther's whole existence.

III

The epistolary form is also particularly well-suited to the
treatment of individual freedom and social patterns.
Goethe, of course, uses this form in a way entirely different from that of Cervantes or Richardson. The letters in
*Don Quixote* are inserted occasionally as part of the parody,
as we see in the one to Dulcinea that Don Quixote entrusts
to Sancho or in the letter from Sancho to Teresa, sent from
the court of the Duke and the Duchess. The letters from
Joseph to Pamela in *Joseph Andrews* are likewise parody,
this time of Richardson, who in *Pamela* used the letter in
dead earnestness and even included some of the replies of
the correspondents. But Goethe, as Hans Reiss has shown,
is far more compact and economical than Richardson, and
more concerned with the letters of one person, to enable
the reader to focus on him alone.[18]

Moreover, in order to reinforce meaning, tone, and
mood, Goethe builds in strong transitional devices between some of the letters, but between others we find
abrupt shifts in subject matter or changes in style. Thus in
book one, on 26 July 1771, Werther's letter ends with a tale
told him by his grandmother about sinking ships and
perishing crews; the next letter begins by telling about a
different kind of disaster—Albert has arrived. Although on
a symbolic level the topics of the two letters are similar,
their styles differ. The letter of 26 July contains a lyrical
quality that is missing in the series of abrupt simple sentences that compose the letter of 30 July. Toward the end of

book two, we find fewer and fewer transitional elements between the letters to parallel, one supposes, Werther's growing mental disorder.

Because Wilhelm's replies are never included, Goethe is able to concentrate solely on the development of one character and to probe thoroughly into that character's inner world. As Goethe wrote in *Dichtung und Wahrheit*, an outpouring of inner life will take place only in letters, where it is not directly confronted by anyone.[19] Furthermore, letters with answers from Wilhelm seen only through the eyes of Werther add to the sense of Werther's isolation, more even than a diary, where no reply would be expected by the reader. But although the epistolary form provides emotional freedom for Werther, it also imposes on both Goethe and Werther a rigid external framework whereon the book is structured. Conventionally, a letter is relatively short, that is, by comparison with the chapter units of a traditional novel. Letters have headings, salutations, and conclusions—abbreviated by Goethe to a dateline. In the interests of clear communication, a letter is usually consistent and logically ordered. Moreover, the letter device serves to do away with Goethe and to replace him with Werther as the author of his own book, as Don Quixote was, in a different way, of his. At the same time, the reader becomes in a sense, like Wilhelm, the silent recipient, thus arousing both his sympathies and his regret at Werther's follies. And although the reader becomes involved, he is, like all recipients of letters, removed by distance. All these effects go hand in hand with the epistolary form to which Goethe commits himself.

A third author of the book, in addition to Goethe and Werther, is of course, the Editor, who must perforce conclude the manuscript. The Editor and Goethe, as well as the silent Wilhelm, provide a series of checks and balances for the extremely emotional Werther. One cannot, however, assume that the Editor and Goethe are one; Goethe's attitudes toward his hero appear more subjective than those of the Editor, who attempts to limit himself to the

facts of Werther's final days. Goethe's presence in the letters is occasionally even an ironic one, ironic in a way not
perceived by Werther himself. For example, the utterance
of the cacophonous name "Klopstock" at the very moment
of the flowering of Werther's love for Charlotte ("she put
her hand on mine and said, 'Klopstock'") (p. 22) may be an
indication of Goethe's own mild amusement at the scene.
In the same letter, on 16 June, the Editor, by contrast,
refers to Werther in a footnote "as an unbalanced young
man" (p. 17). There is a distinct difference here between
Goethe's gentle reservation and the Editor's sterner judgment. A number of days later (8 July), it is apparent that
Wilhelm has chastised his friend for unbridled passions
because Werther begins: "What a child I am to be so solici-
tous about a look!" and concludes, "What a child I am!"
(pp. 31–32). Goethe's presence may also be seen in this
remark, for, although it is clear that Werther does not *really*
see himself as a child, it is implied that Goethe may ironically view him as such.

Another interesting evidence of Goethe's presence in
the letters comes on 21 June, when Werther likens himself
to the suitors of Penelope, who killed, dressed, and
roasted oxen and swine as he himself at Wahlheim gathers
his peas, fetches his saucepan and butter, and sits down by
the fire to stir the pot. The reader is, however, subtly reminded by Goethe that the suitors of Penelope were inter-
lopers, an indirect comment on Werther's own situation,
and, furthermore, that it was Odysseus' swine and oxen
that they were roasting, not their own. Perhaps, too, we
should note that swine and oxen have been reduced to
garden peas, suggesting that our hero lacks something of
the heroic mold.

Futher ironic comment from Goethe may be observed in
places where Werther lectures others on faults that he himself possesses. Thus during the visit with Charlotte to the
vicarage at St. (1 July), as we have earlier noted, Herr
Schmidt, the suitor of the vicar's daughter, becomes angry
when Werther appears to pay her too much attention. Like

Parson Adams, tied to the bedpost, Werther begins to lecture the group on the importance of bearing adversity and of controlling one's temper. Ill humor, Werther continues, "resembles laziness, . . . but if once we have courage to exert ourselves, our work runs fresh from our hands" (p. 28), advice Werther himself would have done well to follow in the closing pages of book two. The ultimate mockery in the scene is developed, however, in the next letter (8 August), when we discover that Wilhelm has taken Werther's sermon on resignation as directed at him. Everyone, except the person Goethe shows us to be most in need of it, hears Werther's speech. Ironically, too, Werther's innocent interference in the affair between Friederike and Herr Schmidt finds its larger and more serious paradigm in his interference in Lotte's and Albert's relationship.

Later, on 11 July, Goethe's irony is once more clear in the transitional material between this letter and the next. Werther concludes the letter of 11 July with remarks on "the incredible blindness of men" in their relations with women. The letter of 13 July, which follows, begins: "No, I am not deceived. In her black eyes I read a genuine interest in me and my life" (pp. 32–33).

This running ironic counterpoint established by Goethe in book one gives the reader a point of reference, a sounding board for Werther's sentimentality, but one that differs radically from the objective and research-oriented point of view of the Editor, who tells us in his first full-length passage that he will "relate conscientiously the facts which our persistent labor has enabled us to collect" (p. 95). Goethe's attitude toward his hero appears to be one of amused indulgence in book one. In book two, as Werther's anguish grows, ironic counterpoint is less frequent and is replaced by Goethe's compassion for his hero. The fact that the Editor in book two no longer passes judgment on Werther's behavior but contents himself with simply reporting it indicates his own concession to Werther's pain. It is apparent that Wilhelm's replies become more urgent toward the end of Werther's life; although in book one he had advised Werther to find work at the embassy (20 July) or to return to his drawing (24 July), at the end of book two he suggests that Werther turn to religion (15 November). This is a step that would effect more far-reaching changes in Werther's personality than drawing or a job at the embassy. Wilhelm is apparently a man of good sense, a stable influence; but he is, unlike the Editor, not totally objective. Also he represents Werther's mother. By establishing several different kinds of reactions to Werther's dilemma, Goethe enriches the book so that it becomes more than just an account of a young man's conflicts with the society in which he lives. Instead we have various responses, such as the early amused indulgence of Goethe himself, the active concern and distress of Wilhelm, the disapproval and detachment of the Editor. The reader is thus given a number of different perspectives from which to view Werther's plight, in addition to Werther's own perspective. The epistolary form is then not a delimiting one but one able to provide many variations on the main theme of the book. The ways in which others approve or disapprove of Werther's behavior are rendered subtly in the letters themselves rather than stated outright. In the letters Werther is free to give full vent to his emotions, restricted only by the convention of the form and by the character of his correspondent. Because of the distance between writer and recipient, letter-writing is a suitable vehicle for Werther's emotions, which at nearer range tend to create havoc. Letters are, in fact, one of the few means of communication left to one afflicted with a sense of *Einschränkung*.

IV

Multiple polarities and various paradoxes serve to make up the larger paradox embodied in a sense of *Einschränkung* in *Werther*. Individual freedom in conflict with conventional social structures is bound to involve a multitude of other oppositions. Thus we find in *Werther* a conflict between intellect and the emotions, between the Editor's objective, calm, and superior point of view and Werther's more excitable viewpoint, or the conflict within Werther himself between intellect and passion.[20] Furthermore, the lyric moods in which he revels in his natural surroundings contrast with the emotional states in which his passion for Lotte is expressed. Hans Reiss shows how as the book progresses his "pathological surge of feeling"[21] increases, gradually crowding out the earlier idyllic scenes.

Different styles of writing also characterize Werther's letters. Lyrical style turns into melodramatic prose as Werther's moods fluctuate. Hans Reiss further points out that quasi-lyrical and epic moods are interjoined and that exclamatory and interrogative sentences vary with expository ones.[22] And Elizabeth M. Wilkinson and L. A. Willoughby explain how, in the letter of 10 May 1771, Goethe created "the very semblance of the Neo-Platonic soaring of the soul towards its creator and its sighing despair of ever being able to express the divine affinity it feels."[23] It is "a pure analogue of the felt life within" the hero of the novel, for through the rise of the words followed by the ominous despair of the conclusion ("I shall perish under the splendour of these visions" [p. 3]), we view the seeds of destruction embedded in Werther's ecstasy. All of these contrasting styles reflect the underlying contradiction in Werther's character and thus in his letters. Goethe sets Homer against Ossian; reason against passion; society against the individual; desire against despair.

It is of interest to note that Odysseus' guardian goddess was Athene, goddess of the intellect and of wisdom, and it is to the *Odyssey* (rather than to the *Iliad*) that Werther usually turns. After the famous snub, when Werther is forced to retire from the assembly of Count C., he drives to M. to watch the setting sun and to read a passage in the *Odyssey*. The passage that he reads describes the swineherd entertaining Odysseus (p. 69), a swineherd who in the aftermath of Werther's snub must seem superior to all the fashionable court snobs at Count C.'s. Paradoxically, Homer supports organized society and the family by showing in the following scenes the terrible punishment inflicted on the suitors. Thus Werther turns for comfort to a book that argues the opposite of his own position. Later on it is Aphrodite and not Athene by whom he is governed. Werther is an intruder, not only at the assembly but in the lives of Albert and Lotte. Homer's *Odyssey* provides then for the reader several interesting points of contrast. Odysseus in returning to Ithaca and seeking shelter from the swineherd is reestablishing his home, whereas Werther by intruding at the assembly and in the love affair of two friends sets himself up against the social order. His need for freedom from social restrictions is far better expressed in the unfettered emotions described in *Ossian*, to which he turns frequently in the latter pages of the book. And yet the pathos of his isolated state is emphasized by the comfort he takes in reading of Odysseus' welcome by the swineherd. Goethe's use of the paradox is both subtle and complex.

Another paradoxical element lies in the selection of Lessing's *Emilia Galotti* as the book found open on Werther's desk after his suicide. Some critics have claimed that the play does not fit in any way with Werther's own story and that Goethe included it only because Kestner had mentioned it in his letter to Goethe about the death of Jerusalem. Treatments of the topic are, of course, innumerable. Among them, Georg Lukács's points to the social significance of choosing *Emilia Galotti*, calling it "until now the high point of revolutionary bourgeois literature."[24] Wilkinson and Willoughby see the significance of Lessing's play in Werther's and Goethe's response to its total import, that is, its portrayal of the effects of *Schwärmerei*, "not intensity of feeling, but a tendency to exalt that which is within . . . at the expense of that which is without,"[25] ignoring the claims of the factual situation. Still others see parallel elements in *Werther* and the Lessing drama, which represents for Edward Dvoretzky the *Entblätterung* theme, "the rose prematurely bereft of its petals,"[26] and symbol-izes Werther's loss of identity and his mental attitude in his last days. Somewhat more complex is Leonard Forster's reading of the Prince in *Emilia Galotti* as a Wertherian char-acter.[27] According to Forster, it is because Werther himself saw parallels between himself and the Prince that he chose suicide as expiation for his sin (his love for Lotte). Further-more, killing Albert might leave Werther alone as the Prince was alone at the end of *Emilia Galotti*. Thus the play serves as an object lesson for Goethe's hero. Robert Ittner also feels that there are strong parallel elements, such as Emilia's and Werther's common sense of guilt. Because Emilia wishes to atone for the death of her fiancé, for which she feels twice over guilty, Ittner draws the conclu-sion that the play furnishes a motif for the end of *Werther*, that it suggests that Werther too recognizes his guilt in ignoring the institutions of this world and acknowledges them by sacrificing his life.[28]

I would suggest, on the other hand, that *Emilia Galotti*, like the *Odyssey*, provides a contrary meaning. Rather than guilty and atoning, Goethe sees his hero as quite the op-posite of Emilia. Thus on 21 December Werther tells Charlotte that "I . . . must sacrifice myself for you. . . . One of us three must go" (p. 108); but after this expression of love and sacrifice for Lotte, he does not scruple to place her in the most painful situations—appearing when she does not expect him, involving her in emotional scenes in Albert's absence, and writing her alarming letters filled with references to their "love." The final sign of his lack of true concern is sending to Albert for the pistols, unforgiv-able behavior in one who wishes to spare Lotte pain. His final actions are all directed to involving her emotionally in his suicide—last desperate attempts to draw her attentions from Albert to him, to make her suffer his death. Further-more, he is overjoyed when his boy informs him that it was Charlotte who handed the boy the pistols, not con-sidering the anguish it cost her to do so. It is difficult to reconcile such behavior with atonement or an understanding of the unhappiness he has caused others. As Anna Karenina died hoping thus to win the attentions of Vronsky, so Werther dies in the vain hope of winning Charlotte's affections. Emotional hypocrisy was one of the chief characteristics of "Wertherism," whose devotees pretended concern for others but lavished it on themselves.

Therefore, Emilia Galotti, who recognizes her guilt, serves as the final and ultimate opposite of Werther; she is Goethe's concluding image, inspired by Lessing's play found open on Werther's desk. She makes clear to the reader the irony and pathos with which Goethe himself views those whose egocentric world bears no relationship to the world as seen by those around them. Emilia is seen as one who can make amends, whereas Werther serves only his own interests and sees reality only from his own special perspectives. Emilia's fiancé is dead; he cannot grieve for her as Werther hopes Charlotte will grieve for him. *Emilia Galotti* provides another one of the oppositions with which Goethe constructs the book. It is appropriate and ironic that in his last moments he should turn to Emilia Galotti, a figure who could have, if he had read her right, provided him with a positive solution to his dilemma. Emilia comes to terms with the conflict inherent in "die Einschränkung" in a way that Werther never can.

And finally it is of interest to note that Goethe's idea of morphology in nature fitted perfectly with his sense of artistic form. Form itself, for Goethe, was the principle at work in the living organism, and not simply a receptacle or "purely passive configuration."[29] "Inner structure determines outward shape and outward shape inner structure."[30] Furthermore, by the time he was twenty, he had learned from Herder about "the morphological approach to the study of cultures"[31] derived from Vico in his *Scienza Nuova*, Vico who was to be a profound influence on the structure employed by James Joyce over a hundred years later. The artist, Goethe saw, manifested in his activity the same process accomplished by natural creation, and the laws of creation were inherent within it, not "absolute norms, external to the individual work."[32] Nor is the organism, any more than Werther himself, separable from his environment, that protaean environment in *Werther* which changes in significance and shape, color and tone, texture and meaning with every transformation of the Wertherian mood.

1. Johann Wolfgang von Geothe, *The Sorrows of Young Werther*, Introduction by Victor Lange (New York: Holt, Rinehart, and Winston, 1949), p. vi. Subsequent references to this volume will be cited in the text.

2. See Hans Reiss, *Goethe's Novels*, p. 37.

3. Robert T. Clark, Jr., "The Psychological Framework of Goethe's *Werther*," p. 274.

4. Ibid., p. 275.

5. Erich Trunz, "Altersstil," *Goethe-Handbuch*, p. 564.

6. Reiss, pp. 36–37.

7. Ibid., p. 37.

8. Georg Lukács, *Goethe und seine Zeit*, p. 26. Unless otherwise indicated, translations from German in this chapter are my own.

9. Victor Lange, "Die Sprache als Erzählform in Goethe's *Werther*," in *Formenwandel: Festschrift zum 65 Geburtstag von Paul Bockmann*, p. 264.

10. Ibid., p. 269.

11. Ibid., p. 270.

12. Lienhard Bergel, "Cervantes in Germany," in Angel Flores and M. J. Benardete, eds., *Cervantes across the Centuries*, p. 329.

13. Ibid., p. 318.

14. Ibid.

15. Cf. Reiss, pp. 24–25 and Gerhard Storz, *Goethe-Vigilien*, p. 29.

16. Liselotte Dieckmann, "Repeated Mirror Reflections: The Technique of Goethe's Novels."

17. *Cymbeline*, 4.2.258.

18. Reiss, p. 23.

19. Ibid., p. 57.

20. Ibid., p. 31.

21. Ibid., p. 36.

22. Ibid., p. 31.

23. "The Blind Man and the Poet: An Early State in Goethe's Quest for Form," in *German Studies Presented to Walter Horace Bruford*, p. 50.

24. Lukács, p. 28.

25. "The Blind Man and the Poet: An Early State in Goethe's Quest for Form," pp. 43–45.

26. "Goethe's *Werther* and Lessing's *Emilia Galotti*," p.24.

27. "Werther's Reading of *Emilia Galotti*."

28. "Werther and 'Emilia Galotti,'" p. 426.

29. Elizabeth M. Wilkinson and L. A. Willoughby, *Goethe, Poet and Thinker*, p. 175.

30. Ibid., p. 176.

31. Ibid., p. 174.

32. Ibid.

Chapter Three

A Triad of Images:
Nature as Structure in *Madame Bovary*

Ortega y Gasset points out in *Meditations on Quixote* that "the characters of the novel [unlike those of the epic] are typical and non-poetic; they are taken, not from the myth . . . but from the street, from the physical world, from the living environment of the author."[1] In June 1852 Flaubert wrote to Louise Colet, "I discover all my origins in the book that I knew by heart before I read it, *Don Quixote*."[2] And according to Ortega, Emma may be seen as "a Don Quixote in skirts with a minimum of tragedy in her soul."[3] Both Quixote and Emma are "typical and non-poetic," "taken . . . from the street" and from the environments of their creators. "The consciousness of the human species has expanded since the time of Homer. Sancho Panza's belly has broken the sash about Venus's waist,"[4] writes Flaubert in 1853.

Flaubert's enthusiasm for *Don Quixote* began at the age of ten and persisted throughout his lifetime, as recurrent references to *Don Quixote* in his letters show. While working on *Madame Bovary*, he wrote in November 1852, again to Louise Colet:

> In the matter of reading, I do not give up Rabelais and Don Quixote on Sundays with Bouilhet. What overwhelming books! they grow in proportion to one's contemplation of them, like the pyramids, and one finishes them almost in fear. What is wonderful in *Don Quixote* is the absence of art and that perpetual fusion of illusion and reality which makes a book so comic and so poetic. What dwarfs all other books are by comparison. God, how small one feels! how small![5]

Although Flaubert admires in Cervantes' book the lack of self-conscious artistry, or "l'absence d'art," Flaubert's own artistic devices are more evident, his fusion of illusion and reality is more consciously structured. In another letter written in 1853, he speaks of the importance of understanding "the anatomy of style, to know how a phrase is constructed and what it modifies."[6] In no other novel discussed in this book is an anatomy more diligently and painstakingly created than in *Madame Bovary*. Flaubert's choice of the word *anatomie* is, of course, deliberate. A well-known anecdote is that of Flaubert as a boy perched on the wall of the hospital in Rouen in order to observe his father perform dissections in a nearby building. One cannot help but remember, too, in this context a follower and heir of Flaubert's techniques, James Joyce, who in his skeleton plan for *Ulysses* assigns an organ of the body to delineate each of his eighteen chapters. The purpose of the metaphor is, of course, to suggest that the coherence and unity of the work of art will equal nature's as manifest in the living body.

The mechanism in *Madame Bovary* perhaps most frequently cited is the counterpoint technique developed in the scene at the Agricultural Show in part two. Less attention has been given, however, to the means by which Flaubert fashions coherence within and among the three parts of the novel, building slowly triadic structures within the larger triad of the book itself. In the interests of verisimilitude, and in imitating physiology, Flaubert selects three basic components of life on earth (vegetable, animal, and mineral) as the imagistic gridiron for his novel. For both Cervantes and Flaubert, then, as Ortega tells us, "the form . . . contains the same thing that was in the content, but it presents in a clear, articulated, developed way what in the content was only a tendency or mere intention."[7]

The agrarian or rustic settings of part one articulate the nature of Emma's early experiences at Les Bertaux; of Charles's vegetable existence ("he throve like an oak") as a youth and young married man. The animal images in part two develop the theme of Emma's growing lusts and of the nature of her lovers (Léon—lion; Rodolphe—red); finally inanimate natural phenomena dominate part three, paralleling Emma's growing death wish, fulfilled through a metallic substance, arsenic; and Charles's death scene in which he is pushed over as if he were a puppet by little Berthe, who thinks he is playing. Both Emma and Charles become inanimate objects, like the predominant imagery in part three.

For a writer with the detachment of Flaubert, the image is a particularly fitting device because, as Benjamin Bart shows, it has a "natural place within the character portrayed."[8] Flaubert was, he himself said, "devoured by comparisons as beggars were by lice."[9] D.-L. Demorest offers perhaps the most complete treatment of imagery in the work of Flaubert.[10] Demorest goes beyond the scope of earlier discussions of Flaubert's imagery (such as those by Brunetière, Faguet, Maynial) by studying the grouping of imagery in the works, or the techniques and tendencies apparent in Flaubert's use of imagery. One grouping noted by M. Demorest is that of nature imagery, but he goes little further than to indicate that Flaubert consistently employs banal natural objects "which surround us everywhere,"[11] as M. Brunetière had already shown in his work on Flaubert.

Claudine Gothot-Mersch, in the chapter "Une Symphonie" in her book on the genesis of *Madame Bovary*, writes of the series of structural schemes that give *Madame Bovary* its unity. She goes on to point out that although a study of the technique of contrast in *Madame Bovary* is beyond the scope of her work, the oppositions in the book respond to a tendency in the temperament of the author.[12] One of the structures mentioned by Mlle Gothot-Mersch is that of the triad. *Madame Bovary* is, of course, written in three parts; there is also a relatively obvious grouping of episodes into three stages.

What is not noted is that the nature imagery employed by Flaubert generally falls into three main groupings. These groupings are constantly acting as foils for one another and as foils for the characters themselves. Situations and people in the novel are, as Mlle Gothot-Mersch shows, continually defined by opposition.[13] Water or liquid imagery, one central grouping of the nature imagery, universally symbolizes the vital and flowing quality of experience. Yet Flaubert's water images are often either sentimentalized or muddy, stained or medicated, as a result of man's intervention. Significantly, in table five, given at the end of M. Demorest's work, water imagery far outnumbers all other elemental images listed; Demorest counts a total of 259 water images in *Madame Bovary*.

A second grouping of images, vegetation images (Demorest lists 101 in *Madame Bovary*), symbolizes both fertility and growth. But Flaubert continually contrasts the flowering natural beauty of the Norman countryside with the squalid existences of those who live within its beauty and who convert its grasses to coarse stubble and its flowers to dried bridal bouquets, or who sentimentalize the exotic lemon tree of distant lands.

The third important grouping of natural imagery is that of animals and insects (Demorest lists 205), living counterparts to man himself. The virility and the simple instinctual nature of the animal stand in opposition to man, who harnesses the animal for his own purposes, which are frequently tawdry and lacking in real direction.

These three groups of images are skillfully alternated throughout each of the three parts of the book. Part one predominates in vegetation imagery, part two in animal imagery, and part three in water symbols. But in each part the two groupings that do not predominate provide counterpoint for the central image grouping. The myth of *bovarism* is the myth of sterility and civilized deformity. Natural productivity is constantly seen in the light of man's efforts to pervert its force. At the end of the book, the natural cycle continues although individual man dies as a result of his own misdirected efforts. The central thematic concern of the book—the cleavage between real and ideal, which controls it on many levels (as well as controlling its author)—is seen as a cleavage created synthetically by the mind of man, a schizophrenic pattern appearing also in *Don Quixote*.[14] Neither real nor ideal has meaning for nature itself, which incorporates both in its very being. Emma and Charles Bovary are perhaps grotesque shadows of Don Quixote and Sancho, and they present for the reader two alternative extremes of human behavior, two extremes that Flaubert treats ironically (even scathingly) by means of nature imagery.

It is possible to examine in detail the employment of Flaubert's three groups of symbols. The vegetation images in part one are sometimes arranged so that they form the positive pole of that part with which the negative pole, represented by nature distorted by man, interacts. For example, in chapter one, Charles thrives like an oak; later he imagines the coolness of a beech grove in the country. Yet the stream by which he lives is stained yellow and purple by dye factories; and as he pursues his studies, he is like the mill-horse walking blindfolded in a circle. On old Rouault's farm in chapter two, the houses, occupied by man, are dark stains by comparison, with even the leafless trees and the birds ruffling their feathers in the cold. As Charles's courtship of Emma progresses, the pear trees flower, although old Rouault wishes someone would stew pears for him. In these early chapters, where vegetation images are often used to suggest natural innocence, water and animal symbols are seen in a negative context, contorted by man.

Yet in the wedding scene in chapter four, it is as if all nature, even the vegetation, stands in opposition to this marriage. Coarse grasses and thistles attach themselves to Emma's wedding gown, the birds for long distances are frightened away by the sound of the fiddle, and foaming cider mugs and brimming wine glasses take their revenge on humans rather than on flies.

At Tostes the vegetation imagery, which at the Rouault farm had been a positive force, begins to be replaced by the imagery of Emma's fantasy world in which nature is contorted and idealized. The dried wedding bouquet of the first wife, some scrawny rose bushes, a thorn hedge are all that remains of Rouault's flowering pear, and Emma longs for a fountain and a fishpond to indulge her vanity. As Flaubert points out, her temperament was "more sentimental than artistic, and what she was looking for was emotions, not scenery."[15] Fish and water are both rerouted to this end.

In chapter six, the chapter taking the reader back to Emma's youth, Flaubert relates how she had rejected country life with its lowing herds, its animal-like simplicity, and replaced it by the sea, which she loved only for its storms, and by vegetation, which she loved only when it grew among ruins. In this paragraph the triad of vegetation, animal, and water imagery is clearly apparent. Here it is the passive animal imagery that retains its original innocence, whereas water and vegetation are seen aslant through the eyes of the heroine. Later in the chapter, the three natural elements are all contorted as Emma imagines turtle doves in Gothic bird cages, an "orderly virgin forest" (p. 43), and a sunbeam quivering perpendicularly in water.

A contrasting triad is formed as Emma's sentimental daydreams continue; she conjures up a honeymoon in which "the tinkling of goat bells," "the dull roar of waterfalls," and "the fragrance of lemon trees" (p. 45) coincide. Here it is the combination of the three images that is contrived, thereby sentimentalizing the scene.

From the idealized world of Emma's daydreams, we return abruptly to another world in chapter seven, to the dull landscape of Tostes with its sharp-edged rushes, to boredom ("like a silent spider"), and to sea winds that fill the country with a salt smell. The central animal image at Tostes, however, is Emma's bitch, Djali, representing nature tamed and domesticated by man, yet also yearning for its freedom. Symbolically the dog's Indian name, in addition to its exotic connotations, suggests the distances for which it longs. Flaubert is also obviously aware of the prosaic nature of Emma's name compared with the poetic name of the dog. Like Emma's thoughts, Djali strays, for in captivity she exists in an unnatural mode. Yet unless nature is held captive by man, it can threaten man's very being. The ugliness that Emma sees near at hand in Tostes and in her marriage to Charles is merely the same benevolent captivity in which Djali is held. But like Djali, Emma runs away. The animal imagery, which begins to move into the foreground at this point, leads smoothly into part two where this second image group predominates.

But before this occurs, we turn to Vaubyessard, which offers a curious parallelism with Rouault's farm, which had introduced the vegetation imagery in part one. Vaubyessard points to the close of the circular pattern of this section. The triad at the opening of chapter eight consists of cows, shrubbery, and a flowing stream. The grazing cows represent the same sort of simple bucolic setting that Emma had rejected at Les Bertaux, but which is now exalted in her eyes by its proximity to the château. The variegated shrubbery and the bridge under which the stream flows are, of course, man's improvements on nature. Furthermore, the elaborate dinner prepared at Vaubyessard sharply contrasts with the simple but abundant wedding dinner served at Les Bertaux. Instead of an entire suckling pig, meat is brought on in slices; in place of cider, the marquis serves champagne; and pineapples and pomegranates replace the almonds, raisins, and oranges. What has changed is the quality of the relationship to food, which is less direct at Vaubyessard than at Les Bertaux. The categories of food served are similar, but the means by which they have been obtained differ, adding to their character a romantic appeal. Parallelism, however, is established by Emma herself, who is reminded of the farm at Les Bertaux as she sees the faces of the peasants pressed against the panes. She conjures up the muddy pond, the apple trees, and herself skimming cream with her finger. The ironic contrast with the scene at Vaubyessard is marked. Back at Tostes there are onion soup and veal for dinner, and Emma stares in amazement at fruit trees and flower beds once so familiar.

The use of the triad device enables Flaubert to create a variety of effects. Parallels may exist both within the triad and between triads. Thus the differences noted in the two landscapes are reinforced by the differences in the two meals. Every detail inserted by Flaubert is calculated, so that the reader participates in Emma's mounting frustrations. At the same time, Emma's memories of Les Bertaux stress the muddy pond and her menial task, whereas her vision of Vaubyessard ignores the ugliness of the marquis's father-in-law, Marie Antoinette's lover, who sits dribbling gravy from his mouth.

Next spring at Tostes when the pear trees burst into bloom, Emma finds it difficult to breathe. Man and his institutions are seen to be stunted by comparison with the regular and luxuriant flowering of nature, the pear trees that had been associated with Charles's courtship of her. The liquids in this final chapter of part one consist of camphor baths and valerian drops, concoctions for the ailing, and vinegar, Emma's means of losing weight. The animal, Djali, becomes in Emma's sick imagination a confidante, and to the dog she tells many secrets. The burning of the bridal bouquet at the end is a symbolic rejection of the flowering and growth of the vegetation that dominates part one. It is fitting that this imagery accompanies the announcement of a pregnancy Emma hates. From now on we will note the gradual development of the animal imagery in part two, which is dominated by this image cluster. At the end of part one, portions of the burned bridal bouquet fly up the chimney like black butterflies, suggesting both the metamorphosis in the imagery as well as the metamorphosis in Emma's nature, as she becomes more debased, more animal-like and as the name, Bovary, becomes more and more fitting.

II

Although the animal imagery increases with the intensity of Emma's appetites, part two opens with a nature passage stressing vegetation and tying this part to the one that precedes it. The pastures, the grainfields, and the streams extend below the oaks of the Aragueil forest. This is the same kind of landscape Flaubert has visualized near the marquis's château and has connected with Emma's childhood on the farm. The cider presses also are a link with Les Bertaux. On the outskirts of Yonville, the image triad consists of aspens and hedges, cider presses and distilling sheds, and window panes with a bull's-eye in the center of each. The pear trees are espaliered and scraggly, supplying a note of foreboding and contrasting with the blooming pears found early in part one.

However, the character of the imagery in part two is suggested by the Gallic cock on the top pediment of the town hall. This image, aggressive and assertive, contrasts with the more passive vegetation images of part one and points to the growing sensual nature of Emma's affairs in this part. Furthermore, the name of the hotel in Yonville is Lion d'Or, clearly reinforcing the central motif. Both Léon and the Lion d'Or, however, represent somewhat less virility than the king of beasts. On the main street of Yonville, we encounter a dry goods shop and a pharmacy, the sterile companions of the golden lion. As the Hirondelle (the swallow) pulls up before the inn, we learn that Djali, Emma's greyhound, has escaped. Emma, like Djali, is soon to escape the mold of the dry society that she despises, for with the freeing of Djali comes the freeing of Emma's passions as she stretches out her foot toward the leg of mutton turning on the spit and talks to Léon of idealized natural settings, pastures at the top of bluffs, huge pine trees, roaring streams, and infinite oceans. Although Charles is always on horseback in the course of his work, for Léon "there's nothing more charming than riding. . . . If you have the opportunity, of course" (pp. 91–92). It is clear from these examples that animal imagery plays the central role in part two as vegetation and water symbols take second place. Yet the three kinds of symbols are still usually found in conjunction with one another. Thus from Emma's new bedroom, we have a view of the tops of trees and of moonlight on the river, but inside the room we find the disorder left by two moving men, nature's serenity in contrast to animal-man's confusion.

The wet nurse, in chapter 3, whose role is that of the animal provider for Emma's baby, lives in a house surrounded by a scraggly garden, a walnut tree, and a trickle of dirt water. Returning from her house, however, Emma and Léon walk by a swiftly running river, long grasses bending in the current, and spidery-legged insects poised on lily pads. This particular scene is brightly lighted by sunbeams, a positive force; Emma's sentimental dreams are often lighted by the rays of the moon.

As Emma's passion for Léon grows, both lovers tend hanging gardens in their windows. At the same time, love is compared by Flaubert to an engulfing thunderstorm leaving its pools of rain on roofs, pools that may pose a danger to the house. It is water imagery that accompanies Emma's downfall in part three.

A bouquet of straw and wheat, tied to the peak of one of the gables at the new flax mill, introduces chapter five. This image of dried vegetation sharply contrasts with the hanging gardens, the swift streams, the long grasses that have accompanied the initial phase of the love affair; the bouquet also reminds one of the two dried wedding bouquets in part one. Emma's carnal desires, her inner storms, continue for the moment, but the dried bouquet of vegetation suggests an outcome ironically different from that signified by the earlier image—the Gallic cock.

Chapter six brings us full circle to another April with its flowers, its full streams, and its grazing cattle. It was April when Emma had arrived in Yonville. Nature, imperturbable and indifferent to human activity, continues its fruitful cycle although the cycles of man are full of interruptions and reverses. Although nature flowers, Léon departs for Paris. The Agricultural Show, at which the animal theme receives it culminating emphasis, serves to bridge Emma's two affairs in part two, for Homais announced the event at the end of the chapter in which Léon leaves.

The affair with Rodolphe abounds in various animal symbols. In fact, the emphasis on this imagery increases. After Léon's departure Emma has looked back with "mournful melancholy" at the water and flower scenes that accompanied her romance with Léon, but her hopes are now "like dead branches in the wind" (p. 140). By contrast blood imagery accompanies the meeting with Rodolphe, the forceful and animal spurt of blood from the peasant's arm. The name Rodolphe, of course, connotes red, a different red from that of the blood Emma has been spitting during the depression over Léon's removal. Life and death are curiously knotted in this scene of bloodletting. Both Justin and the peasant faint, temporarily die, as the animal stream gushes forth; but Emma and Rodolphe remain conscious, for their roles are connected with the "undoing" of life.

The Agricultural Show represents the obvious climax of the animal theme in part two. Even the townspeople at the show are described by Flaubert by means of animal symbols. The legs of Binet seem to contain all of his vital energies, like the legs of a horse; or Homais's reverse-calf shoes represent the character of the apothecary, an "inside-out" animal who poses as a man of civilization. Water and vegetation are overwhelmed in this chapter by a proliferation of human animals and domestic beasts, even though the pediment of the town hall has been looped with ivy, a sign of perennial plant vitality. Pigs, calves, cows, rearing stallions, mares are lined up to be judged by a group of gentlemen who advance with heavy step. Horses and Hippolyte (a name derived from the Greek word for *horse*) go off together toward the stables. And Emma and Rodolphe, sitting on the second floor of the town hall, half listen to the speeches, while Rodolphe argues that casting off the animal skins of savage ages cost man more disadvantages than benefits. The planting scenes cited by Monsieur Derozerays are accompanied by Rodolphe's eulogies of the instinctive animal man and by the imagery of water as he compares his inclinations and Emma's to two rivers at their confluence—another variation of the nature triad basic to the imagery of the novel. The merging of man and animal is made total by the appearance of Catherine Leroux, who through living among animals has taken on "their muteness and placidity" (p. 170). Yet Catherine Leroux is an authentic figure by contrast with the studied savage reversion suggested by Rodolphe. Her life has been one of service to man and to animal; Rodolphe's and Emma's aim is temporary gratification of both vanity and the senses. Man's fireworks, like those stored in Monsieur Tuvache's cellar (*vache*, of course, meaning cow), are damp and will not go off.

Homais's article, which concludes the chapter, combines once again all three nature images. The topic is, of course, the Agricultural Show, but a show transformed by his pen beyond recognition, a show festooned by garlands of flowers and attended by crowds rushing "like the billows of a raging sea" (p. 173). Flaubert makes it perfectly clear in this chapter that authentic animal existence has no relation to the sick and contorted image made by social man. Catherine Leroux with her fifty-four years of service wins her medal by means far more honorable than Homais's methods in winning "la croix d'honneur." The animal imagery in this chapter counterpoints the activity of man in the same way that the vegetation imagery at Les Bertaux and La Vaubyessard counterpointed the petty idealisms displayed by humans who inhabited these places and who tampered with nature for their own selfish and narrow ends. Yet man is finally defeated in his foolish pursuits, whereas nature, like Catherine Leroux, persists, and the cycle of seasons produces ever new vegetation, new foals and calves, and spring freshets. These for Flaubert stand in stark contrast to the fevered imaginings and cerebrations of Emma Bovary and her lovers in their sterile and short-range affairs. The irony of this chapter is sharp because of the abrupt animal-man contrasts brought out by the well-known counterpoint technique. The very name *Bovary* suggests that these contrasts were to be of major importance in Flaubert's novel.

After this point in part two, animal imagery commences

gradually to recede in favor of water imagery, which is to dominate part three. (In the same way, the dog Djali in part one foreshadowed the animal theme in part two.) Although the lovemaking between Emma and Rodolphe is connected with horseback riding, their union takes place in the woods, in the midst of vegetation, by a little pond. Emma's blood flows like a river of milk. Earlier in the scene Emma looks as if she were swimming "under limpid water" (p. 180). It is a sense of becoming submerged that overcomes Emma in the final portion of the book and that makes the water symbolism appropriate for part three. It should be noted in this connection that, according to M. Demorest's table 5, water is the dominant nature image in the entire book.

The waning pleasures of Emma's love affair with Rodolphe are compared in chapter ten to the ebbing of the water of a river. At the same time, the yearly gift of a turkey and an accompanying letter from M. Rouault remind Emma of foals whinnying and galloping in the fields, of bees and beehives. M. Rouault has planted a plum tree under Emma's window at Les Bertaux, but in Yonville-L'Abbaye, Lestiboudois rakes up the cut grass. Although at the Agricultural Show and in the lovemaking scene horses had played an immediate and vital role, now foals are memories for Emma, as are the bees. Likewise the new plum tree is far removed from Emma's present window under which not planting but cutting and raking (performed by the sexton who will dig Emma's grave) is taking place. Furthermore, the cock to be sent by M. Rouault will be a dead cock. The ebb of water is symbolically removing both plant and animal life, all growth, from Emma and her environment. The cock imagery is particularly appropriate at this point, for it recalls the Gallic cock on the pediment of the town hall at the beginning of part two, an image used to prefigure the more virile nature of this section. However, it is clear by chapter ten that the cock is doomed to die, and that by next year Emma may need more than M. Rouault's gift of a dead bird.

The horse imagery, which has been part of the entire

episode involving Rodolphe, forms the basis, indirectly at least, of the next chapter concerning the operation on Hippolyte's foot. Horses appeared at the Agricultural Show; Emma and Rodolphe rode out to the consummation of their affair. Now an operation is about to be performed on a man whose name bears at least two associations with horses. *Hippos* is, of course, the Greek word for horse, Furthermore, Hippolytus in Greek mythology was dragged to his death by horses after Theseus had petitioned Poseidon for punishment. The use of the name Hippolyte suggests complex but unmistakable mythical overtones. Hippolyte himself is hardly more than a horse, very like the horses he tends. Moreover, like his mythical forebear, he receives an unjust punishment at the hands of the gods. The modern Phaedra is Emma Bovary, who is using Hippolyte for her own selfish and vain ends. Hippolyte is maimed as Hippolytus had been killed. Dark liquid oozes from his leg. This operation symbolically injures the very root of his existence, for to the horse the leg means survival, and he is destroyed when his legs no longer perform. The operation and the ensuing amputation also symbolically indicate the excision of the thematic concern with animals in part two.

In the evening after the amputation, Emma meets Rodolphe in the garden on the lowest step of the river stairs. As Brunetière has pointed out, Flaubert's nature imagery is often so banal that it goes unnoticed. Yet after the animal screams of Hippolyte, which have rent the village that day, the simple and idyllic conclusion involving a garden and a river provides welcome relief. Although the horses of pain and passion have been stilled, the passive garden and river persist and remain as backdrop for the imprudent enterprises of man. The animal, the dominant concern of part two, is destroyed or maimed when it is used as it has been by Emma for her own vain ends. And yet ironically it is this very animal that serves man most faithfully. Rather than frightened horses, it is the raging sea of Poseidon, the sea of passion, that will cause Emma's death. (Still, the myth element remains. Out of the sea comes the bull [symbol of lust] that terrifies the horses; it is, thus, the sea that is the source of death in the myth, also. The irony is that Emma has offended not Aphrodite but Athena.) Meanwhile the river threatening and writhing like a serpent flows in the background at Emma's last meeting with Rodolphe, although their memories are concerned with the silent rivers, the perfumed syringas, and the prowling night animals they have seen in earlier days. After Emma's desertion by Rodolphe, she feels as if she were on a pitching ship. She develops an aversion to her garden and has it re-landscaped; her horse is sold.

The tumult of a storm at sea (the kind of storm she had dreamed of in the safety of the convent) descends upon Emma in the final chapter of part two. The animal-man is now in the clutches of Poseidon as the double basses at the opera (cf. the operation) remind Emma of the cries of ship-wrecked sailors "against the tumult of a storm" (p. 252). And yet the animal motif is not entirely submerged, for among the crowd at the opera Emma meets Léon (lion). The elements of the nature triad—vegetation, animal, and water—will continue to interact in part three. M. Demorest has called Flaubert's writing of *Madame Bovary* a "new and perilous voyage of discovery."[16] Surely Flaubert's complex use of imagery proves Demorest's point. Rarely in novels do we find such a conscious and calculated use of common objects to enrich thematic patterns.

III

The waters of part three are not, however, always the crashing and tumultuous storms of Emma's youthful dreams. Still, the tempest evoked at the opera is skillfully carried over by Flaubert into chapter one of part three through the comparison of the carriage in which Emma and Léon make love to a ship tossing at sea. (At the same time, Flaubert echoes the scene of lovemaking in part two, for horses have carried Emma and Rodolphe to that scene as horses now draw Emma and Léon.) Accompanying the image of the sea and completing the triad are the torn bits of paper (thrown from the cab by Emma) that are compared to white butterflies alighting on a field of red clover. The sea image here, however, is the dominant image—the butterflies and the clover evoking merely postoral quietude. (The white butterflies may also recall the black butterflies that floated up the chimney as Emma burned her bridal bouquet and so suggest the theme of another metamorphosis.) Thus Emma's resolution to reject Léon is discarded, as are the vegetation and animal symbols of part one and two, in favor of the tossing cab, the stormy sea, to which the heroine abandons herself. This final love affair with Léon is accompanied not by images of growth and life, plant and animal, but by the inanimate elements.

However, instead of romantic storms at sea, the liquid imagery in part three is often of a medical or chemical nature, as the function of Homais's Capharnaum becomes apparent. The liquids of chapter two are the acids and alkaline solutions of the pharmacy. The chapter opens with a description of jelly-making in the village, not with the boiling ocean but with the sticky, boiling jelly of the kitchens of Yonville. This picture corresponds to the pictures of foaming cider in part one, but the temperature of the juice is now at the boiling point. The arsenic, with which Justin absentmindedly threatens the lives of Homais and his family, could have combined with the juice to bring destruction. This boiling cauldron of liquid is the dominating image of the chapter, rather than the maimed Hippolyte, who stumps in with Emma's bags, or the fragile violets brought by Léon. Vegetable and animal life now play secondary roles by comparison with the role of liquids in part three.

Chapter three of this section is full of water imagery. The hotel where Emma and Léon stay is on the riverfront. At dusk they drift downstream (suggesting the direction of their affair) on a river polluted by great oily patches. The river flows toward the ocean, but Emma and Léon land on

an island where vegetation imagery once more predominates, the grass, the poplars, and the breeze in the
branches, reminiscent of part one, as if Emma's progress
toward death, toward the ocean, were temporarily halted.
Left behind in the city is the barking of dogs, the animal
theme of part two that has been associated with Rodolphe.

When the lovers next meet, it is in Yonville during a
thunderstorm. Again the suggestion of inundation by
water occurs, and the scene takes place, of course, in the
garden.

But in the city where Emma goes to take her "music
lessons," the trees are leafless, and Rouen has "the static
quality of a painting" (p. 299). The islands in the river look
like huge black fish, and smoke pollutes the air as oil has
polluted the water. In the city, nature is despoiled as the
result of man's presence. But the three galloping horses
that draw the Hirondelle bearing Emma into the city take
us back to the imagery of part two, and the bed in the form
of a boat, in which she and Leon sleep, to the tossing cab,
now unyoked, at the beginning of part three. Liquids flow
not only in the rivers and fountains in chapter five but in
the running sores of the blind beggar and in the perspira-
tion of Emma as she hurries through the streets of Rouen.
Finally the triad of absinthe, cigars, and oysters (liquid,
vegetable, animal)—smells in the rue Nationale—symbolizes in microcosm the larger imagery pattern in the book.

As adultery begins to pall, Emma's thoughts return to
the protective elms near the convent of her youth and to
her rides in the forest. Vegetation scenes and animals exist
now only in memory, and "the leaden river shivered in the
wind" (p. 331). It is as if even the water shivers before the
coming storm that will engulf Emma. At the beginning of
her desperate search for money, she is threatened once by
crowds, pouring out of the cathedral like a river, and again
by prancing black horses, driven by a man who reminds
her of the vicomte. Nature itself seems to collaborate in her
downfall, for Emma has long courted the destructive forces
of life. After her attempt to borrow money from Rodolphe

fails, night falls and crows fly overhead, dismal harbingers of her death.

Although arsenic is the immediate means of Emma's suicide, the entire section describing her death is dominated symbolically by the imagery of the storm at sea. The convulsive movements that accompany Emma's final hours, her heaving body and rolling eyes, her gasping breath and her flowing tears, become a horrible parody of the romantic storms at sea she has envisaged and of the scenes of passion with her lovers. The storm reaches its peak in the death scene, and Emma's ship at last shudders and succumbs to the furious waves. Flaubert writes: "everything seemed drowned by the monotonous flow of Latin syllables" (p. 369).

In the final chapters of the book, it is clear that nature continues to be employed by man in foolish ways to abet his vanity. Thus Charles's desire for three coffins, one of oak, one of mahogany, and one of lead, exemplifies man's frivolous attempt to forestall decay and separation. For ironically, the arsenic that was chosen by Emma for her destruction is related to the lead chosen by Charles as a means of preserving her body. Likewise the herbs, the camphor, the benzoin, and the chlorine water contributed by Homais are futile gestures, as is the holy water sprinkled by the priest. These pharmaceutical and religious panaceas seem trivial beside the joyous sounds of spring that accompany Emma's burial.

Here, once again, the three elements of the nature triad are united, as colts bolt off under apple trees, and dewdrops shimmer on the thorn hedges. Nature persists and recurs, indifferent to, and despite, man's failures. Appropriately Emma's bier moves through the cemetery "like a boat pitching at every wave" (p. 383). The sea of passion that has submerged her cannot rest until her body is interred, but meanwhile spring is rejuvenating the earth with new vegetable life, new animal life, and fresh streams of water, beside which the holy sprinkler of Bournisien seems like a gaudy trinket. The destructive imagery of the ocean accompanies Emma's burial to the very end, when Charles drags himself toward the grave "as though to be swallowed up in it with her" (p. 384).

With Emma's death a final sterility seems to settle on human activity in the last chapter. The natural cycle continues as Charles sits grieving in his arbor, but the blind beggar (the animal) is locked up to satisfy Homais's political ambitions; Homais designs even the grass in his garden to reflect his own glory, the Legion of Honor; and Charles's mind is flooded by futile memories. The capping irony is the cotton mill where little Berthe is sent by her aunt to work. It is as if the vegetation symbolism of part one were here purposefully revived in the form of a dead fiber (like the dead wedding bouquets and the bouquet of wheat and straw on the flax mill) to remind the reader of the sterile nature of Emma's legacy. Moreover, the dry goods dealer, M. Lheureux, has had a hand in luring Emma to her destruction.

The details studied in the course of this chapter, numerous as they are, simply serve to indicate the tremendous conscious complexity of Flaubert's techniques. More still could be said, but proof here is sufficient to show the skill with which Flaubert manipulated these three image groups. In reading *Madame Bovary*, one has a feeling, as M. Demorest has well expressed it, "a little like that which one has in listening to a very beautiful and substantial new symphony played by an intelligent and sympathetic orchestra under a genius as director."[17] The same judgment could be made, of course, of *Don Quixote*.

1. Ortega y Gasset, *Meditations on Quixote,* p. 127.

2. Gustave Flaubert, *Correspondance 1850–1859,* 13:203. Unless otherwise indicated, translations from French in this chapter are my own.

3. Ortega y Gasset, p. 162.

4. Flaubert, *Correspondance,* 13:379.

5. Ibid., pp. 251–52.

6. Ibid., p. 407.

7. Ortega y Gasset, pp. 112–13.

8. Benjamin F. Bart, *Flaubert*, p. 351.

9. Ibid., p. 350.

10. D.-L. Demorest, *L'Expression figurée et symbolique dans l'oeuvre de Gustave Flaubert*.

11. Ibid., p. 426.

12. Claudine Gothot-Mersch, *La Genèse de "Madame Bovary,"* p. 224.

13. Ibid., p. 223.

14. Marianne Bonwit, "Gustave Flaubert et le principe d'impassibilité," p. 286.

15. Gustave Flaubert, *Madame Bovary, Patterns of Provincial Life,* trans. Francis Steegmuller (New York: Modern Library, 1957), p. 41. Subsequent references to this volume will be cited in the text.

16. Demorest, p. 418.

17. Ibid., p. 480.

Chapter Four

Spatial Patterns in *The Brothers Karamazov*

As Ludmilla B. Turkevich tells us in her essay "Cervantes in Russia," Dostoevsky was deeply impressed by *Don Quixote*."[1]

> "A more profound and more powerful work than this one [*Don Quixote*] is not to be found," he says. "It is the finest and greatest utterance of the human mind. It is the bitterest irony that only man could express." It is the key to life showing "how man's purity, wisdom, simplicity, benignity, manliness, and finally his great mind . . . go to waste, go without benefit to mankind and are even turned to ridicule . . . only because these highly noble and lavish gifts . . . lack but one final gift—namely the genius to manage and to guide all this power along the road of truth and not of fantasy and madness, along the path that is for the benefit of humanity."

Dostoevsky must have seen that his predecessor, Cervantes, unlike his character Don Quixote, did not lack the genius "to manage and to guide" his own powers of creation, nor did Dostoevsky himself fail to manage his. Despite the verdicts of nineteenth-century English criticism (Matthew Arnold, in particular) or of Henry James in America, Dostoevsky's novels are models of precise structure and craftsmanship. One noteworthy essay on the form of *The Brothers Karamazov* by Victor E. Amend suggests musical parallels such as theme, subordinate themes, counterpoint, and modulations to describe the careful development of this novel. In brief, the unifying theme, "man's search for God the Father,"[2] is extended, according to Amend, by three subordinate themes, each concerned with one of the brothers. These themes play against each other in contrapuntal fashion until the novel ends *fortissimo* with a restatement of the central theme in the "manner of the best romantic composers."[3]

Whereas the structure of *Crime and Punishment* reflects the psychological crisis in the life of Raskolnikov, the structure of Dostoevsky's later novel *The Brothers Karamazov* reflects instead the spiritual crisis in the lives of the brothers, Dmitri, Ivan, and Alyosha. As a result of their careful structuring, both books, from the Russian realistic movement, give evidence of an architecture that has rarely been surpassed in the history of the long novel.

According to Robert Louis Jackson, "A certain formal aptitude in the arts may have been indirectly stimulated through his studies in drawing and draughtsmanship in the Engineering School."[4] Dostoevsky's almost geometric sense of order is also noted by Edward Wasiolek, who remarks on the "compartmentalized chaos" to be found in the notebooks. "One discovers," he writes, "almost a geometric symmetry in the disposition of the notes."[5] An examination of the original pages of the notebooks shows this to be consistently true. In the same way, we observe in studying the architecture of *The Brothers Karamazov* that certain geometrical or spatial forms control its structure or become objective correlatives, serving to sharpen meaning in the entire development of the book. Wasiolek takes note of the "subtlety, psychological and ideational," that "often intervenes between notes and novel: ideas are refined, structural relationships are discovered, introduced, made more complex."[6]

Polar opposition is a concept in which not only distance between opposites but interaction of opposites are inherent. Thus the poles in a battery interact to produce electricity, or the north and south poles of a planet complement one another magnetically. Such a concept underlies the epigraph to *The Brothers Karamazov*: "except a corn of wheat fall into the ground and die, it abideth alone: but if it die, it bringeth forth much fruit" (John 12:24). The opposites, death and life, are thus united in the act of creation, in the falling of the seed and in its regeneration.

Another form of creative opposition is that of the triad or

triangle (exemplified by Dostoevsky's troika) in which three points instead of two stand in relation to one another. Dostoevsky makes most obvious use of this form in the triad of the three brothers, representing body, mind, and spirit. It is reminiscent, of course, of the Christian trinity and the creative interaction of those three elements—father, son, and holy spirit. Any triangle is given definition by means of, and according to, the position of its three points. Thus an act by any one of the brothers changes or modifies the triadic structure. Smerdyakov, who stands apart from the triangle, a point in isolation, a half-brother, is unable to interact creatively because he lacks both peers and counterparts. As Robert Lord points out, "The interplay of these characters and their separate worlds is of a 'polyphonic' kind, more like an interweaving than a blend."[7]

The third spatial form, that of the sphere, inherent in *The Brothers Karamazov*, embodies the solution toward which the entire book moves. In the sphere there is no opposition, only coherence. In it we find concentricity, layer upon layer, overlapping and underlapping, and all points on the surface of the sphere are equidistant from its center. It is represented by the onion of Grushenka, which acts as objective correlative. It will be shown that oppositions, either polar or triadic, in each book ultimately dissolve in favor of a spherical reality that is expressed in the message of the conclusion in the epilogue when "hand in hand" the boys shout in unison, "Hurrah for Karamazov!" In almost all the twelve books of *The Brothers Karamazov*, we find, then, a slowly developing concentricity, incomplete and sometimes indistinct in the earlier books but soon, by books six and seven, reaching a full expression through the subject matter and the imagery.

In this connection, a scholar of Russian literature, Marina Bergelson Raskin, of Purdue University, writes to me:

> I think that the aesthetic sense of the sphere, the spheric, round shape, is inherent in the Russian culture. In old Russian paintings, for instance, the fluid, plastic, rounded line was

84

very important, reaching its peak of perfection in Andrei
Rublev's "Trinity," which graphically represents an ideal
sphere.

Original Russian architecture, which was highly developed
before the Tartar invasion, then practically disappeared, and a
few centuries later started to develop in a very different direction, was also spheric. Unlike Western church architecture (all
the early cathedrals were built in the shape of the cross, when
seen from above), the Russian churches of the 10th–12th centuries were round. Traditionally, it was important to design a
Russian church in such a way that one could go through all the
aisles and complete a circle.

Of course, the typical rounded dome of the Russian church,
the 'bulb' (or, in Russian literally, 'onion') is another interesting example.

I am not a specialist but if I were an anthropologist I would
probably want to explore the connection between the old
Russian painting and architecture, on the one hand, and
Russian folklore, on the other, where the narration is always
circular, as compared to other national folklores (Icelandic, for
instance) where it is linear.

It is perhaps appropriate to note here that Christianity came
late to Russia, in the 9th century, and while the country was
still pagan—which, of course, it always remained in many
senses—people worshipped Yarilo, the Sun, and one can see
its round shape in the cultural monuments of the time.

To introduce a very different theme, a Russian writer of the
last century, Leskov, wrote in a lengthy passage on female
beauty stating that the Russian idea of a nice-looking woman is
very different from the European one. We Russians, he said,
do not care very much for the features, for the face, as long as
the nose is upturned and the face is full, but everything must
be round, all the shapes, all the curves, because 'roundness
brings merriness to the eye.'

To summarize, it is difficult to say whether Dostoevsky uses
the spheric design in *The Brothers Karamazov* intentionally and
consciously, as a creative device, or because it simply permeates the culture, and his taste and aesthetic sense as part of that
culture, and thus finds its way into the novel.

Keeping Marina Raskin's important perspectives in
mind, let us turn now to the close study of structural patterns in *The Brothers Karamazov*. Book one displays at once,
in its opening and concluding chapters, one and five, the

polar opposition between Karamazov and the monastery, that is, between old Fyodor and Father Zossima. The temptation of Satanic pride is one to which old Fyodor has fallen prey whereas self-abnegation, self-conquest, and submission to God's will characterize the Elder. Two kinds of fatherhood are thereby contrasted, that of Karamazov, abject, vicious, and senseless, and that of Zossima, someone on earth who was "holy and exalted." Edward Wasiolek has remarked that "behind the opponents, circumstances, issues, and programs of history, Dostoevsky confronts something primal, universal, and personal: the Elder Zossima and Father Fyodor, the spiritual father and the earthly father, the beautiful, kind, unselfish, self-sacrificing father and the ugly, cruel, taunting, predatory father. Dostoevsky had been writing his 'fathers and children' at least since *The Idiot*."[8]

In the same book, book one, the first meeting of the three brothers is effected, establishing the underlying triadic shape of the novel. The character of each brother is firmly set in separate chapters of book one—Dmitri, the sensualist; Ivan, the intellectual; and Alyosha, the spiritual force. At the end of book one, a gathering of the Karamazovs in the cell of Father Zossima is proposed, an early attempt (even though suggested in jest by old Fyodor) to achieve unity and coherence within the family. Thus book one, which is sometimes cited as a kind of overture in which all the central melodic themes may be found in embryo, moves as the work as a whole moves from oppositions (dual and triple) toward the sphere of human concord.

Book two likewise moves from discord toward an attempted gathering together of forces, but it is an "unfortunate" gathering, as the title of the book tells us. Oppositions abound as the old buffoon Fyodor sets foot in monastic surroundings. Complementing him is the female buffoon, Madame Hohlakov, who serves as a contrast to "the peasant women who have faith." Furthermore, in the triad of brothers, Dmitri, Ivan, and Alyosha, each one is by himself involved in a contrariety: Dmitri, torn between Katerina and Grushenka—a young lady of good family and an enchantress; Ivan in his dialectic, torn between state and ecclesiastical control; and Alyosha drawn between monastic life and life in the outside world. Father Zossima, in bowing to Dmitri and saying, "Good-bye! Forgive me, all of you!",[9] attempts to form a spherical whole of these conflicting forces; but the meaning of his gesture is lost on those present, and the scene is summed up in Miüsov's remark, "I can't answer for a madhouse and for madmen" (p. 85). In bowing to the sinner, Father Zossima suggests, as the Devil impishly later tells Ivan, that good and evil are interdependent, that "suffering is life" (p. 780). He who suffers, suffers for other men, taking upon himself the cross that someone must carry. And in asking their forgiveness, he implies that he like them is prey to human frailty and error. In other words, as Father Zossima has told Ivan, it is not the fact of suffering in itself that is important, but the way that one integrates that suffering into life. "Thank the Creator," he says, "who had given you a lofty heart capable of such suffering: of thinking and seeing higher things" (p. 80). But despite the Father's wisdom and compassion, dissension and malice intensify in the group, and culminate in the ironic "second coming" of old Fyodor, who returns unexpectedly to heap further calumny upon the holy fathers.

Books three, four, and five form a triad in themselves, each one developing more fully a single brother Karamazov and his particular conflict. At the same time, however, each of these three books presents significant polar oppositions that deepen and enrich the characterization of each brother. In book three, for example, "the sensualists," old Fyodor and Dmitri, are seen to be of different and opposing natures, different sorts of sinners. Fyodor, who has raped the half-wit Lizaveta in the gutter, is of a different stripe from his son Dmitri, who in quoting Schiller's "Hymn to Joy" is at least aware of the "vision of God's throne" even though consigning himself to the in-

sects. He is, therefore, redeemable; and in his three confessions to Alyosha, taking up three chapters of book
three, lie the beginnings of his salvation.

Two other contasting characters in book three are
Grushenka and Katerina, who both play major roles in
Dmitri's "confessions." Agafya is a woman of loose conduct who offers her services "freely without asking for
payment" (p. 130); Katerina, on the contrary, is "a person
of character, proud and really high-principled," a woman
of "education and intellect" (p. 131). However, the opposition created by these two women becomes not productive
but counterproductive because they are not true polar opposites, but share the same self-centeredness in different
guise. In Katerina's forced bowing down to Dmitri, we find
the opposite of Father Zossima's voluntary bowing down
at the monastery. Perceptively Ernest Simmons points out
that "she continually lacerates herself in welcoming
Dmitri's insults, and that her submissiveness and self-
abasement have their roots in her towering pride."[10]
Katerina's pride thus contrasts with the holy father's humility, and it is her pride that finds a parallel in Dmitri's
egoism. Likewise Grushenka's coquetry and vanity find a
parallel in Dmitri's sensuality. Self-centered in different
ways, the two women despise one another, and both are
using Dmitri with frivolous intentions. Both women want
to save Dmitri from himself, but Katerina's offer to marry
him is a self-inflicted punishment, like Father Ferapont's
self-directed flagellations. On the other hand, Grushenka's
later commitment to Dmitri is in the nature of understanding, reciprocity, and interdependency, coming after the
scene of her redemption with Alyosha. Simmons takes
note that "generosity, a wide soul, and a capacity to suffer
seem to effect a synthesis in the contending forces of her
nature."[11] It is a synthesis that Katerina is not likely to
achieve.

Dmitri, in lavishing on Grushenka money stolen from
Katerina, exhibits not selfless giving but egoism and fear,
fear that old Fyodor will prevail and win Grushenka as a

result of his ability to pay her. His continual shaming and humiliation of Katerina come from the same need to dominate and the same egoism. It is only when he hears Grushenka's selfless offer to go into exile with him, to expiate their mutual guilt, that the vicious circle of prideful acts is broken and his egoism is stripped from him. What Dostoevsky is showing us here in the mutual relations of these three characters is that sin begets sin, that Katerina's need for abasement encourages in Dmitri a cruel need to dominate, and at the same time Grushenka's coquetry whets Dmitri's towering passions. Furthermore, the self-centeredness of the two women, though different in nature, is mutually stimulating. It is only in the polar opposition of Alyosha as he listens to Mitya's confession, saying finally, "I believe that God will order things for the best" (p. 144), and later as he offers an "onion" to Grushenka that the redemption of the sensualists is achieved.

In book four, devoted to the Alyosha theme or the spiritual life, other polar opposites operate. Father Ferapont, imprisoned in his cell, is the exact opposite of Alyosha as he freely walks through town. Furthermore, the punishments and deprivations Father Ferapont inflicts upon himself contrast with the unsolicited "punishments" that Alyosha receives from the schoolboys when they stone him; from Katerina, who calls him "a little religious idiot" (p. 277); and from the Snegiryov family, whose cottage he visits. Dostoevsky is showing us that, in creating his own punishments, man arrogates the role of God and lives in Satanic pride. On the other hand, Alyosha's lacerations serve only to increase his humility. At the end of the book, he withstands the captain's prideful wrath at being offered money; although "inexpressibly grieved," he simply bends to pick up the two crumpled notes, to smooth them out, and to return them to Katerina. Caught between the prides of two proud people, he makes no move to retaliate, nor has he retaliated for any of the other insults shown him in book four. As Alyosha bends to pick up the notes, we find another symbolic bowing down to a sinner.

In culmination, in book five, Ivan's book, we find the famous polar opposition between pro and contra, Christ and the Grand Inquisitor, an opposition underlying the entire political history of our times. In his poem Ivan describes the reappearance of Christ in sixteenth-century Seville. In the "breathless" night, the Inquisitor is brought to Christ's cell, and the celebrated colloquy, or rather soliloquy, begins. Christ's silence is like His response to Pontius Pilate when He countered in Matthew 27, "Thou sayest." Rather than oppose the Inquisitor with words, Christ places on his "bloodless aged lips" a soft kiss. Passive and active resistance are also contrasted here, the essence of passive resistance lying in its silent insistence that the aggressor bear the full responsibility for his acts. By creating a vacuum that must be filled by the aggressor, the passive resister condemns or challenges his enemy to create a world that is at least livable for himself, and if, for himself, of course, for other men. He succeeds, then, in replacing original oppositions with others that are more creative.

In the conversation between Alyosha and Ivan that follows the poem, we find a good example of what Bakhtin calls "contrapuntal inner dialogue." "The speech of one character throws into relief the covert dialogue inherent in the speech of another."[12] Alyosha's questioning of Ivan brings out clearly Ivan's hidden desire to do violence to his father. For instance: "And the old man?" (p. 312), queries Alyosha. (Which old man, the Inquisitor or Father Fyodor?) "The kiss glows in his heart, but the old man adheres to his idea" (p. 312), Ivan replies. (That is, to burn Christ tomorrow.) "And you with him, you too?" (p. 312), cries Alyosha. (Will you, too, commit murder?" And later on the same page Alyosha sums up Ivan's position: "'Everything is lawful,' you mean? Everything is lawful, is that it?" (That is, with sophistry you justify the killing of old Fyodor?) Such contrapuntal dialogue is mentiond simply in passing as another subtle stylistic use of the powerful tension created by the fact of opposition.

Triads, too, figure prominently in Ivan's poem. Christ's

three temptations in the wilderness are repeated in the three questions posed by the Inquisitor:

> Dost Thou know that the ages will pass, and humanity will proclaim by the lips of their sages that there is no crime, and therefore no sin; there is only hunger? (P. 300)

> Is the nature of men such, that they can reject miracle, and at the great moments of their life, the moments of their deepest, most agonising spiritual difficulties, cling only to the free verdict of the heart? (P. 303)

> But Thou mightest have taken even then the sword of Caesar. Why didst Thou reject that last gift? (P. 305)

Bread, mystery, and authority provide for the believer a threefold security, a triangle of certainty, three points that act together to circumscribe and to stablize his life. Given the means of sustenance, given safe conduct in the face of the inexplicable, and given arbitrary rules, the man of faith is prepared for every exigency. There are areas into which man may not for his own good venture.

However, Ivan's poem contains a basic inconsistency: the incompatibility of the position of the main speaker, the Inquisitor, with the fact that a poem that inherently questions this speaker exists at all. The very existence, then, of the poem speaks in justification of Christ.

## II

Various oppositions discovered in book five and the two previous sections find a kind of tentative resolution in the next two books dealing with "the Russian Monk" and Alyosha. Books six and seven act as a pivot for the novel as a whole, proposing that a strength achieved through faith in God can answer the dilemmas of all three brothers. Whereas the first five books have presented problems to be solved, the last five show how these problems may or may not be worked out. In the two core books, six and seven, Brother Markel, Father Zossima, the mysterious visitor, and Alyosha all provide concentric experiences (that is,

forming a sphere) that enlarge on and foreshadow the solution. It is on this surface that the two halves of the novel
may be implanted, like two hemispheres.

Brother Markel, after mocking the season of Lent and
the Church, upon falling ill from consumption begins going to church and becomes "bright and joyous, in spite of
his illness" (p. 343). The young Zossima, disappointed in
an affair of the heart, challenges the husband of his beloved to a duel, and then in a fit of frustration and cruelty
beats his orderly in the face. Unable to endure his own
crime, he faces the first shot in the duel, then throws his
pistol away. Soon after, he resigns his commission and
enters a monastery. The third convert, Mihail, the mysterious visitor, also rejected by his beloved and unable to bear
the thought of her marriage to another man, kills her. One
of his serfs is accused and sentenced. Mihail, like
Raskolnikov in *Crime and Punishment,* confesses publicly;
but, unlike Raskolnikov, he is believed by no one and dies
perhaps as a result of his unexpiated guilt. This triad of
experiences in book six opens the route that all three
brothers must pursue in his quest for salvation. Markel is
perhaps a surrogate for Dmitri; Zossima for Alyosha; and
Mihail (whose problem is not worked through) for Ivan.
Dialectics and religious exhortations compose book six,
chaper three, dealing with the unifying and cohesive force
of prayer, love, and faith and giving concentricity to the
stories of these three converts.

Book seven enlarges and focuses the experiences of the
foregoing triad by describing the doubts and then the reaf-
firmation of faith of Alyosha. A polar opposition is early
set up in book seven when the holy Father Zossima's body
begins to decompose. Physical process is not to be expected from the corpse of a holy elder, and the entire
monastery, as well as the community, is in an uproar.
Appropriately, it is the onion, spoken of by Grushenka in
chapter three, that is to resolve the problem of the rotten
odor coming from Zossima's corpse. The onion symbolizes
for Grushenka the tiniest gift possible, yet an authentic

gift. Furthermore, the onion is a root (that is, a source of life); it is spherical and it is concentric, consisting of layer upon layer (something like an egg, also a source of life). Like the elder's body, the onion stinks. All of these attributes cause the onion to become in this book the objective correlative for salvation, which may not be achieved in solitude and apart from the earthy stink of life. Father Zossima has continually urged his pupil to go out into the world, and the old woman in Grushenka's story ruins her chance for salvation when, as she is being pulled out of the burning lake of hell by means of an onion, she kicks others away and thus breaks the stalk. Like the corn of wheat of the epigraph, the onion must be buried in the earth of this world in order to take root. Within the earth it achieves its full spherical and concentric shape and its pearl-like consistency and color. Furthermore, the onion is hardy and grown the world over since primitive times, making it a suitable universal symbol for the concept of salvation.

It is through the onion spoken of by Grushenka (and the title of chapter three) that Alyosha's doubts about Zossima's death are resolved, and he discovers "a true sister, I have found a treasure—a loving heart" (p. 422), in other words, emotional concentricity. The unity embodied in the onion is dealt with in a different way in chapter four, "Cana of Galilee," in which Christ in effect marries soul and body by using his spiritual powers to turn water into wine. Symbolically the water associated with baptism is thus turned into the wine associated with communion, the communion of souls. Baptism is a ceremony of initiation whereas communion is a ceremony of shared participation among peers in the life of the Church. Thus by turning water into wine, Christ symbolically inspires not only communion between the wedded couple at Cana but communion in all ideal human relationships. Book seven moves then from the doubts inspired by Father Zossima's stinking corpse toward resolution in the spherical perfection of the ceremony of marriage and of Holy Communion. The wine of Holy Communion in essence represents

Christ's blood, the ultimate sacrifice in the achievement of salvation.

III

The final five books of *The Brothers Karamazov* move toward establishing among the characters the spherical unity embodied and foreshadowed in books six and seven. Dmitri moves to stage center in books eight and nine. His desperate search for money at the beginning of book eight culminates in his visit to Madame Hohlakov in the chapter called "Gold-mines." We find here a mocking use of the principle of polar opposition. If by burial and descent into the earth we ensure ourselves of new fruits, as the epigraph promises, Madame Hohlakov's suggestion to Dmitri that he should go to the gold mines to make his fortune (simply because she is too parsimonious to lend him money) is no less than sheer hypocrisy. She assures him that she has come to the conclusion, "That's a man who would find gold" (p. 467). Ironically enough Mitya is later sentenced to the mines (though not to gold mines). Also ironically he is destined to "find gold" in the sense of religious salvation, but Madame Hohlakov's mention of the gold mines to ensure monetary salvation for Mitya is foolish avarice. For the orthodox Christian, wealth is incidental in the search for the salvation of the soul.

Dostoevsky's grotesque sense of humor rests in itself on a polarity. Continually we find in his comic relief an element of incongruity. The intensity of such characters as Madame Hohlakov (or Katerina Ivanova in *Crime and Punishment*) contrasts sharply with the petty quality of their minds, a point made by Rakitin in his "hymn" to Madame Hohlakov's swollen foot (pp. 718–19). Both women are on the verge of imbecility, and yet Dostoevsky invests both with a self-importance that causes them to behave like termagants. Aware of this polarity, the reader at the same time must pause, for he finds himself in the position of the insensitive characters in Cervantes' book who laugh at Don Quixote, another half-mad misfit. Furthermore, these

94

two women are without a mission and thus in theory more
pitiable but in practice more laughable than the Don. Such
humor is grotesque because we ridicule and yet pity such
characters in the same breath.

Polar oppositions turn, as books eight and nine develop,
into a triad of ordeals that Dmitri must undergo, a progres-
sive loss of pride during the preliminary investigation immediately after his arrest. During these ordeals Dmitri is to
learn the meaning of false pride, a pride that consists of
only his own angle of vision.

The first ordeal in chapter three of book nine concerns
his relationship with Grushenka. For the first time, we see
him humble, meek in his awareness of her love and sacrifice for him. "How can a clumsy, ugly brute like me, with
my ugly face, deserve such love, that she is ready to go
into exile with me?" (p. 564). This ordeal provides for
Dmitri a recognition of Grushenka's point of view, as well
as an acceptance of himself as worthy of another's love, as
a human being like everyone else, corruptible but also capable of achieving salvation. Able to bear his dual nature
for the first time, he says to the investigators: "Gentlemen,
forgive me! But now I am comforted" (p. 564).

Dmitri's second ordeal concludes in further loss of false
pride. As the questioning has continued, Dmitri has become sullen. When he talks of a possible penalty for breaking Grigory's head, he hopes for six months, but "without
loss of rank" (p. 567). However, toward the end of the
scene, a feeling of nausea overcomes him, and he tells his
interrogators of a recurrent dream he has of someone
hunting him in the dark. He now realizes that "I am a wolf
and you're the hunters" (p. 572). Parallel to the first ordeal,
where he had seen himself as a "clumsy, ugly brute," he
now compares himself to a crafty and rapacious animal. It
is a step in his loss of a rank that is counterfeit, and he
advises himself, "Be patient, humble, hold thy peace"
(p. 572).

The culminating ordeal, the third one, consists of further
humiliation for Dmitri when he is asked at the end of the

investigation to take off his clothes so that he may be searched. To this, too, he must patiently submit. Such a triad of ordeals turns Mitya's thoughts from gratification of his immediate needs, which has motivated his behavior with Grushenka up until this time, toward a sense of other people's humanity and a sense of his own humanity, in that, like all of us, he shares traits in common with the brute and with the wolf. As Edward Wasiolek points out, "One cannot love what is ugly until one has recognized the ugliness within oneself. Dmitri's regeneration begins when he cries to all at the preliminary investigation: 'We're all cruel, we're all monsters, we all make men weep, and mothers and babes at breast, but of all, let it be settled here, now, of all I am the lowest reptile.'" As the Elder Zossima had prostrated himself before Dmitri in the opening scene, now Dmitri symbolically prostrates himself in order to "crush by humility the impulse to judge and consequently to crush the impulse to commit murder in one's heart."[13] It is the sign of his redemption.

In chapter eight of book nine, Mitya's dream of the weeping babe and his response to this dream provide the concentricity, the spherical shape and the unity, that resolve the various oppositions depicted thus far. Mitya "wanted to do something for them all, so that the babe should weep no more" (p. 616). It is a sign of Mitya's concern for others, coming on the heels of Grushenka's real concern for him in her promise to share his exile. It signifies a mutuality and the beginning of a new life for them both: "He longed to live, to live, to go on and on, towards the new, beckoning light" (p. 616).

The same basic process is repeated in different guise as we trace Ivan's efforts to achieve salvation. Dostoevsky begins by setting up various polar oppositions between two of the boys, Kolya and Ilusha, younger surrogates for certain brothers Karamazov. Kolya "could beat the teacher . . . at arithmetic and universal history" (p. 626), like Ivan, who "began very early, almost in his infancy . . . to show a brilliant and unusual aptitude for

learning" (p. 13). Ilusha is, on the contrary, first characterized by his intense loyalty and devotion for his father, like
Alyosha's for Father Zossima, but unlike Alyosha he resorts to stabbing his opponents with a penknife when the
latter taunt Captain Snegiryov. In his use of violence, he
approaches Dmitri, despite the difference in motive.
Shortly after his conflict with the other boys, Ilusha falls ill,
but his devotion and concern for his father, the Captain,
do not flag. Rather than being sorry for himself, he cries,
"'Father, father! How sorry I am for you!'" (p. 680). Like
Dmitri's, Ilusha's humility increases as his ordeal progresses: "'Father don't cry, and when I die get a good
boy,'" he exclaims (p. 680). The parallel between Kolya
and Ivan is also only approximate, for as Ilusha's health
worsens, Kolya takes on characteristics of Alyosha in his
care of, and love for, his sick friend, Still, in his precocity,
which fosters both conceit and impiety, he remains an
Ivan, so that Alyosha at one point says to him, "'Kolya,
you will be very unhappy in your life'" (p. 677). The
autonomous development of character in *The Brothers
Karamazov*, as exemplified in Kolya and Ilusha, makes clear
Bakhtin's point about "the plurality of independent and
unmerged voices"[14] in Dostoevsky's work.

Yet despite all the complicated parallels and oppositions
operating in the depiction of the boys, Smerdyakov retains
the same role in both the main plot and the subplot, as the
perpetrator of violence designed to kill. Of Ilusha's attack
with the penknife Kolya has remarked that "'the wound
was a mere scratch'" (p. 650). The bite on Alyosha's finger
and the bruises from the stones thrown by Ilusha are also
relatively minor. Furthermore, these acts of violence are
directed by a missionary zeal against opponents more
powerful than Ilusha, persons who could easily crush him,
like an insect, were they so minded. On the contrary, the
violence unleashed by Smerdyakov is directed against
helpless dogs that in their hunger will snatch at anything
resembling meat. Their subsequent torment is out of all
proportion to the motive that inspires Smerdyakov—per-

verted amusement. It is worth noting that the trick has been taught to Smerdyakov by the evil father, old Fyodor. On the other hand, the good father, Captain Snegiryov, has taught loyalty and compassion to Ilusha by the Great Stone where he wishes to be buried. Two kinds of violence are contrasted in this particular opposition: one that can be overcome and transcended and one that, like Ivan's god, "tortures children [and animals] as Fyodor has tortured his."[15]

Ivan's three interviews with Smerdyakov, paralleling Mitya's three ordeals at the preliminary investigation, act as the focal point of book eleven, in contrast to the various polar oppositions developed in book ten. Unlike Mitya's three ordeals, however, Ivan's three interviews, rather than freeing him from guilt, serve to involve him progressively in the murder of his father and in the evil world of Smerdyakov. At the end of the first interview, he and his half-brother make a pact, Ivan agreeing to say nothing of Smerdyakov's ability to sham a fit in return for Smerdyakov's silence about the conversation at the gate (book five, chapter six). This complicity deepens at the end of the second interview, when, finally convinced by Smerdyakov's argument that he tacitly had condoned the murder of old Fyodor, he exclaims, "I share his guilt for I put him up to it (p. 751).

The third and last interview is accompanied by interesting parallels with Dmitri's dream of the babe. At the opening of chapter eight, Ivan meets a drunken peasant whom he pushes down onto the ground and leaves to freeze, partly because the peasant is singing a song about going away to Petersburg, reminding Ivan of his departure for Moscow on the eve of his father's murder. After Smerdyakov's accusation, "'You are the real murderer, I was only your instrument'" (p. 758) and his confession, Ivan plans that they will appear together at the trial to give evidence against themselves. Partly to assuage his growing guilt, he returns and helps the freezing peasant, providing him with a doctor and some money. But Dmitri's concern for the crying babe, his mark of salvation, has been *preceded* by public confession; Ivan's concern for the peasant is accompanied by his remark, "'Everything together tomorrow'" (p. 771), as he decides not to go to the prosecutor that night. In actuality, of course, Ivan's public confession never takes place, forestalled by Smerdyakov's suicide and his own dementia. Thus his concern for the peasant is only a step toward the salvation that Dmitri accomplishes, a step nullified by subsequent events. The three interviews with Smerdyakov have served to seal securely his doom.

And finally the spherical form, the unity or concentricity, with which Dostoevsky endows episodes that are worked through to completion, is not evident in the last scene of book eleven, describing (in contrast to Dmitri's dream of the babe) Ivan's nightmare of his conversation with the Devil. In fact, no real polarity is even set up, as in the Grand Inquisitor scene, for the two protagaonists, Ivan and the Devil, seem to be carbon copies of one another, as Ivan himself realizes when he cries, "'You just say what I am thinking . . . and are incapable of saying anything new!'"(p. 776). This sterile relation stands in sharp contrast to the fruitful opposition found, for example, in the conversation between Father Zossima and Ivan at the unfortunate gathering. Ivan questions the Devil and receives his own answers. Together they suggest the heresy that God's existence is dependent on the existence of the Devil: "'No, live, I am told, for there'd be nothing without you'" (p. 780). Together they predict the appearance of a man-god in a thousand years, joyous in extending his conquest of nature by his will and by science instead of in dreams of heaven. Frustrated by one who serves only to put into words the temptations of his own logic, Ivan flings a glass at the intruder. Rather than reciprocal concern and harmony, this relationship is a mockery of such states; Ivan's hatred of the Devil is his hatred of himself.

At the end of the nightmare, a loud knocking is heard; it is Alyosha, who brings news of Smerdyakov's suicide, thereby blocking the road to confession and redemption that Ivan had proposed to follow on the morrow. Instead of concentricity and unity, we find at the end of book eleven only self-hatred, disruption, and anguish. The God in whom he believes—that is, the Devil—and he are one.

In chapter three of book twelve, we find a spherical image that must open the discussion of this final book. One of the important but little-emphasized objective correlatives in the novel is the pound of nuts given by Dr. Herzenstube to Mitya when he was a boy. These nuts (concentric like onions in that they consist of layers, that is, shell and kernel) are unexpectedly of use to Mitya in his defense. The fact that he has been grateful to the doctor (whose name means "room of the heart") and has remembered to thank him after twenty-three years have passed is a point in Mitya's favor. Nuts are seeds that, like the corn of wheat of the epigraph, must be planted in the earth in order to grow. By planting these seeds of compassion, Dr. Herzenstube has, then, symbolically assured Dmitri's salvation. It is the one act of love that Dmitri can remember in his childhood.

The prosecutor's speech, however, in chapter six assumes a triadic structure as Kirillovitch analyzes the character of each brother in turn: Ivan as a brilliant young intellectual "who has lost all faith in everything" (p. 847); Alyosha as an idealist, likely to degenerate into a gloomy mystic or a blind chauvinist (p. 848); and Mitya as one who combines good and evil, a lover of Schiller but a brawler in taverns. All of this finds its objective correlative in Gogol's troika, "galloping to an unknown goal" (p. 845). If drawn by Gogol's heroes, Kirillovitch argues, "it could reach no rational goal, whoever might be driving it" (p. 845). (It will be remembered that Dmitri's frenzied trip to Mokroe in search of Grushenka had been accomplished in a troika.) Kirillovitch, by means of this image, spells disaster for the Karamazov triad. It is a triad that as prosescutor he depicts as interacting destructively rather than creatively, no matter who might hold the reins, even Gogol.

However, the defense lawyer, Fetyukovitch, sets up a

polar opposition, that between the good father and the bad father, which serves to counteract the argument of the prosecution. It also brings to full circle the contrast between the two fathers effected in chapters one and five of book one. "'Such a father as old Karamazov cannot be called a father and does not deserve to be,'" he exclaims (p. 902). By contrast, he states that "'the father is not merely he who begets the child, but he who begets it and does his duty by it'" (p. 903). The basic opposition here is the same as that between Father Zossima and old Fyodor at the unfortunate gathering. The suggestion is that the prosecution is wrong and that it *does* matter who holds the reins in the driving of the troika. The driver may be one who neglects his responsibility or one who nurtures it. If a responsible driver is found, the goal of the troika will be a rational one, according to Fetyukovitch. It is the role of the father, not his children, to provide such guidance. The driver, not the horses, must determine the destination of any troika.

Dmitri's sentence of twenty years in the mines provides a final image of concentricity that rounds out book twelve. Like the corn of wheat, the onion, and the nut, Dmitri must be buried beneath the earth in order to be reborn. Within him he bears the seeds of his redemption. "'Go greet him on his way into the darkness,'" Alyosha admonishes Katerina (p. 921).

In the last chapter of the epilogue, it is, however Ilusha, Kolya, and Kartashov, the new generation, who become the "resurrected" ones and the focus of the conclusion. Because of their experiences with Alyosha, the Karamazov name will be reborn. "And always so, all our lives hand in hand!" (p. 940). The stinking root of the onion has produced its tiny crown of white flowers in this centering of common effort, this unity, created by the responsible fatherhood of Alyosha in directing the course of these admiring "sons."

"'Karamazov, we love you!' a voice probably Kartashov's cried impulsively" (p. 939).

1. Ludmilla B. Turkevich, "Cervantes in Russia," in *Cervantes across the Centuries*, p. 365.

2. Victor E. Amend, "Theme and Form in 'The Brothers Karamazov,'" p. 240.

3. Ibid., p. 252.

4. Robert Louis Jackson, *Dostoevsky's Quest for Form*, p. 213.

5. Fyodor Dostoevsky, *The Notebooks for "The Brothers Karamazov,"* p. 135.

6. Ibid., p. 14.

7. Robert Lord, *Dostoevsky* (Berkeley: University of California Press, 1970), p. 201.

8. Wasiolek, pp. 10–11.

9. Fyodor Dostoevsky, *The Brothers Karamazov*, trans. Constance Garnett (New York: Modern Library, 1950), p. 85. Subsequent references to this volume will be cited in the text.

10. Ernest J. Simmons, *Dostoevsky: The Making of a Novelist*, pp. 339–40.

11. Ibid., p. 341.

12. Lord, p. 205.

13. Wasiolek, p. 12.

14. Mikhail Bakhtin, *Problems of Dostoevsky's Poetics*, p. 4.

15. Wasiolek, p. 11.

Chapter Five

## Dostoevsky's *Crime and Punishment* and Kafka's *The Trial*

The polar opposition or contrapuntal structuring inherent in *The Brothers Karamazov* may be seen also in Dostoevsky's earlier novel *Crime and Punishment*. Although he does not work out his structures with quite the compunction and care we find in *The Brothers Karamazov*, it is clear that Dostoevsky intended in *Crime and Punishment* to form a counterpoint alternating between two aspects of Raskolnikov's psychological adjustment: his relationship to mother, sister, and mother surrogates and his relationship to the authorities of the state, the police and detectives, and to various father figures. If one can generalize, perhaps dangerously, one sees that parts one, three, and five deal largely with the former relationship; parts two, four, and six with the latter; and the epilogue, consisting of two chapters, hints at solutions and reconciliations within the tortured conscience of the hero, showing him finally perhaps that these two problems are actually one, or at least closely related, and revealing to him the true motivation for his crime (a motivation he has sought vainly to discover throughout all six parts).

Briefly, in summary, the emphasis in part one is on Raskolnikov's thoughts of the old pawnbroker and her sister; the crucial letter from his mother revealing Raskolnikov's painful family ties to her and Dounia; his abandonment of the drunken girl; his dream of the tortured mare; and his murder of Alyona Ivanovna and Lizaveta. In part three, Raskolnikov's mother and sister arrive in Saint Petersburg, and we are able to observe this triadic family relationship at close range. In part five the role of Sonia becomes paramount in Raskolnikov's life in his confession to her, foreshadowing the resolution of his ambivalence toward the mother and consequently toward other women.

On the other hand, in part two Raskolnikov makes his first visit to police headquarters and faints in fear of punishment for his crime. Razumihin, a nurturing father-brother, tends him in his illness. We meet here, too, several fathers *manqué*: Luhzin, who lives only for himself; Zametov, a father confessor, who does not listen to what Raskolnikov is trying to confess; or Marmeladov, who dies having lived and drunk at the expense of his daughter's virtue (much as Raskolnikov feels he may now exploit Dounia's). In part four the relationship with the police is observed at close range and in detail (as in part two his relationship with his mother and sister had been), particularly through the developing game of wits he and Porfiry Petrovich engage in. And in part six the dilemma with the authorities begins to reach a resolution in Raskolnikov's bowing down at the crossroads and subsequent progress to police headquarters to confess his crime. (Svidrigaïlov's terrible end in this part is, of course, that of another father *manqué*, the ultimate object lesson for the hero.)

The contrapuntal treatment of these two themes in the six parts of the novel is, of course, not quite so neat and exact as this brief summary may suggest, but in general it applies. Furthermore, within each part we find shorter sections exemplifying the same counterpoint; for example, in part three Raskolnikov's first visit to Porfiry coming on the heels of Sonia's first visit to Raskolnikov's room. However, the approach to structure will be slightly different in this chapter from earlier approaches. Dostoevsky's structures in *Crime and Punishment* will be examined in full detail in the light of a novel that followed his, Kafka's *The Trial*. Whether or not direct influence is involved is not the question. Suffice it to say that curious and intriguing parallels can be shown to exist between the general structuring of the two books, and it is of no little interest to study Dostoevsky's techniques and themes transposed and adapted possibly to a twentieth-century, post-Freudian novel.

Franz Kafka's admiration for Dostoevsky is a well-documented fact. Dostoevsky is mentioned seven times in *The Diaries*, all seven of the entries coming in the years 1913–14; it was in 1915 that Kafka worked extensively on *The Trial*. In his biography Max Brod mentions that during the period 1912–17 Kafka read in "the Bible, Dostoievski, Pascal, Herzen, and Kropotkin."[1] Furthermore, Brod, in writing of the genesis of *The Castle*,[2] mentions Dostoevsky. And Mark Spilka in his article on *The Metamorphosis* and in his book on Dickens and Kafka draws important parallels between the two authors.[3] In 1973 Ronald Gray called attention to a similarity between *The Trial* and Dostoevsky's *The Double* and to the possibility that Kafka's aphorism, "How . . . oppressive it is to have even the faintest conviction that our life in time will eventually be justified in eternity," could have been inspired by Ivan Karamazov.[4] And Kafka's letter of 2 September 1913 to Felice mentions his admiration for Dostoevsky.[5] Finally, there is Gustav Janouch's report: "When Kafka saw a crime novel among the books in my brief case he said: 'There is no need to be ashamed of reading such things. Dostoievski's *Crime and Punishment* is after all only a crime novel. . . . At the heart of action is a mystery, which is gradually brought to light. But is there a greater mystery than truth?'"[6]

The subject of justice and punishment could hardly fail to remind a writer familiar with Dostoevsky of Dostoevsky's first major novel. *Crime and Punishment* does seem, in fact, to have a direct bearing on *The Trial*, and because we know that Kafka read Dostoevsky, it is fruitful to reread *Crime and Punishment* with *The Trial* in mind.

Doing so makes one aware of new ways of looking at Raskolnikov. It is possible to see in the police of *Crime and Punishment* an embryo of the same force represented by the court and its officials in *The Trial*. It is also possible to see definite parallels between the women figures in the two novels.

Many excellent psychological interpretations exist dealing with *Crime and Punishment* and *The Trial* individually, but there is no detailed study that connects the two books as examples of the same psychological syndrome. Among the interpretations are Edna C. Florance's "The Neurosis of Raskolnikov,"[7] which discusses both the incestuous and homosexual inclinations of Dostoevsky's hero, and A. Bronson Feldman's article dealing with father love and the character of Svidrigaïlov.[8] On the other hand, Selma Fraiberg's essay "Kafka and the Dream" sees that Kafka in his work is in "hopeless pursuit of the crime and the judgment,"[9] and Simon Lesser discusses the source and the sense of guilt in *The Trial*.[10]

On the psychological level, then, light is thrown by means of the comparison backward on *Crime and Punishment*. Writing with an awareness of Freudian psychology, Kafka develops the Oedipal situation in which K. is caught and points overtly to K.'s dependency on various women as well as to his fear and anxiety concerning the court (a father surrogate). If K. is indeed a later Raskolnikov, perhaps we can find a clarification through K. of Raskolnikov's long sought after and vexing motive. What follows is an attempt to reassess Raskolnikov in terms of K. and his trial. The nature of the motive also makes clear why both Raskolnikov and Dostoevsky have difficulty in recognizing it themselves.

*The Trial* may be seen as a retelling of Dostoevsky's plot in terms of the inner world of the dream and of the unconscious. Both books have in common the two central themes mentioned earlier: the confrontation with authority and the relationship of the son to the mother-sister image, ancient subject matters familiar from the time of the mythical world of "Oedipus Rex" to the modern world of "Tonio Kröger," Thomas Mann's story, which Brod tells us that Kafka "loved."

Although Kafka's and Dostoevsky's books open at apparently different points, one with an arrest, the other with the commission of a crime, both acts serve the same function in that through them the heroes experience traumatic blows. The existence of each hero is suddenly and dramatically altered by these acts. K.'s mechanically ordered day as a bank executive is invaded by the agents of his trial in the same way that Raskolnikov's reasoned superman theory is disturbed by his murder of the pawnbroker. However, the appearance of the warder in K.'s bedroom suggests that the trial is from the beginning an inward one for K., the warder a projection of K. himself and of K.'s conscience. The novel is to describe, thus, the confrontation of K. with his own identity and his self-condemnation. Likewise Raskolnikov's central problem is his own guilt, which appears to exist *before* the commission of the murder, as can be seen from his otherwise inexplicable generosity to the Marmeladovs, from his reaction to his mother's letter, or in his dream of the mare. It is as if he himself were somehow personally responsible for Sonia's, Dounia's, or the mare's plight. Raskolnikov's basic problem is his search for a solution to his case. That is, both heroes are seeking a resolution of their own tangled relationships to their societies.

To repeat, this relationship is basically twofold—to the authoritarian world of the father figure and to the protective world of the mother figure. The father figure for both Raskolnikov and K. is threatening, cruel, and austere. For Raskolnikov he is represented by the nameless men who exploit Sonia; by Svidrigaïlov, who has insulted Dounia; by the man who is following the drunken girl; by Luzhin, whose motives in proposing to Dounia are purely selfish; and later by the police. All these figures are summed up in Raskolnikov's dream of the man who beats the mare to death. For K. the father figure is the court and its officials. They invade his privacy as well as invading, uninvited, the house of Frau Grubach and the room of Fräulein Bürstner. Again these officials may be seen as projections of K.'s own wishes, for at the end of the first chapter, it is K. himself who "invades" Fräulein Bürstner's room. Furthermore, this same projection theory may throw light on Raskolnikov's motive, for the men who exploit the women in the opening section may be seen as projections of Raskolnikov. Both Raskolnikov's and K.'s anxiety about the father figure is partially related to anxieties about their own behavior in reference to the mother figure. Killing the pawnbroker and the sister is a kind of token killing and removal of two figures (mother and sister) who threaten Raskolnikov as sexual objects. K. is unnecessarily apologetic to both Frau Grubach and Fräulein Bürstner for the visit of the officials; Frau Grubach seems to take such things for granted, however, and Fräulein Bürstner immediately suspects that it is K. who has mixed up her photographs, further confirmation of the theory already advanced. For both Raskolnikov and K., the father figure is personally threatening as well as threatening to the mother-sister; Raskolnikov and K. both fear and desire authority; they also both fear and desire the sexual relation with the mother-sister. It is these conflicts that lead Raskolnikov up the stairs to accomplish the murder act, and it is these conflicts that lead to K.'s arrest and to his self-accusation.

The protective and advisory role of the mother, which K. seeks in Frau Grubach, Fräulein Bürstner, and in all the other women he meets, is parallel to the role in which Raskolnikov places his mother and sister, who literally "support" him, and later Sonia, who becomes his spiritual support. The Inspector in chapter one advises K. to "think more about yourself," but both Raskolnikov and K. seek answers from others and particularly from women on whom they are dependent. The problems of both persist, for having reached physical manhood, they both still relate, as if they were children, to the mother image; and they are both unable to identify with, or even conceive of, a benevolent authority, but see authority only in terms of brutality and force. Thus the opening sections of the two novels present strikingly similar situations that comment in different ways but with like discernment on the criminal or psychopathic personality, on its motivations and behavior patterns. Crime, it is suggested, is often the result of self-punishment, and trials are the result of deep and unresolved conflicts with a society.

II

The parallels continue on into part two of *Crime and Punishment* and chapters two and three of *The Trial*, which deal with the immediate effects of the opening actions. Both heroes are called to appear before the officials. Raskolnikov is called to police headquarters, not knowing the reason for his summons and for another reason than the murder. K. goes for his first interrogation by the court, not knowing of what he is accused. K. is asked by the court if he is a house painter;[12] for a while it is the house painter that the police in *Crime and Punishment* suspect. Raskolnikov faints when he overhears his murder discussed; K. later faints in the stuffy atmosphere of the law offices. Raskolnikov is aided in his subsequent illness and delirium by his friend Razumihin, who himself takes a lively interest in the murder story; K. is assisted during his fainting spell by the Clerk of Inquiries. Luzhin's arrival in town to claim his prize is parallel to the appearance of the law student who carries off the woman of the courtroom to the Examining Magistrate.

All of these parallels further develop the two central themes, the relation to authority and to the mother-sister figure. But Kafka is writing of an inner level of experience, whereas Dostoevsky is depicting the everyday realities of the existence of Raskolnikov. Thus the empty courtroom that K. discovers on his second visit is inwardly the same sort of experience that confronts Raskolnikov when he learns that Nikolay, the house painter, has been accused. Raskolnikov scarcely speaks in part two, chapter four, for his courtroom is also empty, his accusers having turned their attention elsewhere. The frustration Raskolnikov feels at being denied his accusers is vented in the next chapter on Luzhin, toward whom he directs all the fury he could wish directed against himself. He tells Luzhin to "go to hell"[13] while at the same time rejecting Luzhin's forgiveness, stating that he is not ill. He feels cheated of

Luzhin's retaliation and tries every means to provoke him, for he himself has also exploited Dounia in as selfish a manner as Luzhin's. Unable to bear the empty courtroom, Raskolnikov attempts to confess to Zametov and later to the people outside the pawnbroker's house. In both instances he partially succeeds, awakening a flash of insight that Zametov apparently rejects and convincing one of the onlookers at the murder scene.

In the same way, K. is unable to bear his empty courtroom, as evidenced by his immediate penetration of the Law Court Offices to find his accusers. When even here they do not materialize but he is confronted by others who also await their trials, he succumbs to his fainting fit as his only remaining means of gaining attention. Raskolnikov's fainting fit on his first visit to police headquarters similarly draws attention to him as well as drawing the early suspicions of Ilya Petrovich, to whom Raskolnikov at the end makes full confession of the crime.

Thus the immediate effects of the arrest and of the murder center chiefly on a seeking of punishment from the very authority both heroes fear. Both simultaneously want to remove themselves from the environs of their accusers and to remain in these environs. At the end of his scene with the crowd, Raskolnikov is flung into the street by the porter. K., also unable or unwilling to leave under his own power, is helped to the door by the Clerk of Inquiries. Both heroes are impotent to deal with the ravishers of the women. Raskolnikov shadow-boxes with Luzhin, who treats Raskolnikov as a sick man or an invalid, and K. is able to muster no serious opposition to the student who carries off the woman of the court; yet both Dounia and the woman have themselves offered assistance to the protagonists.

III

Dostoevsky's part three and chapters four and five of *The Trial* continue to develop on parallel lines. Dounia gains the protection of Razumihin as Fräulein Bürstner is now protected by a friend who moves in with her. Emotionally and psychologically left to themselves, the two heroes turn to a series of self-lacerations, K.'s on an inner level, Raskolnikov's on an outer level.

Raskolnikov's conversation with his mother and sister in chapter three involves several humiliations starting with his penitence and moving to his irritation and to his recalling of his masochistic love for the hunchback girl, soon to be transferred to the prostitute Sonia. Both women are flawed beings. Immediately thereafter Raskolnikov visits Porfiry and engages in the first round of the cat-and-mouse games that repel as well as attract him. He then dreams of a macabre reenactment of the murder, returning to the scene as K. does to the lumber room. Similarly K. is involved with the whippers in another back room of his consciousness. Franz and Willem, the victims, are obviously projections of K. (One of them is given Kafka's own first name.) K.'s attempts to free them is anything but decisive, and his only solution is finally to slam the door, that is, to shut out the results of the punishment that he feels he deserves, that he both desires and does not desire. The whipping scene may, of course, represent also sexual pleasure, derived from the sadomasochistic and homosexual nature of the proceedings, and subsequent guilt feelings. Sexual overtones are also present in Raskolnikov's dream in which the old woman (a mother figure) is loudly appreciative of the act of murder. On the second evening, K. finds the lumber room exactly the same as it had been on the first evening; Raskolnikov in his dream also returns to a reenactment of the crime (although a distorted one). Again K. slams the door to repress the scene as Raskolnikov in self-protection tries to scream and awakens to find Svidrigaïlov by his sofa.

The attentions of the authorities (in part two) and of the mother-sister figures (in part three) have been diverted elsewhere, and the heroes are confronted with the necessity for creating their own punishments and their own protections. K. finds this inner world of self "smothered in dirt" (p. 111), and in Raskolnikov's dream there is "a smell of mortar, dust, and stagnant water" (p. 270). This is an ugly mirror world in which the hero is isolated and where he must face his self-accusations to which society's accusations may have little relationship. However, neither hero succeeds in these passages in discovering what the real self-accusations are. Raskolnikov dreams of murdering an old woman who is thoroughly enjoying every blow of the axe, "simply shaking with mirth" (p. 272), yet Raskolnikov does not grasp the meaning of her behavior in the dream. In the same way, K. slams the door on the scene in the lumber room. Why did he abandon Franz and Willem is a question he might have asked.

IV

Having carried the protagonists into a world where they have no one but themselves to confront, the two authors begin to work toward their dénouements in part four of *Crime and Punishment* and in chapters six and seven of *The Trial*. The doubt that exists concerning the order of Kafka's chapters must concern us here for a moment. I have used Brod's order throughout this discussion fully realizing that this order may not have been Kafka's intended order. The similarity of the situations in which the two heroes are placed does not depend on exact order of development, however. Both Brod and Uyttersprot agree that material in chapters six through ten belongs within these chapters. The first five chapters stress the increasing isolation of K., a descent into a lower world, culminating in the lumber room scene, which both Brod and Uyttersprot place as chapter five. Whether or not Fräulein Bürstner's friend moves in with her earlier or later makes little difference to my thesis that K. is step by step estranged from all outer contacts. The actual order in which this is accomplished makes less difference than the fact that Dostoevsky and Kafka both are concerned with this process of estrangement in the opening halves of their novels.

From this point on, both authors establish new connections for their protagonists, the old ones having been severed. Each hero has faced himself in the nightmare world of his personal hell, Raskolnikov in his dream and K. in the lumber room. Each has turned his back on these ugly scenes of self-revelation, and each has failed really to comprehend their import.

New relationships that now arise in the two novels (and here too the exact order is of little importance) bear some striking similarities. First two pseudo-father figures appear almost as if to mock Raskolnikov and K. Raskolnikov awakens from his dream to find Svidrigaïlov by his sofa, Svidrigaïlov who at once proclaims his similarity to Raskolnikov, a similarity Raskolnikov is loath to acknowledge. Raskolnikov rejects Svidrigaïlov and his schemes even though Svidrigaïlov's intentions are apparently philanthropic and to Dounia's and Raskolnikov's advantage. Likewise K.'s uncle arrives upon the scene to offer help to K. Both father figures are aware of the "cases" and both offer advice. But the lawyer to whom the uncle takes K. turns out to be no more helpful than Svidrigaïlov's offers of assistance.

Other new relationships are Raskolnikov's growing attachment to Sonia and K.'s to Leni. Sonia in reading the Lazarus story from the Bible points the way to rebirth for Raskolnikov as Leni does with her advice to K.: "'You're too unyielding, that's what I've heard.' . . . 'You must confess to guilt'" (p. 135). Later the whole burden of Sonia's advice to Raskolnikov is that he should confess. Nor can one overlook K.'s kissing of Leni's deformed hand, reminding one of Raskolnikov's love for "deformed" women (for the landlady's daughter, a cripple, and for Sonia, a prostitute).[14]

In the fairy tale, the kissing and consequent transformation of deformity represent the redemptive power of love, but in these novels the kiss is offered largely narcissistically. However, the new relationships with women that the heroes form are by and large more valid than the earlier ones. Although Raskolnikov sees Sonia chiefly as a mother figure and K. sees Leni chiefly in terms of her helpfulness to him, both relationships are potentially normal. For once we see K. exhibiting compassion for another person. However, Sonia is far more positive and influential than Leni, and this in turn emphasizes the generally more negative posture of the twentieth-century novel. From now on, whereas Dostoevsky works toward a resolution, Kafka works toward a conclusion.

Nothing illustrates this more clearly than the new relationships to authority that each hero adopts. Raskolnikov's visit to Porfiry immediately after the Lazarus scene with Sonia is less in the nature of a social call than his first one when he had been accompanied by Razumihin. Although he still has the excuse of the pawned watch, it is clear in his begging for certainty from Porfiry that he is about ready to abandon pretense and to come to grips with the real issue—his crime. On the other hand, K. after chapter three never again seeks out the authorities, and his relationship to the lawyer engaged by his uncle is cavalier and indifferent, even though his name, Huld, signifies grace. It is this grace that in chapter eight he dismisses entirely. Furthermore, Raskolnikov's relation to the authorities is partly sustained by him, whereas they assume largely passive roles, waiting for Raskolnikov to come to his own confessional. K.'s relation to authority, on the other hand, becomes more and more passive and fortuitous. He dismisses his lawyer, he meets the priest in the cathedral through no desire on his part, and he is escorted forcefully to his death. Never, like Raskolnikov, does he give himself up.

Not only a mock father figure, Svidrigaïlov may be seen as a double for Raskolnikov, representing the corrupt and evil side of Raskolnikov's nature. Both commit crimes and both are in the process of suffering for these crimes. The painter, Titorelli, may stand in the same relation to K. or as another projection. He possesses the same flaws that we find in K., although in different degree. The girls who flock about his door are like the girls (the woman of the court or Leni) with whom K. has passing and superficial encounters. Superficial sexual pleasure is suggested by the painter's name. Svidrigaïlov, it will be remembered, also has a penchant for young girls. Furthermore Titorelli has betrayed his art by painting what he is told to paint, although he has not seen the subject. K. has betrayed life in the same way and goes to the bank merely from habit, not because of the involvement with his work there. Titorelli mentions "postponement" of K.'s case, a solution that has long been K.'s own apparent one in his sidetracking of all the essential questions of his trial. The two stunted trees in the pictures that K. buys are perhaps Titorelli and K. himself seen in the light of the death (sunset) they are courting. If so, they are fitting mementos of K.'s visit. But whereas Raskolnikov transcends his double, Svidrigaïlov, K. does not manage to move beyond the stage represented by Titorelli with his flock of girls and apparent strong homosexual leanings. These two corrupt figures offer another kind of relationship entered into by the protagonists in these portions of the books leading toward conclusion and redemption.

In summary, this section shows the heroes, after their futile confrontations of self, beset by mocking offers of assistance from basically hostile father figures, turning to Leni and Sonia for strength and advice, still bargaining and temporizing with the authorities, and confronting their own evil natures disguised in the figures of Svidrigaïlov and Titorelli.

V

Dostoevsky's fifth part and Kafka's chapter eight both serve to slow the action before the two catastrophes. Dostoevsky brings to a conclusion the story of the Marmeladov family. Marmeladov has been another double for Raskolnikov, another figure whose relation to women was entirely a mother-son relationship and whose relation

to authority has always resulted in punishment. Left behind is Marmeladov's daughter, Sonia, who will transcend
the lonely role her stepmother was forced to play with
Marmeladov. It is to Sonia that Raskolnikov confesses his
crime in this section, thus setting in motion the redemptive
pattern.

Likewise in *The Trial* the story of Block, the tradesman,
effectively blocks the action temporarily. Like K., Block is a
client of Lawyer Huld and like all Huld's clients is involved
also with Leni. He is dried up and shriveled, perhaps a
foreboding of K.'s own possible future state. Neither
Marmeladov nor Block has succeeded in a solution of his
case. Marmeladov dies an alcoholic, and we leave Block
trembling in terror before the remarks of Lawyer Huld and
turning to Leni for support.

VI

The cathedral scene in *The Trial,* whether it appears as
chapter nine (as in Brod's order) or earlier (as Uyttersprot
claims), serves the same function as Raskolnikov's three
major encounters with Sonia in *Crime and Punishment*—
first the Lazarus scene, then his confession to her, and last
the scene in which she gives him the wooden cross to
wear. Both heroes are told parables that directly relate to
their own plights and suggest solutions. The parable of the
doorkeeper suggests that K.'s answer is near at hand and
awaits only his own positive action, a sense of personal
responsibility and an abandonment of his casting about for
answers outside himself. He must take the initiative without waiting for permission to enter.

The story of Lazarus provides a similar answer for
Raskolnikov; he need only ask of God to be forgiven and
resurrected, but he must ask. He must take the initiative.
This is clearly brought out in the confession to Sonia in
part five where she urges him to stand at the crossroads
(symbolizing the way of the cross as well as a new life, a
right-angle turn) and say, "'I am a murderer!' Then God

will send you life again" (p. 407). It is only in the final
meeting with Sonia in part six that he agrees to wear the
cross; still at the crossroads, he is unable to confess, and at
his first try at the police station he flees, returning shortly
to tell Ilya Petrovich, "It was I killed the old pawnbroker. . . ."[15]

Both heroes are told the way their salvation lies, and for
both the priest's words to K. are relevant: "It is not necessary to accept everything as true, one must only accept it as
necessary" (p. 276). Raskolnikov confesses more because it
is necessary than because he feels confession will lead to a
solution, and K. accedes to his executioners because he
"suddenly realized the futility of resistance" (p. 282).
Raskolnikov, even to the end, is never sure of his real
motive in committing his crime, nor is K. any surer of what
he has done. The full meaning of their trials escapes both
heroes. In his meetings with Sonia in part five, Raskolnikov casts about in real torment for his motive and concludes that he murdered himself, not the pawnbroker, that
the devil murdered her; and in the final scene in part six,
he is no closer to understanding himself. He is merely
taking the way prescribed to him by society. Both heroes
must bow to necessity, one to imprisonment, the other to
execution, but neither receives more than a glimpse of the
true reason behind his punishment.

The reader, however, is aware that both suffer from a
common sickness. Raskolnikov's real confession comes in
his final words to Dounia. They are an admission of his
unconscious incestuous drives: "Oh, if only I were alone
and no one loved me and I too had never loved any one!
*Nothing of all this would have happened*" (p. 504). And K. is
warned by the priest that help from women is not the right
kind of help. In the final chapter when Fräulein Bürstner
appears in the square, K. at last recognizes the futility of
resistance.

For the first time, it does not matter whether it is
Fräulein Bürstner or not. In other words, the need for protection from the mother figure is receding, and K. now

recognizes that he must make his own choices—in this instance, the acceptance of an absurd fate. In the same way in *Crime and Punishment* in the final scene in Haymarket, although Sonia is among the crowd, Raskolnikov goes alone into the police office reflecting, "If I must drink the cup what difference does it [motive] make?" (p. 510). Raskolnikov, too, has accepted an absurd fate.

K. dies like a dog, and Raskolnikov languishes in prison with other common criminals. Dostoevsky's epilogue is, of course, intended to convey the possibility of a new life for Raskolnikov. K.'s life, on the other hand, ends with the thrust of the knife, although a window had been opened before he died. Dostoevsky, in other words, offers a solution; Kafka can only describe the plight of man caught in the toils of the law of his conscience and unable to extricate himself. He depicts the absurd acceptance of an absurd punishment, whereas Dostoevsky suggests that in the acceptance of the absurd punishment lies the possibility of a "gradual regeneration, of his passing from one world to another" (p. 532). The real crime in each book is the crime of Oedipus, and the real punishment lies in the trials given Raskolnikov and K. by their own consciences. But since, as was stated earlier, *The Trial* is an inward account of crime and punishment, the thrust of the knife may represent no more than Raskolnikov's exile to Siberia, and the open window may stand for the kind of solution toward which Raskolnikov is moving.

But beyond this and in summary, the books are archetypically akin for we read here of the disturbances caused by an overdependency on the mother and a contest with the father. Moreover, in the modern novel represented by both books, the archetype suggests not a simple representation but a representation that is anti-archetypical. The story is the same but with a difference. The father figure, the Laius, who in Sophocles' play is never seen but is represented as an individual (or Claudius in *Hamlet*), is replaced by bureaucracy in the two modern novels. Big Brother,[16] the state, with whom the individual must contend, is no longer within reach of the hero who struggles with it. This means that the modern hero, caught in Oedipal toils, faces a new collective father figure, one at once more threatening, more vague, and more stifling, and one who can no longer be killed by a stroke at the crossroads. Acceptance for the modern hero means then the acceptance of absurdity, not a father with whom a common identity is possible.

The contrapuntal structuring of *Crime and Punishment* (paternal and maternal relationships, Laius and Jocasta) as well as the whole forward thrust of Raskolnikov as a character may be fully appreciated when evaluated in the light of Kafka's *The Trial*. It is little wonder that Dostoevsky has been acclaimed as the forerunner of twentieth-century fiction.

1. *Franz Kafka: A Biography*, p. 153.

2. *Franz Kafka Today*, pp. 161–64.

3. See Mark Spilka, *Dickens and Kafka* pp. 90, 270, 277.

4. Ronald Gray, *Franz Kafka*, pp. 107, 192–93.

5. In this letter Kafka terms Dostoevsky a "true blood-relation" (*I Am a Memory Come Alive*, p. 95).

6. Gustav Janouch, *Conversations with Kafka: Notes and Reminiscences*, pp. 93–94.

7. In *"Crime and Punishment" and the Critics*, pp. 57–77.

8. "Dostoevsky and Father-Love Exemplified by *Crime and Punishment*."

9. In *Art and Psychoanalysis*, pp. 21–53.

10. "The Source of Guilt and the Sense of Guilt—Kafka's *The Trial*."

11. Philip Rahv, *The Myth and the Powerhouse*, p. 113.

12. Franz Kafka, *The Trial*, trans. Willa and Edwin Muir (New York: Alfred A. Knopf, 1968), p. 50. Subsequent references to this volume will be cited in the text.

13. Fyodor Dostoevsky, *Crime and Punishment*, trans. Constance Garnett (New York: Modern Library College Editions, 1950), p. 151. Subsequent references to this volume will be cited in the text.

14. The same motif appears in *The Brothers Karamazov* (part three, chapter three) when Alyosha calls Grushenka "'sister" and Grushenka is touched in much the same way as Leni is in this scene. One thinks also of Alyosha's attachment to Lisa, a cripple.

120

15. The importance of these three scenes is indicated by their positions in their respective sections: chapter four in parts four and five and chapter eight in part six. See Louise Dauner's article in *Modern Fiction Studies* for the significance of the number 4 in *Crime and Punishment*.

16. It is significant that George Orwell's *1984* also deals with a hero involved with a paternal bureaucracy. Furthermore, Winston like both Raskolnikov and K. has a neurotic relation with mother and sister figures. See Marcus Smith, "The Wall of Blackness: A Psychological Approach to *1984*," *Modern Fiction Studies* 14 (Winter 1968–69):423–33.

## Chapter Six

## The Interplay of Circular and Spiral Form in Mann's *The Magic Mountain*

In "Voyage with Don Quixote," Thomas Mann describes his reading of Cervantes' book during a sea voyage to America, interspersing comments on the novel with his impressions of the trip; the essay cannot help but remind one a bit of the way in which Cervantes himself interwove his various literary digressions with his observations on his hero's trip. Did Mann intentionally equate himself with Don Quixote? Mann's comments on Cervantes' novel are not, however, always complimentary. Reading the book in Tieck's translation, he was, of course, subject to a romantic interpretation, and he saw Cervantes as "the 'ingenio lego' who is not conscious of either his art or his fundamental convictions."[1] Mann writes, "It is precisely because they [E.T.A. Hoffmann and Cervantes] were artists in and beyond art that they came so dangerously near to the ironic dissolution of form."[2] Furthermore, he preferred the 1605 *Don Quixote* to the second part, seeing in the first part a naïveté and unpretentiousness without any conscious plan. "The second part has no longer the happy freshness and carelessness of the first," he writes, "which grew into a book of a whole people and of all humanity" *"par hasard et par génie."*[3] When form does appear, then, in Cervantes' work, Mann judges it to be too scrupulous or self-conscious to count.

The conclusion of *Don Quixote* also disturbed Thomas Mann. He is dissatisfied with the conversion of the hero to sanity at the end and is shocked by the callousness of Don Quixote's friends after his death, failing to see as Leo Spitzer[4] suggests that Cervantes' "prosaicness" in these scenes was doubtless a deliberate attempt to satirize the sentimentality and elaborate literary devices writers of fiction employed in his day. As Cervantes so often demonstrated, his main purpose in *Don Quixote* was to destroy those writers of romance who denied reality.

Several times throughout the essay, Mann describes his own artistic stratagems in his Joseph books, always to Cervantes' disadvantage. Thus he sees the humor he himself creates (for example, in the scene where Joseph, sitting by the well, compares his real body with the ideal body with which the centuries have endowed him) as superior to what he judges to be often amorphous buffoonery in Cervantes' novel.[5]

It is clear, then, that Mann in his own work would wish to follow a different artistic course from that which he had observed in the reading of *Don Quixote*. It also must be clear, however, from earlier portions of this critical work that Cervantes' book was far less unstructured and formless than Mann judged it to be in the Tieck translation. Like Flaubert, Mann admired Cervantes' naturalness and lack of self-conscious artistry. At the same time, these qualities disturbed his Germanic sense of symmetry and form. Mann, the ironic German, did not appreciate the irony in his own employment of an art form whose structural foundations had been laid by a novelist Mann judged to compose with no conscious plan.

Thomas Mann's novel *The Magic Mountain* is often cited as an example of what critics call the "philosophical novel,"[6] the dialectic between Naphta and Settembrini giving partial support to this opinion, as does the book's contribution to metaphysics and to various views on the relation of appearance and reality. Mann's entire philosophy of process is an important underlying factor in the book, and, in order to give this philosophy body, he uses frequently various circular patterns within his story. In fact, the circle is the main objective correlative of his philosophy of time. Mann himself was aware of these facets of his work, for he wrote, "It passes beyond realism by means of symbolism, and makes realism a vehicle for intellectual and ideal elements."[7]

Erich Heller has pointed out that the circular motion of time has determined the form of Mann's work.[8] Everything in the book moves in circles. Up and down, to and fro, have no real significance because as parts of circles they are easily confused or reversed. Everything returns to its starting point in one way or another. But it is not the closed circle of repetition, Nietzsche's "ewige Wiederkehr," that Mann celebrates (despite his earlier admiration for Nietzsche), for by 1924 the closed circle had become for Thomas Mann the equivalent of "measureless monotony" or routine (p. 547). In the ocean of time, one must chart a direction, but first one must abandon watch and compass in order to do so. Such abandonment is equivalent to the process of breaking out of a circular into a spiral reality. The hands of the watch, the routine of the Berghof, the needle of the compass—all describe closed circles, but true human activity is described in spiral form. Thus the early dualism established by the rudimentary conflict between Clavdia and Settembrini (between body and mind) gives way in chapter six to the more complex dualism between Naphta and Settembrini (between this world and the next), to be subsumed in the elaborate figure of Mynheer Peeperkorn, representing both Christ and Dionysius, in effect all the earlier points of view wrapped in one. Each episode transcends the previous one. At the same time Hans Castorp's own spiraling development, instead of following these exterior occurrences on the mountain, springs from three interior events, three germinal scenes (in the sections called "Snow," "The Fullness of Harmony," and "The Thunderbolt") that mark his progress in life and its resolution. The two spirals are, of course, not independent of one another; instead Mann establishes a contrapuntal effect.

The first circle of experience in which Hans is involved covers five chapters of the book, concluding with the Walpurgis Night scene. Within these first five chapters, we find also a myriad of lesser circles and spirals that are freely used by Mann as exponents of his philosophy of reality.

Hans's arrival at Davos-Dorf is the result of the spiral progress of the train into the higher regions of the Swiss Alps: "The train wound in curves along the narrow pass" (p. 4). The closed circle of experience that Hans is tentatively leaving is, however, symbolized by the christening basin (and plate) found in the title of chaper two. The christening basin forms, of course, a perfect circle of gilded metal, resting solid "on a round base" (p.22). Furthermore, we learn that it had been in use "for a round hundred years" (p. 21) ("seit rund hundert Jahren").[9] Already the names of seven successive owners have been engraved on the back of the plate. Each time a new child has been held over the gilded bowl, the same words exactly have been spoken by the minister and the water has flowed over each child's head in "precisely the same way" (p. 23). Presumably one day Hans's name would be added to the list on the back of the plate, and his child would in turn be held over the basin in "precisely the same way." The reality described by this objective correlative is a frozen reality. Hans's grandfather has little use for the new, although Hans himself is often troubled, when observing the bowl, by a sense of *both* change and duration. His thoughts presage his own fate, which is, of course, to break out of the magic circle of the seven owners of this antique bowl. The fact that the one hundred years of its use are "round" suggests that they end exactly where they began. Hans's arrival, then, at the Berghof by means of a train that wound in spiral fashion up the mountains augurs for Hans a new beginning, a new direction, and perhaps even new growth. Even thirty-four, the number of his room at the Berghof, symbolically breaks in two the number seven[10] (which for Mann represented a completed cycle), associated with the christening basin and plate. It is a well-known fact that Mann was fascinated by numbers and their possible mystical or symbolic significances.

In chapter three a different kind of circle is invoked, one that springs from the cyclical repetition inherent in myth. As Frederick J. Hoffman wrote: "The repetitive value of myth, as it appears and reappears in various guises and disguises, constitutes its true historical importance. The succession of such mythical occurrences causes a suspension of historical time, in favor of a time governed by racial, unconscious rhythms."[11] Hans Mayer made the same point in different words: "For mankind there is no end. At the heels of a dying epoch, follows a new beginning."[12] Thus we find ourselves in the third section of chapter three in the circles of a Dantean hell, ruled over by Satana (or Settembrini) and judged by a modern Minos and Rhadamanthus (Hofrat Behrens and Dr. Krokowski). Ascent and descent become suddenly reversed as Herr Settembrini informs Hans that his trip *up* five thousand feet was "only seeming" (p. 58). The past described in this section is unlike the closed circle of tradition found in chaper two, for Mann shows us that myth and legend are capable of modification as the wheel of fate turns. Hans in repeating the experience of Dante in "descending" to hell finds a new Virgil (Settembrini) to act as guide. This modern Virgil recites Latin verse with an Italian pronunciation, but summons Hans in words taken from his predecessor: "Let us go together, our way is the same: the 'path on the right that shall lead to the halls of the mightiest Dis'" (p. 62).

The particular Satana (also Settembrini) discovered in these "lower" regions is a humanistic one, drawn from Carducci, a Satan of rebellion against blind authority represented by the modern judges Minos and Rhadamanthus. "There is a good deal up here that is positively mediaeval" (p. 61), Settembrini further informs Hans. In fact, Hofrat Behrens, who is subject to melancholia, and Dr. Krokowski, always clad in black, have established a kind of medieval Chamber of Horrors at the Berghof, according to Hans's new friend, who also insists that the directress, Frau Adriatic, must first have seen the light of day in the thirteenth century.

The circular reality proposed in this section of the book is abstract or theoretical, not expressed by means of an ob-

126

jective correlative like the christening basin. Nevertheless, as we know from his Joseph books, Mann was strongly drawn to the idea of cyclical return, of generation upon generation working through the same experiences and returning always to the same point, sometimes, of course, with a difference. One of the basic principles behind the Joseph books was the revolving sphere of Sumerian-Babylonian mythology.[13] In his essay "Voyage with Don Quixote," Mann had remarked that as a teller of tales he had reached the stage of myth: "I would humanize it, would seek, in my unlimited contempt for the soulfully and wilfully barbaric, a rapprochment between humanity and myth."[14] Thus Dante himself in his descent to hell merely followed creatively many legendary predecessors, and Mann's Satana springs from antecedents without number (for example, the devils of Ivan Karamazov, Faust, and Milton). For Mann a recognition of the historical and mythical past living within us all was a creative recognition, leading to a sense of role as well as to the urge to reconstruct this role on one's own terms, thus preventing experience from becoming a closed circle. At the end of chapter three, Settembrini (Satana, Virgil), sensing Hans's initial infatuation with the ailing Frau Chauchat and fearing just such a closed circle of experience for his "Dante," urges Hans to leave the Berghof, but without success. Hans glances into the next room and his eyes fall on the full face of Clavdia Chauchat, once more triggering a half-formed memory of his schoolboy friend, Pribislav Hippe.

As a result chapter four is permeated with the imagery of the closed circle. To begin with, Hans's sense of time fades, confronted by the closed circle of routine that takes its place and that is followed punctiliously day after day at the Berghof. Complete uniformity is achieved as the hours "scurry by like dead leaves" (p. 105). The endless repetitions of the Mexican lady, "Tous-les deux," provide another kind of deadly closed circle. Furthermore, Hans has now become fully cognizant of Clavdia's similarity to Pribislav Hippe, and he relives with her his schoolboy infatuation. "How remarkably like her he looked," he thinks, "like this girl up here!" (p. 123). And to pick one more closed circle at random, we find the sun and the moon, one rising, the other setting, "from day to night and back again to day" (p. 154) in the scene that Hans remembers from his past when he rowed upon a lake in Holstein.

"A continuous present, an identity, an everlastingness" (p. 183) are described in chapter five in the first section entitled "Soup Everlasting." Another section is entitled "The Dance of Death," the circular dance suggesting the real motivation behind Hans's and Joachim's new and sudden interest in the moribund, for it is perhaps an attempt by means of empty repetition of form (the visits, the flowers, and the condolences) to conquer the death that they, too, must ultimately face. As Hans says at the beginning of the enterprise, "It will do me good" (p. 295).

In the final section of chapter five, "Walpurgis-Night," we complete the first large circle of Hans's experience on the magic mountain, for the ascent of the Brocken implied in the title carries us back to Hans's ascent of the "magic mountain" in chapter one. The carnival season, the festival, for Mann is fraught with significance, for through such points inserted into the normal and monotonous round of existence, transcendence (or *Steigerung*) can be achieved. "A feast is an anniversary," Mann wrote, "a renewal of the past in the present."[15] Only by returning to a specific point (for example, this festival marking the beginning of summer) can one assess and master one's life because such points provide us with contrasts and comparisons, and, like the risers of a staircase, with perspective. Mann refers to them as always alchemistic (p. 725). But at this festival, Hans achieves no such *Steigerung* because he manages merely to repeat fruitlessly with Clavdia the school scene in which he had asked Pribislav Hippe for a pencil, without learning from it or seeing it in perspective. Mann's use of the *Leitmotiv* in this scene, the pencil and Clavdia's "Kirghiz eyes," is, as Erich Heller points out, a "literary symptom of a metaphysical belief towards which he inclined."[16] For through the *Leitmotiv*, Mann creates a sense of reenactment or return in time. The pencil here suggests the circular nature of reality, and Hans's love for Clavdia will be as unyielding of results as his love for Pribislav had been.[17] Faust, too, on his famous Walpurgis-Night had danced with a young witch. The summer promised by Hans's infatuation with Clavdia becomes, therefore, a blighted one, and the departure of Clavdia from the Berghof means that Satana's pupil must seek elsewhere for his answers.

## II

Another circle of experience begins shortly thereafter for Hans Castorp with the coming of Herr Naphta to the village. His arrival coincides, of course, with another festival, the summer solstice or Midsummer Night, the beginning of another round. Mann writes, "But the motion by which one measures time is circular, is in a closed circle; and might almost equally be described as rest" (p. 344), suggesting that the experience of Hans at present is also a closed circle, and it continues to be as he listens tirelessly to the endless, fruitless, and repetitive debates of Naphta and Settembrini that lead to no resolution.

However, toward the end of chapter six we find Hans lost in a snowstorm and returning again and again "tipsy" and "giddy" to the same hay hut. "You went in a circle, gave yourself endless trouble under the delusion that you were accomplishing something, and all the time you were simply describing some great silly arc that would turn back to where it had its beginning, like the riddling year itself" (p. 487). The double significance of this statement is clear when we consider Hans's present predicament as well as the nature of human reality. Circular reality is further underlined as Hans once more remembers giving "the ailing Clavdia Chauchat back son crayon—his, Pribislav Hippe's, pencil" (p. 489).

Nevertheless, his near brush with death in the snow turns out for Hans to be his first successful escape from the closed circles in which he has been imprisoned into a new round of spiral reality. After his dream he knows that, as in the snow, he has "wandered lost with Settembrini and Naphta" (p. 495). Because of this symbolic experience of "descent" into the grave (his dream of witches dismembering a child), despite the heights on which he has wandered, Hans is reborn and now recognizes that the position of *Homo Dei* lies neither in the "mystic community" of Naphta nor in the "windy individualism" of Settembrini, but somewhere in the middle. "Only love, not reason, gives sweet thoughts" (p. 496), yet love "always in silent recognition of the blood-sacrifice" (p. 496). As R. Hinton Thomas points out, Hans experiences in the chapter "Snow" "the deeper essence of time, quality as against quantity."[18]

It is Joachim, less fortunate than Hans, who, in the final section of this chapter, fulfills the prophecy of the opening page, of time as a "closed circle." We learn that Joachim must "give up his soldier's career and return to the horizontal" (p. 502); and one day the same train brings him back that had brought Hans, the same time of year, the first days of August. "It has just begun" (p. 502). Years had passed, "very eventful yet 'the sum of nothing'" (p. 502).

Likewise we learn that Clavdia is returning, and Settembrini taunts Hans with: "Your Beatrice is returning? Your guide through all nine circles of Paradise? I must hope that you will not scorn the friendly hand of your Virgil" (p. 519). Both Virgil and Beatrice have led Hans to fruitless repetitions.

But it is Joachim's life that in its single-minded devotion to the military describes the perfect closed circle of experience. His last thoughts as he lies dying concern writing an application for an extension of his leave, and the Hofrat sums up his life with the cryptic "Honour was the death of him" (p. 539). Did Mann, intimating still another closed circle, have in mind Brentano's hero Kasper?[19] As a final tribute to the "ewige Wiederkehr": "It had been decided to take Joachim home" (p. 539).

In the new circle that begins with the return of Clavdia, accompanied by the Dutchman, Mynheer Peeperkorn, Hans has the opportunity to put into practice the lessons he has learned from his dream in the snow in chapter six. As a result Mynheer Peeperkorn and Hans become "brothers," Hans having passed the period of probation. "Let us give free rein to brotherly feeling" (p. 611), Peeperkorn proposes. And after Peeperkorn's suicide, Hans and Clavdia become brother and sister (like Alyosha and Grushenka in *The Brothers Karamazov*)[20] as he moves to kiss her on the forehead, a kiss he had been unable to bestow in Peeperkorn's presence. *"For the sake of goodness and love, man shall let death have no sovereignty over his thoughts"* (p. 497).

Peeperkorn himself, of course, in his majestic hypocrisy and hubris ("he regarded himself as the instrument of God's marriage" p. 624), is a grotesque synthesis of all opposites. He thereby neutralizes all experience, for not even his admirers can hear him as he orates by the thunderous waterfall, thunder drowning out thunder. This figure represents the ultimate in meaningless circularity. His final signature before his suicide is to wave his beaker "half-circle before the assembled guests" (p. 621). Although Mann uses the word *dynamic* to describe him, it is a dynamism directed to empty forms and fetishes, that is, to no real end, a wasted power.

It is in the section of chapter seven called "The Fullness of Harmony," however, that Mann's answers to Hans's interminable questions about life may be found. It is a reinforcement and a rounding out of the insight granted to Hans in the "Snow" section and serves as the culminating point in the book, offering a positive philosophy of love in answer to life's problems. When Hans becomes manager of the gramophone, we are provided with a fascinating new objective correlative for Mann's concept of reality. The grooves of the gramophone record (or the moving needle of the machine) describe a spiral pattern, inward to the vortex, the still center, thus combining the principles of Castorp's two mentors, both essence and existence. We are consequently involved with a process of circular reality whereby the needle continually returns to the same point, but a point removed by a fraction of an inch in its course toward the still center. As we have said, it is this spiral form that for Mann denotes progress away from the closed circles of experience described in the flatlands and in the monotony of the Haus Berghof. The spiral allows for what Mann calls *Steigerung*, or "heightening." It was a principle that Mann probably had from Goethe, who saw it as an intensification. *Steigerung* was not for Goethe a sense of ascending process but "the mechanism of concentration and refinement."[21] It is in this sense that Hans achieves the "fullness of harmony," both the intensity and the ability to give form to his dream of perfection.

In essence what we find in this section, "The Fullness of Harmony," are five different records, each one providing Hans with new perspectives by repeating various cycles of his own life on the mountain. The passage from *Aida* replays the experience of Clavdia and Hans, buried alive on the mountain as Radames and Aida had been buried beneath the temple. It is a Freudian principle that repetition of experience through art may help one to mastery of experience. "The Afternoon of a Faun" retells Hans's early days in the sanatorium as "goat-legged" he pursued both Clavdia and research into biology, anatomy, and physiology. *Carmen* revives the story of Joachim and Marusja as does the Prayer from Gounod's *Faust*, while at the same time the Prayer mirrors the brother-sister relationship that has developed between Hans and Clavdia. The fifth record, a song by Schubert, however, provides the ultimate answer for Hans and for Mann. The linden tree stands at the center of process "am Brunnen von dem Tore," the spring and the gate representing life and its challenge. The hero of the song rejects the delusion of peace and rest offered by the tree's sheltering branches.

Instead he elects the tension of life, the wind blowing straight in his face, death as a part of a life process, for life feeds on life.

> Die kalten Winde bliesen
> Mir grad' in's Angesicht
> Der Hut flog mir von Kopfe
> Ich wendete mich nicht.[22]

> (The cold winds blew
> Straight in my face
> My hat flew from my head
> I did not turn.)

Form and civilization, Mann writes, "always in silent recognition of the blood-sacrifice" (p. 496). "Ah, it was worth dying for the enchanted *lied!*" (p. 653).

Mann deplores the faked repetition, the trumpery of Joachim's return in the séance scene—those who would tamper with the phenomenon of the circle, using pretense and deception to make a mockery of natural process. Although Mann was often drawn to experiment with the séance himself, he appears in this section,"Highly Questionable," to be thoroughly disillusioned with its mimicry. Joachim sits with "hollow, shadowy cheeks, warrior's beard and full, curling lips" (p. 680); and Hans is able only to whisper, "Forgive me!" (p. 681), as his eyes overflow with tears.

The third and final experience of *Steigerung* that Hans undergoes comes only at the end when he completes the large circle of his seven years on the magic mountain and descends to the flatland, but not as the Hans Castorp who had arrived with his book on ocean steamships in the first pages of the novel. It has taken the thunderbolt (the title of the final section) of World War I to crack open the closed circle of these seven years of his life and to change them to spiral form. He returns down below in a new role, one denoting penance and a sense of community or social cognizance, as we see him on the battlefield "limping on his earthbound feet" (p. 715), and humming Schubert's song:

> "And loving words I've carven
> Upon its branches fair—"

According to Mann, "World War I forced us out of the metaphysical and individual stage into the social."[23]

In the last paragraph, the "dream of love," discovered both in the snow scene and in the "Fullness of Harmony" section, is restated in Mann's farewell address to his hero; it is the third playing of the central theme of the book. For out of the "rainwashed evening sky" (p. 716), out of disease, suffering, and death, comes their opposite, the "fiery glow" of Love. Freud had preceded Mann in showing how Thanatos and Eros play against one another in our lives. "There is as it were an oscillating rhythm in the life of organisms: the one group of instincts [Thanatos] presses forward to reach the final goal of life as quickly as possible, the other [Eros] flies back at a certain point on the way only to traverse the same stretch once more from a given spot and thus to prolong the duration of the journey."[24] We discover here in summary the conflicting forces that have beset Hans Castorp in the hermetic atmosphere of the magic mountain. "For man himself is a mystery, and all humanity rests upon reverence before the mystery that is man" (p. 729).

1. Lienhard Bergel, "Cervantes in Germany," p. 346.

2. Thomas Mann, *Essays of Three Decades*, p. 442.

3. Ibid., p. 436.

4. Leo Spitzer, "Thomas Mann y la muerte de Don Quijote."

5. *Essays of Three Decades*, p. 442.

6. See Herman J. Weigand, "The Magic Mountain," p. 164.

7. Thomas Mann, *The Magic Mountain*, trans. H. T. Lowe-Porter (New York: Alfred A. Knopf, 1960), p. 726. Subsequent references to this volume will be cited in the text.

8. Erich Heller, *The Ironic German*, p. 239.

9. Thomas Mann, *Der Zauberberg* (Berlin: S. Fischer Verlag, 1976). p. 33.

10. Harry Slochower writes of the importance of seven as a symbol in *The Magic Mountain*, the number seven representing the completion of a

cycle. *Three Ways of Modern Man* (New York: International Publishers, 1937), p. 98.

11. Frederick J. Hoffman, *Freudianism and the Literary Mind* (Baton Rouge: Louisiana State University Press, 1957), p. 218.

12. Hans Mayer, *Thomas Mann: Werk und Entwicklung* (Berlin: Volk und Welt, 1950), p. 227. My translation.

13. See Margaret Church, *Time and Reality: Studies in Contemporary Fiction*, p. 158.

14. *Essays of Three Decades*, pp. 455–56.

15. Ibid., p. 425.

16. Heller, p. 194.

17. See Church, p. 149.

18. R. Hinton Thomas, *Thomas Mann: The Mediation of Art*, p. 110.

19. See Clemens Brentano, "Vom braven Kasperl und dem schönen Annerl," *Werke* (München: Carl Hanser Verlag, 1963), 2:744–806.

20. See chapter four on *The Brothers Karamazov*, section two.

21. Elizabeth M. Wilkinson and L. A. Willoughby, *Goethe, Poet and Thinker*, pp. 192–200.

22. Wilhelm Müller, "Der Lindenbaum," stanza 5. Set to music by Schubert in 1827. My translation.

23. Thomas Mann, *A Sketch of My Life*, p. 58.

24. Sigmund Freud, "Beyond the Pleasure-Principle," in *A General Selection from the Works of Sigmund Freud*, ed. John Rickman, M.D. (Garden City, N.Y.: Doubleday and Company, 1957), p. 162.

Chapter Seven

How the Vicociclometer Works:
The Fiction of James Joyce

Georges Borach, Joyce's language pupil in Zurich, records in his journal on 1 August 1917 that Joyce had said to him the evening before in the Pfauen Café: "The most beautiful, all-embracing theme is that of the Odyssey. It is greater, more human than that of *Hamlet, Don Quixote*, Dante, *Faust*."[1] One is, in fact, hard put to find references to Cervantes' work in either *Ulysses* or *Finnegans Wake*. In *Ulysses* Don Quixote is mentioned twice, in the "Scylla and Carybdis" episode where Stephen sees himself as Don Quixote as he looks down "on a wide headless caubeen, hung on his ashplanthandle over his knee. My casque and sword," and later, on the same page, where George Moore and Edward Martyn are compared to Don Quixote and Sancho, Moore described as "A knight of the rueful countenance here in Dublin. With a saffron kilt?"[2] In *Finnegans Wake* the references to Cervantes' novel are equally rare. In book two, chapter one, Shem "had his tristiest cabaleer on" and is "donkey shot at? or a peso besant to join the armada?"[3] And Shaun becomes "Sin Showpanza" with Isabel, of course, cast in the role of "dulsy nayer." Another reference in book three, chapter three, designates John MacDougal of County Mayo (Saint John of the fourth Gospel) as "Johnny my donkeyschott."[4] It is perhaps a clue to Joyce's reaction to Cervantes' novel that he casts Stephen, George Moore, Shem, and Saint John as Don Quixotes. Shem is the Penman; in the words of Anthony Burgess, he is "the man who can make the dead speak but is totally incapable of coming to terms with the living."[5] And even though James Joyce (Shem = James) often sees himself in this role, his heroes, Odysseus-Bloom and HCE, are Everyman, not simply one spokesman in "a sort of tragicomic dialectic."[6]

135

It is clear, therefore, that we must look elsewhere for direct influences on the architecture of Joyce's fiction. As heir of fictional techniques since the time of Cervantes, Joyce, like Mann, of course, is indirectly in debt to his sixteenth-century predecessor; for Joyce it was Flaubert, in particular, who acted as intermediary. Scholes and Kain mention Joyce's debt to Flaubert's "realism,"[7] and David Hayman notes that Flaubert was one of several predecessors to furnish Joyce with "theories, images, points of style and an occasional sequence of sense."[8] Both Hugh Kenner[9] and Richard Cross have devoted book-length studies to relationships between the works of Flaubert and Joyce. Cross's fifth chapter deals with similarities in the spatial form of *Madame Bovary* and the "Nausicaa" episode in *Ulysses*, and Cross notes that *Madame Bovary* "takes its place in the great tradition of parodic fiction stemming from Cervantes."[10]

The importance of structure was paramount for an artist of Joyce's temperament and mental capacities. Some pattern had to be found to contain the multitude of allusions, facts, and fancies that crowded Joyce's mind. A tightly structured work like *Madame Bovary*, described once by Proust as even "lacking in air,"[11] was doubtless one of the prototypes Joyce observed with interest in planning his own work. There is no question about Joyce's admiration for Flaubert; Ellmann mentions it time and again in his biography, although Joyce was said to prefer *Madame Bovary* to other works by Flaubert.[12]

The particular pattern to which Joyce turned for the purposes of structure was, of course, that of the Ages of Man as described by Giambattista Vico in *Scienza nuova* (1725), a powerful source and influence throughout Joyce's career.[13] Despite the work of the "new criticism," of various deterministic schools of thought, of psychological criticism, of studies of craftsmanship or of social or psychological development, without source study one must ignore revealing literary relationships such as those between *Crime and Punishment* and *The Trial*, between *Don Quixote* and

*Joseph Andrews* or *Madame Bovary*, between *Tristram Shandy*
and some of the novels of Virginia Woolf. A good source
study provides one with material for understanding both
the work influenced and the source. It enables one to place
the work influenced in a literary context, to define it and its
goals through such context, and to decide thereby how it
succeeds and how it may fail.[14] In addition, Jorge Luis
Borges has shown how awareness of source may enlarge
understanding of the source itself: "Every writer," Borges
claims, "*creates* his own precursors."[15] In "Pierre Menard,
Author of the *Quixote*," Borges points out that Menard, in
"composing" the *Quixote*, has enriched "the halting and
rudimentary art of reading" through deliberate anachron-
ism and that attributing *Imitatio Christi* to Céline or James
Joyce is "sufficient renovation of its tenuous spiritual indications."[16] Thus he would argue that in attributing the
*Scienza nuova* to James Joyce, one may gain insights into the
writings of Vico as well as into Joyce's own work. Norman
O. Brown has recently demonstrated this point with con-
creteness in his *Closing Time*, in which he juxtaposes passages from Vico and *Finnegans Wake*, creating a three-way
dialogue with himself as moderator and chorus.

*Genesis* is *Natura*
the nature of nations is their *nascimento*                                    *NS*,
                        the way they were born        147–48

culture is nature
the nations have a natural law which is their nature        *NS*,
                        the way they were born   311

the Vico Rd is the Nascimiento Rd                                    *FW*, 452
                  (below Big Sur

the way they were born
the birth trauma
        (Otto Rank
determines their character[17]

Intriguing critical possibilities for reinterpretation of both
source and counterpart exist if one can introduce Borges's

theory of mutual interaction of literary works into the field of criticism.

Studies of Vico and Joyce have, however, been largely limited to *Finnegans Wake*. One may consult my own extended treatment of this subject in *Time and Reality*.[18] It has also been my contention that Joyce used Vico in his work much earlier than has usually been acknowledged, and the examination of *Dubliners* and *A Portrait* in the larger context of a gradually unfolding Viconian pattern, traceable in Joyce's entire canon, will demonstrate Joyce's significant debt to Vico as well as Vico's significant debt to Joyce.

II

James Joyce stated that in *Dubliners* he tried to present Dublin "to the indifferent public under four of its aspects: childhood, adolescence, maturity, and public life. The stories are arranged in this order."[19] In examining *Dubliners* under these four categories, one can plainly see the patterns and strategies of Joyce's later four Viconian cycles emerging. Seen in this light, *Dubliners* may be viewed as evidence of Joyce's quadrilateral frame of mind as early as 1903, a frame leading to a ready acceptance of Vico's philosophy in his later works.

Croce's restatement of Vico, "Man creates the human world, creates it by transforming himself into the facts of society,"[20] has a deep relevance for *Dubliners*. Although one can only speculate as to the exact date when Joyce became aware of Vico, it would seem that this date may perhaps be earlier than 1911 rather than later, even though Ellmann does not mention Vico until describing Joyce's conversations with Paolo Cuzzi from 1911 to 1913. At least by the time "The Dead" was written in 1906 and 1907, Joyce had had opportunity as "an exile" in Rome to discover Vico. He may perhaps have added it as the final story in *Dubliners* to act as a *ricorso* for the collection. At least we can state with some certainty that Vico's philosophy, whenever Joyce did discover it, reinforced rather than altered his patterns of thought. It is possible to construct, as the discussion that follows shows, a Viconian pattern for *Dubliners*.

The first three stories may be seen to portray not only childhood but a foreshadowing of Vico's first age, the Divine Age or the Age of the Parents. It is viewed from many perspectives, among them the religious, the psychological, and the mythical. The gods in Joyce's Divine Age are our parents and elders, all singularly warped and all incapable of providing in any meaningful way the guidance or solace demanded of our gods. Especially paralyzed is Father Flynn in "The Sisters," haunted by guilt of simony. About him hangs an aura of evil; his face, even in death, is "truculent" and his nostrils black and cavernous passages to the underworld. The "education" he gives the boy turns the child in his uncle's words into a Rosicrucian, the pedantic and esoteric taking precedence over the vital and free. The boy experiences a sense of freedom once Father Flynn is gone; he has been rapt into a foreign world "where the customs were strange."[21]

Attending the priest are "the sisters," Nannie and Eliza, spinster women who have devoted their lives as nurse and mother figures to Father Flynn. Nannie is the generic for nurse; Elizabeth was the mother of John the Baptist, and ironically the name *Elizabeth* means "consecrated to God." The consecration and service of these "sisters" (both in the religious and secular sense) is betrayed by their brother's sale of their birthright. These representatives of the divine—Father Flynn and "the sisters"—in Joyce's Divine Age must serve as earthly gods for the young boy; that Joyce attaches importance to the religious overtones of the story is clear in his title.

The psychological overtones of the title are perhaps even more telling. As well as a story of holy father and sisters, this is a tale of a father surrogate and of brother and sisters. It is Father Flynn who takes from the uncle the role of earthly father for the boy, encouraged by the aunt who sends High Toast to Father Flynn. It is Father Flynn who turns the boy's mind from the physical to the spiritual arena. But the parent figures in this instance are both flawed ones. Although the uncle's point of view can be seen as pedestrian, unimaginative, and mundane, the priest's can be seen as guilt-ridden and distorted by a powerful superego. The chalice he has sold, although in his sister's words "it contained nothing," is symbolic of his role as a priest and consequently of his relation to both religion and life. The cup that traditionally holds the Blood of Christ, the grail of the quester legend, stands for the virtues that are the essence of Christian perfection. Having bartered his birthright and his role in society, Father Flynn withdraws into a life of infantile security watched over by mother and nurse figures. It is to this paralytic that the boy turns for guidance and for companionship.

The story may be seen on the mythological level as the myth of the quester hero in reverse. The irony directed against the priest turns the story into an "anti-myth." Rather than a knight in search of the grail, Father Flynn has sold and lied about the grail with which he was entrusted. Rather than moving toward discovery and insight, Father Flynn travels away from these goals, shutting himself up in the dark in his confession box and then retiring to a childlike dependency in the home. Joyce's ironic Divine Age is well served by Father Flynn.

The second "divinity" in Joyce's *Dubliners* is the pederast of "An Encounter." Like a god he appears out of nowhere and becomes the center of interest for the truant boys. This god is a seductive god, full of salacious talk. The leadership and guidance of the teachers whom the boys have deserted for the day is parodied by this man as are the virtues of the gods.

On the psychological level, this mock father figure represents a narcissism that uses even children for its own ends. The boys meet a series of frustrations. First, Leo (Lion) Dillon, associated in their minds with the Wild West, chickens out of the adventure, and the siege at Smoothing Iron fails to materialize as a result of Leo's absence. After crossing the Liffey, they are again frustrated, this time by the escape of the cat. The man, on the contrary, moves not away from them but in their direction. Instead of the hunters the boys become the hunted. The father figure, rather than protector, is seen as ravager. Faced with this threat, the "I" must reluctantly turn for protection to his contemporary, Mahoney. The father figure would use the young for his own selfish ends.

Mythologically, "An Encounter" is yet another inversion of the quester tale. Seeking adventure and "wild sensations" of explorers of the West, the boys move step by step away from real adventure and into an underworld of perverted desire. Crossing the Liffey is symbolic of a journey into the dark regions. The legend on the stern of the Norwegian vessel is undecipherable, for the boys are in a strange and foreign land like the one introduced by Father Flynn to the boy in "The Sisters." Dublin's Divine Age, the Age of the Parents, is once more viewed by Joyce as a dark age.

The same mock-religious figures (the priest, who leaves his money to institutions and his furniture to his sister; the indifferent and sadistic uncle-father) appear in "Araby." Psychologically, the story revolves again around a boy with a desire for adventure and for the exotic, a boy who is thwarted and frustrated by the adult world. The legend is that of another search, unfulfilled. Added to this pattern is for the first time an idealized romantic interest in the opposite sex. Neither the stimulus of adventure nor of love is able to overcome the deadening weight of the parent and of the divinity, who hover near the child. Joyce's Divine Age is filled with divinities who gainsay, mislead, and try to pervert their would-be idolators. The boy in "The Sisters" is perhaps least aware of this failure in leadership. The other boys face it and are either frightened by it as in "An Encounter" or filled with self-reproach as in "Araby."

Disillusionment with the divine leads into the next age, the Heroic Age, or Age of the Sons, sons fostered by the kind of parents seen in the first three stories. But these sons are not Christ figures, nor are they heroes in their own right; anything but this. A daughter and seven sons are viewed in the next eight stories covering Joyce's two categories of adolescence and maturity, which coalesce in the Viconian plan into one category or cycle, the Age of the Sons.

It is appropriate that the cycle starts with a name that suggests Eve. Eve is both offspring and wife of Adam. She stands then as a suitable transition figure between the Age of the Parents and the Age of the Sons, having a share, so to speak, in each age. Eveline, in Joyce's story, is a wife surrogate for the man who is her father, but the relation in the story is both suppressed and destructive. The story also serves as an excellent example of the *effect* of the Age of the Parents on the Age of the Sons and thus as a logical transition between the two parts.

On the religious level, the sons in the Heroic Age are anything except Christ figures or Christian knights. Jimmy Doyle in "After the Race" sells his birthright in a way different from that which Father Flynn has chosen. He gambles it away to two Frenchmen on an American yacht, that is, to foreigners. Lenehan and Corley are hardly the "two gallants" suggested by the title. The word *gallant* connotes chivalry, especially toward one's lady. Joyce's gallants exploit instead of serve their "lady." On the other hand, Mr. Doran of "The Boarding House" rather than exploiting is the *object* of exploitation by "the Virgin Mary" (Polly) and her mother, Mrs. Mooney. Joyce's Dublin has sullied and defiled the Christian values to which it gives lip service.

Young adults fare no better than adolescents in this Heroic Age. Little Chandler is unable to play the role of parent or earthly father. Still seeking for a strong father substitute himself, he readily accepts the leadership of both his wife, Annie (grace), and the false god, Ignatius Gallaher (Galahad). Gallaher's superficiality and self-centeredness are not apparent to Little Chandler, who is blinded by his idolatrous devotion to what he thinks

Gallaher represents. Nor is Farrington in "Counterparts" able to assume a responsible role in either his business or personal worlds. Rather than ministering to those who need his support, he drinks away the family income while his son is forced to minister to him, to cook his evening meal, and to receive blows complementary to those inflicted on Farrington by the outside world. Equally helpless to save others, another anti-Christ, is Joe Donnelly in "Clay." Manipulated by his wife, he can only shed impotent tears at the realization of Maria's (Mary's) plight at the hands of Mrs. Donnelly. The younger generation now fails the older generation as the older had once failed the younger. And finally Mr. Duffy in "A Painful Case" is a far cry from Tristram, associated with Chapelizod, Mr. Duffy's home. He seeks in Mrs. Sinico a mother figure and like Joe Donnelly is incapable of saving the one he loves. All these persons in the Age of the Sons may be seen as antitheses of the Christ of the New Testament. Rather than preaching and spreading the word of God, these "sons" sell and deny their predecessors. "Love thy Neighbor" becomes "Exploit thy Neighbor." Unable to minister to others, these figures seek to be ministered to. Engrossed in their own petty concerns, they are impotent to become saviors of this world.

Psychologically and mythically, the Age of the Sons is the age of the Oedipus and Electra complexes. Eveline is as incapable of leaving her father as Mr. Duffy at the end of the section is of abandoning the interpretation he holds of Mrs. Sinico as a mother figure. The two gallants seek support, monetarily, from a female figure. Little Chandler, like them, is unable to identify with the father. Lost in his poetry, he allows his child to cry helplessly. Arrested at the same infantile level, Farrington is also unable to identify with benevolent authority and rebels against it (his employer) while at the same time exercising a childish and brutal authority in his home. Others, like Joe Donnelly, do not outwardly resist the aggression they despise, but cower before it and weep in their impotence.

The support and guidance denied the children in the Divine Age, the Age of the Parents, produces in turn young persons unable to assume their roles as parents and leaders in the Heroic Age. An angry and bitter irony runs through all eight stories in this section: Joyce is telling us that our Christs have become anti-Christs, that our sons have remained infants, and that our Galahads and Tristrams retain no traces of their heroic prototypes.

In Vico's Human Age (the Age of the People) the councils of this society are equally inept. Individuals, like those impotent and weak persons in the Age of the Sons, make up the three committees that appear in the three stories in this section. Parnell, like God, is dead. Hynes once celebrated his death in a poem that now he does not want to remember. On the religious level, the committees represent an ironic version of the disciples of Christ after His death. The politicians in "Ivy Day in the Committee Room" engage in idle and vain talk; their candidate is "Tricky Dicky Tierney." And Hynes, whose poem on Parnell arouses a reaction of sincere emotion, is suspected of being a spy, a Judas to the cause. None of the other members of the committee engage in anything but futile and inconsequential political activity, being more interested in the stout that they consume, ironically parallel to the communion wine.

The committee, *Eire Abu*, in "A Mother," ostensibly formed for the encouragement of the Celtic Revival, is a shadow committee composed apparently only of secretary and assistant secretary. It lacks both funds and good taste. Such a committee can foster only a false culture based on empty promises and mediocre art. Even Mr. Holohan's name has an empty ring.

Furthermore, the self-appointed committee in "Grace" is incapable, unlike the Apostles, of producing grace for the sinner. Lacking the "power" to save (despite the name of its leader), it falls back on a meaningless religiosity based on form and propriety. The qualities of Mr. Cunningham and Mr. M'Coy are clear from their names. Mr. Kernan becomes "the victim of a plot."[22]

Without leadership the committees may be seen on a psychological level as representing the nadir of group activity. Unable to identify with each other because they have no central figure with whom to identify, twentieth-century Dubliners pull away from one another in many directions. Even the priest, Father Purdon (*perdu*), betrays the "good" intention of the committee in "Grace" by preaching allegiance to Mammon, and Hynes is suspected of having betrayed the cause of *his* committee. Without real leadership for their society, the venture of Mr. Holohan and Mr. Fitzpatrick in "A Mother" turns into slapstick comedy.

Dublin collectively in the Age of the People is singularly lacking in direction. As in the other ages, Joyce has shown us that failure lies in the inability of modern man to assume fatherhood, either in image or in person. The committees viewed here are united by no Round Table nor do they have a sense of the discipleship found in the Apostles. Parnell, unlike Christ, cannot rise from the dead because his followers have let his spirit die. Politically and culturally Ireland is betrayed, and even religious grace is denied Joyce's Dubliner.

The *ricorso* is introduced by a modern Gabriel, reminder of the angel of the annunciation, who arrives late at his aunts' social affair. Unlike his predecessor's, Gabriel Conroy's speech "takes up the wrong tone." At the end Gabriel's entire world collapses as he recognizes the pettiness and futility of his existence, the superficiality of Miss Ivors and her kind who trumpeted the Celtic Revival, and the untruth of his marriage to a woman who has for years harbored a secret love. But Michael Furey lies dead, and all Ireland, indeed the universe, lies dead under the "faintly falling" snow. The bang of the *ricorso* is a whimper born of Gabriel's frustration.

Nevertheless, Joyce's employment of the Viconian pattern is even in *Dubliners* far more complex than the discussion thus far has indicated. Wheels move within wheels, gears mesh, and series of concentric circles emerge. Enlarging on Vico, Joyce believed that the four cycles existed within each other and concurrently and that complexities of movement characterized every instant. One might live psychologically in the Age of the Parents as one lived socially in the Age of the Sons. Thus "Clay," which tells us through Joe Donnelly and his wife of the Age of the Sons, of the Heroic Age, at the same time deals with the Divine Age in the Central figure, Maria, a parent figure who is now manipulated by the younger generation. Having repressed her own desire for motherhood, she has nursed her nephews and has, like Father Flynn, betrayed her chalice. This parent figure is seen as a witch by those on whom she now depends, and she can offer them only a dozen mixed pennycakes, having symbolically left her "wedding cake" on the tram.

Similarly in "A Mother," although the central issue is the Age of the People, public life, and the *Eire Abu*, the Divine Age, the Age of the Parents, is also present in the figure of Mrs. Kearney, just as Mrs. Mooney and the Age of the Parents had been present in "The Boarding House," representative of the Age of the Sons. These mothers both exemplify the grasping, greedy, and destructive parental attitude discovered earlier in the pederast of "An Encounter." Both mothers are willing and ready to sacrifice their own daughters to expediency, greed, and false pride. The parent cycle is imposed as well on "A Little Cloud" by means of Gallaher, an indifferent and self-centered "parent," similar to the uncle of "Araby." Thus the types whom we meet in one age are often repeated and superimposed on other ages and act as commentaries upon one another as Mrs. Mooney and Mrs. Kearney are vilified by the implied comparison with the pederast of "An Encounter."

In "The Dead" many of the figures we have met are reassembled at the Misses Morkan's annual dance, *dance* with its connotations of circular movement, of *ricorso*. We meet in different guises and circumstances Joe and Maria (in Gabriel and the Misses Kate and Julia); the *Eire Abu* (in Miss Ivors); the boy of "Araby" (in Michael Furey). All are drawn together in this final scene of life in Dublin, like the planets redrawn into the sun. This sun, formed by the dancers, will once more explode to shape a new Divine Age, a new Age of the Parents.

III

The years 1911 to 1914, when Joyce was working on the final text of *A Portrait*, were years when, according to his pupil, Paolo Cuzzi, "Joyce was also passionately interested in this Neapolitan Philosopher," Vico. Cuzzi at this time talked to Joyce about Freud as well, but Joyce, although he listened carefully, said "that Freud had been anticipated by Vico."[23]

Of all the structural and mechanical systems that Joyce employed in his works, Vico's was perhaps the most comforting and germane to the Joycean temperament. Formal orders, and as many as possible, encompass and control everything he wrote. As A. Walton Litz points out, "these neutral but controlling designs" were Joyce's means of ordering his diverse materials.[24] A number of structures have been found in *A Portrait*, and most of them are ones Joyce may have consciously employed. They coexist, suggesting human development on various levels. Basically the structural studies divide into three categories: (1) the studies of scholars like Grant Redford[25] and Thomas E. Connolly,[26] who see the structure of *A Portrait* as governed by the aesthetic principles developed in the final chapter of the novel; (2) the studies of Robert Andreach[27] or Thomas Van Laan,[28] who propose a structure determined by the spiritual stages through which Stephen moves; and (3) the argument of Richard Ellmann[29] and Sidney Feshback[30] for the process of physical gestation as an organizing principle in *A Portrait*. Other more general studies stress imagery[31] or motif[32] as a major means of producing unity in the book.

As I have shown with *Dubliners*, the Viconian pattern is one that fits in with the natural framework of Joyce's thinking. Appropriately, the term "vicociclometer," used in *Finnegans Wake*, suggests not only Vico but also the instrument to measure arcs of circles and revolutions of wheels. As William York Tindall asserts, to replace Christianity, Joyce needed a system that would give him a sense of order; according to Tindall cyclical recurrence became Joyce's substitute for metaphysics.[33] Furthermore, the Viconian system—with its parallels in the natural cycle of the four seasons of the year and in the cycle of the development of man through childhood, adolescence, and maturity to death—is one that appealed to Joyce as universal. The possibility of cycles existing within cycles at different levels of interpretation allowed for the complexities and ambiguities that teased and attracted the subtle Joycean mentality. This section will examine, then, the Viconian structure that perhaps enables us to view *A Portrait* in a new light, especially in its relation to *Ulysses* (which Ellmann tells us Joyce had been preparing himself to write since 1907 and which, according to Ellmann, "extends the method of *A Portrait*";[34] and in relation to the theories of Kenner, Tindall, Robert Ryf,[35] and others concerning the continuity to be found in the Joycean canon. As it is in *Dubliners*, the Viconian pattern in *A Portrait* is worked out on the religious, psychological, and mythical levels.

Vico's Divine Age (Joyce's Age of the Parents) may be seen as the basis of chapter one as it was the basis for the first three stories in *Dubliners*. The key to the Viconian structural pattern appears as early as page 13 where we read, "That night at Dalkey the train has roared," "roaring and then stopping; roaring again, stopping."[36] Vico Road is, of course, located in Dalkey as we learn in the "Nestor" episode in *Ulysses*. Furthermore, the cyclical pattern of the roaring and stopping of the noise is suggestive of Vico. The gods of Joyce's Divine Age are again, as in *Dubliners*, threatening figures, figures like Stephen's father with his hairy face, the older boys at Clongowes, the quarreling elders at Christmas dinner, and Father Dolan.

On the religious level, God the Father and the priests at the school are warped and angry gods, demanding cruel payment from the consciences of their young charges. Father Arnall and the prefect of studies, Father Dolan, with his pandybat, combine to inflict unjustly shame, agony, and fear on Stephen. And Father Conmee, who at the end of chapter one is viewed by Stephen and the other boys as a savior and protector, sees, we later learn, the whole incident of Stephen's beating as amusing. These are the figures of spiritual authority who dominate Stephen's life at school in this Divine Age.

In his psychological relation to the adults at home and to the older boys at school, Stephen fares scarcely better. In his infancy he fears his father and in his childhood is left "terror-stricken" by the violence of the argument over Parnell at Christmas dinner. Dante refers to Parnell as "a bad man" (p. 16), and yet Mr. Casey sees him as "My dead King!" (p. 39). For the boy, therefore, this national figure is an ambiguous leader. The older boys at school provide even less real leadership. Their names, Rody Kickham, Nasty Roche, and Cecil Thunder, connote violence and filth. And Wells, another older boy, shoulders him into the slimy ditch, causing him to become ill. Both physical and mental torture are inflicted by these "gods," even though Rody Kickham keeps a pair of greaves in his locker (reminiscent of knightly armor in a heroic age). Meanwhile, stalking the halls of the castle is the ghost of an earlier and nobler time, a real leader, a marshal in a white cloak, who had received his death wound on a battlefield near Prague and who seems to say *"drive away from it* [the castle] *all"* injustices (p. 19). Such leaders exist, however, only in Stephen's fantasies.

The movement into the Age of the Sons, Vico's Heroic Age, is heralded in the last sentence of chapter one by the "pick, pack, pock, puck" of the cricket bats "like drops of water in a fountain falling softly in the brimming bowl" (p. 59). This sound has been a punctuation device throughout the entire latter section of this chapter, indicating that time is about to overflow into a new age of human development. The pock of the corks in "Ivy Day in the Committee Room" likewise has punctuated the movement toward the climax when time overflows and Hynes recites his poem on Parnell. In the same way the "Sirens" episode in *Ulysses* is filled with clacks, taps, claps, pops, suggesting a falling apart or breaking up of continuity in the movement of the episode toward the new Age of the Fathers, the "Cyclops." As Joyce uses this sound at the end of chapter one of *A Portrait of the Artist*, it may be seen as a Viconian sign of the coming of a new age of adolescence, and of the "heroic."

The decline of the Age of the Parents is clearly apparent on the first page of chapter two where Uncle Charles is relegated to the outhouse to smoke his villainous black twist. Furthermore, we discover the key to cyclical recurrence on the next page in Stephen's run around the park (a familiar image in *Finnegans Wake*) as Mike Flynn stands timing him near the railway station (reminiscent of the train that roars and stops in chapter one). Trains recirculate and, therefore, are often Viconian images for Joyce. The Age of the Sons in *A Portrait* is at first one of sentimental idealisms and Bovaristic daydreams (unlike that in *Dubliners* where the heroic is mocked by the crassness of Lenehan and Corley and the innocence and stupidity of Jimmy Doyle and Bob Doran), for this is the adolescence of "the artist." Stephen reads about, and identifies with, the Count of Monte Cristo and dreams of a Mercedes of his own. He founds a gang of adventurers and imitates Napoleon's dress. He sees himself as a kind of "Childe Stephen" (connoting both heroism and immaturity). When the family moves, he circles the square timidly for a time, but soon regains momentum. The myth and the romance are closely related in this chapter to Stephen's psychological development, and the religious element is pushed temporarily into the background. His Mercedes materializes in E. C., the girl he is with on the tram (the symbol of recirculation), and even his school bears a romantic-sounding name, Belvedere. At his school Stephen takes the chief part in a play, a farcical role like that of Quixote himself; yet all the actions of Stephen as hero are ineffectual and unproductive, and the play leaves him with a sense of wounded pride and fallen hope.

The relationship between son and father continues to deteriorate, for on the trip to Cork, Simon declares, "I'm a better man than he is any day of the week" (p. 95); and Stephen is "wearied and dejected by his father's voice" (p. 92). This is what Joyce meant when he told Paolo Cuzzi that Vico anticipates Freud, for in Vico's Heroic Age the younger generation and the older reenact the rivalry inherent in the oepidal dilemma. At the end of chapter two, Stephen's mock-heroic attempt to usurp the role of the father in the home with thirty-three pounds, his prize money, and to rescue the family, also fails. And his dreams of his Mercedes are, in the last pages, actualized in the arms of a prostitute. Ironically, the heroic age of the artist is finally embodied in Stephen's iniquitous cry of abandonment, "a cry which was but the echo of an obscene scrawl which he had read on the oozing wall of a urinal" (p. 100).

The Age of the People (the Human Age) is seen in chapter three of *A Portrait* (as it had been in *Dubliners*, in the story "Grace") in terms of "religious" communion with one's fellowmen. The new age is introduced by the December dusk that tumbles "clownishly after its dull day" (p. 102). Like Mr. Kernan, Stephen is enjoined to a retreat and to confession. The torments ensuing on disobedience are made clear to him. Alone he moves toward religious community, attempts to reach outside himself and to attach himself to a larger social segment. An old woman with a "reeking withered right hand" (p. 141) directs him to his confessional as the warped characters in "Grace" had directed Mr. Kernan. Stephen feels that he has entered into another life, the body of our Lord and the community of saints. And yet the dreams of religious community found in chapter three turn out to be no more conclusive than the sentimental daydreams that had haunted Stephen in his Heroic Age.

For a short time, however, Stephen finds communion and symmetry in the church until he recognizes, in chapter four, in a revelation paralleling Vico's *ricorso*, that his destiny is to learn apart from others. "He would fall. He had not yet fallen but he would fall silently . . . falling, falling but not yet fallen, still unfallen, but about to fall" (p. 162). Then he crosses the bridge over the stream of the Tulka. The imagery recalls "The Dead," the *ricorso* of *Dubliners*, with its sense of falling and the falling snow. Stephen's sudden and stark recognition is one of death, emptiness, and restriction (symbolized by the window cord) in the life of the priesthood. Like Gabriel Conroy's, this life now seemed "grave and ordered and passionless" (p. 160). The emphasis in the first part of the chapter is upon sundering ties, first with his mother as he moves toward the university and "a new adventure," then in the crossing of bridges (two times in six pages, pp. 162–67), indicating his entry into new worlds and the changing direction of his existence. The final epiphany, his name Dedalus as prophecy, prefigures a new father figure in the mythical Daedalus, a replacement for Simon, and a new direction in the turning tide and the crane-like girl who will replace Mercedes. This new Daedalus symbolizes the artist as does the crane, which is capable of flight. The tide begins to flow in, and Stephen feels "the vast cyclic movement of the earth" (p. 172) revolving toward a new Divine Age or Age of the Fathers attendant upon this *ricorso*. Joyce's material quite naturally falls into the Viconian pattern partly because Vico's plan is primordial and archetypal of a lived life. In "To live, to err, to fall, to triumph" (p. 172), Vico's entire schema is submerged.

Perhaps one reason that critics have overlooked Vico in *A Portrait* is that it contains five chapters, rather than four. But in a book about a young man in search of a father, two

rounds of the Age of the Fathers are appropriate. Nevertheless, the second Divine Age, despite the high hopes of
the artificer in the preceding *ricorso,* is as sterile and restrictive in its own way as the priesthood toward which the
first cycle had moved. The new cycle begins with the gods
of the university, the fathers who teach literature, art, and
philosophy and under whose authority Stephen now finds
himself. Hugh Kenner suggests that this fifth chapter is
perhaps "a suspended chord,"[37] and it may indeed be a
cord linking *A Portrait* with the "Telemachia," the first
three episodes of *Ulysses.* This may be the Age of the
Fathers to the new Age of the Sons found in the
"Telemachus" episode. The Divine Age of the university
leads, however, to a Heroic Age of abstraction, theory, and
teleological systems. Viewing Joyce's entire canon, then, in
the light of Vico, we can see close parallels between
*Dubliners* and *A Portrait* as well as the final chapter of *A
Portrait* as a background for the opening of *Ulysses.* The
middle section of *Ulysses* may also be modeled on a
Viconian pattern, and the "Nostos," then, leads into the
giant *ricorso* of *Finnegans Wake,* just as the fifth chapter of *A
Portrait* leads into *Ulysses.*

    The new gods in chapter five are figures like the Dean
and other professors, Stephen's literary models, Aristotle
and Aquinas. And yet the Dean teaches without joy and
his literal and matter-of-fact mind serves the marketplace
rather than the creative arts. The fires that he lights are
made from coals and twisted papers. Stephen mocks these
gods of the marketplace as he imagines them "ambling and
stumbling, tumbling and capering, kilting their gowns for
leap frog" (p. 192). They exhibit a stupid and dogged failure to understand the meaning and purpose of the arts.
Nor can Stephen countenance the false gods of the other
students like the Tsar in whose name the petition for peace
is being circulated. Furthermore, the gods of aesthetics,
Aristotle and Aquinas, lead Stephen into complex and
abstract theory that is easily drowned out by even a dray
loaded with old iron. Rhythm, Stephen finds, "is the first

formal esthetic relation of part to part in any esthetic whole" (p. 205), reminding us of the rhythm of part to part imposed by Joyce's reliance on Vico. The rhythm of structure is also implied in Aquinas's *Consonantia*, which Stephen apprehends in theory. Yet in this world of abstraction, the artist is eventually, in Stephen's own words, "refined out of existence" (p. 215).

Toward the end of chapter five, we are again moving toward a new Heroic Age, the Age of Telemachus. The bird imagery once again suggests the possibility of escape, not only from the fathering principles of nationality, religion, and language, but also from the whole elaborate ideology of the fathering university as is implied in Stephen's thoughts of Swedenborg, who sees that birds have not perverted the order of times and seasons by intellect (p. 224). The cyclical pattern of Vico is subsequently suggested by reference to birds going and coming and building unlasting homes (p. 225). The conclusion to this Age of the Fathers becomes, then, *Non serviam* and flight as Stephen listens to the call of ships and appeals once more to the mythical artificer, Daedalus. However, the gods of the university have been abandoned in no real sense, for the knife blade of Stephen's intellect is the basis for his new nickname Kinch in *Ulysses*, and the "ineluctable modality of the visible" and other metaphysical concerns are the main subjects of Stephen's thoughts and conversation throughout the "Telemachia." Whereas the first cycle had led to a spiritual stasis, this second cycle leads to an intellectual stasis, "anesthetic emotion . . . raised above desire and loathing" (p. 205), as Stephen had defined it earlier. Even with the girl at the end he turns on his "Spiritual heroic refrigerating apparatus" (p. 252).

We leave Stephen, then, in the last pages of *A Portrait* as "a young man" on the verge of departing from his second Age of the Fathers. Joyce has promised us no more. He is a young man lacking the understanding and compassion to refrain from quarreling with his mother on the score of religion, lacking insight into his own motivations (Cranly tells him, "Your mind is supersaturated with the religion in which you say you disbelieve" [p. 240]), and dependent on the empty forms of an aesthetic and metaphysical system. And yet he does not fear his exile and goes into it with high hope, perhaps recognizing in his diary that in hoofs hurrying in the night one hears the eternal patterns of all journeys through the ages of the divine, the heroic, and the human.

For Joyce is saying in *A Portrait*, through Vico, that the Divine Age, the Age of the Fathers, may influence the development of the entire cycle so that in the end (the fifth chapter) new gods must be sought to replace the meaningless, empty, or shoddy ones who produce only barren repetition of experience. Repetition of experience must lead to mastery of experience, not to return for the sake of return. Freud has made the same point. It is to this end that Stephen has sought in chapter five for the original father, "the old artificer," the Daedalus who had fashioned both labyrinth and wings, both nets and the means of freedom from those nets. But the tragedy represented in *A Portrait* is that Stephen has found fatherhood neither in the sacred font of the church nor in the ivory tower of the university.[38]

Joyce's concept of the epiphany and its use in *Dubliners* is closely akin to his concept of the Viconian *ricorso*, a moment—a period—when old things fall apart, disintegrate, and when with eyes burning "with anguish and anger" one sees the vain illusions of one's life laid bare and there is nowhere to go, except phoenix-like to be reborn. The "shaft of shivery" and "cloudclap" in *Finnegans Wake* metaphorically serve the same purpose as do "time's livid final flame, the shattered glass and toppling masonry" of *Ulysses*. In writing in *A Portrait* about Stephen's studies of Aristotle and Aquinas, Joyce says: "His thinking was a dusk of doubt and selfmistrust lit up at moments by the lightnings of intuition, but lightnings of so clear a splendour that in those moments the world perished about his feet as if it had been fireconsumed" (p. 177). The concept of the creative power of lightning, or fire from heaven, lies deep in our mythic roots, for example, in the belief in the first Egyptian dynasty that the sacred Apis had been born of a cow impregnated by lightning, as depicted on the walls of the Serapeum at Memphis.

Even more interesting is the way that Joyce integrates his Viconian schemes of organization into the substructures of his books; I would like briefly in this section to examine the function of the *ricorso*, the flash of lightning, in the substructure of *A Portrait*.

Joyce manipulates the Viconian Ages in complex ways so that, as in the telephone circuits of a large city, impulses, patterns, may run independently and counter to one another at the same time as they run parallel, providing both continuity and radical discontinuity on the heels of each *ricorso*. The *ricorso* provides a kind of electrical shock to process, shattering it and provoking at the same time new process. For example, in chapter one of *A Portrait* the glint of Eileen's "fair hair" streaming out behind her like gold in the sun leads to Stephen's insight: "By thinking of things you could understand them" (p. 43); the crack of Father Dolan's pandybat leads to an epiphany in which Stephen (like the boy in "Araby") burns with "shame and agony and fear"; the "pick, pack, pock, puck" of the cricket bats (a parallel and yet polar image to the pandybat) leads to the overflowing of the brimming bowl in chapter two.

In chapter two it is imagery, such as the kiss he gives E. C. or the kiss of the prostitute, which was "too much for him" (p. 101), or Heron's cane cutting at Stephen's legs, which acts like a flash of lightning forking into a truck, splitting the substance of oak or ash so that new shoots may spring from the devastation.

Chapter three, in which Stephen considers joining the community of saints, is sharply punctuated by utterances of hellfire and damnation by the preacher. Stephen emerges from the chapel "his legs shaking and the scalp of his head trembling" (p. 124). Hell torment follows hell torment in this chapter until Stephen vomits after his dream and is remade: "Another life! A life of grace and virtue and happiness!" (p. 146).

The flash of insight in chapter four when Stephen sees the crane girl is, of course, the culminating one for the book thus far and in this chapter of *ricorso*—and too well known to bear further describing.

It is the burgeoning disconnections of chapter five, in crescendo, the fragments and flashes of which it is composed, which—in a new Age of the Fathers (with the fathers of the university now replacing those of the church and home), of indoctrination into a new mode for Stephen —show us Joyce's increasing stylistic reliance as he approaches *Ulysses* on the pattern of discontinuity, of *ricorso*, of breaking up and reorganization and reestablishment. The style of chapter five, like the style of much of *Ulysses*, is full of interruptions, of interjections. In fact, the discussion between Stephen and Lynch is actually a resumption of an interrupted conversation begun a few nights earlier. The earsplitting whistle of Simon Dedalus opens the chapter, interrupting the washing scene between mother and son; on the way to the university, Stephen hears a mad nun screeching "Jesus! O Jesus! Jesus!" and he shakes the sound out of his ears and hurries on. Eleven strokes of a clock make him think of MacCann, then that he is late for the lecture. The word *ivory* shone in his brain, and sparks and fire abound as the Dean lights the fire or as Stephen sees in his eyes the spark of Ignatius' enthusiasm. Later a long dray loaded with iron drowns out Stephen's words "with the harsh roar of jangled and rattling metal" (p. 209). One could go on and on with such examples of sharp blows to the senses, of streaks of lightning, of thunderclaps of sound, and they are all closely related to the Viconian *ricorso*, to the epiphany, even obliquely to the radiance of Aquinas—the apprehension of *quidditas*, or the *whatness* of a thing. Richard Pearce, of Wheaton College, suggests to me in a letter that in chapter five "what we get is a greater quantity of detail, much apparently irrelevant, coming in fragments and flashes and with a sense of speed."

I should like to suggest then that in maturing as an artist Joyce began to see radical discontinuity as a creative stylistic device to produce not only the insights of his characters but to stimulate those of his readers and himself. The *ricorso*, opening as it does new possibilities of development, is at the same time a product of situations in a previous cycle of experience. It thus serves as a symbol of both the continuity and discontinuity of process. The montage, the film-clip quality of chapter five, leads toward a new stylistic mode for Joyce, a period in which *ricorso* began to function as the very fabric of his craft, which was at the same time enunciating the credo that only when the old order has been reduced to ashes or when the sea falls "below the line of seawrack" (p. 170) can new life arise and can the tide begin to turn "flowing in fast to the land with the low whisper of her waves" (p. 173). The epiphany of *Dubliners* stresses the disintegration of old patterns, the radiance of Aquinas stresses the whatness of a moment or thing, but the *ricorso* of Vico is oriented toward the *recon*struction of patterns and toward the future.

IV

The comparison between *The Magic Mountain* and *Ulysses* is a fascinating one, for both novels use the thunderbolt as conclusion to process, as the inductor to the still center. And like Mann, Joyce puts the emphasis on process itself, not on the attainment of stillness. Joyce's interpretation of Vico lies, of course, at the heart of his work; and again through Vico, we may trace in *Ulysses*, my exemplar here, a spiral process somewhat similar to Mann's as elaborated in *The Magic Mountain*. The difference lies in that Joyce's pattern rests on Vico's notion of the rise and fall of empires—a pattern visible throughout human history—whereas Mann's spiraling reality rests more upon a

Jungian concept of the collective unconscious, of the repetition inherent in myth and, before that, in nature itself.

It is not only in the minutiae, sentences and words, but in the larger structure of *Ulysses* that Vico may be seen. Joyce wrote in a letter to Harriet Weaver that the circumstances of his own life were what forced him to accept the theories of Vico.[39] More than a historical theory, Joyce sees in Vico a psychological progression, the circumstances of human lives. As Richard Ellmann points out, Joyce sees Vico's divisions not as chronological divisions of ideal history but as psychological ingredients that combine and recombine. "I use his cycles as a trellis," Joyce said.[40] As such, Vico's influence does not lead to an abstract pattern, but is closely connected with character development, the vine that grows on the trellis.

Vico's three ages were a cycle of decline, somewhat different from Joyce's cycles. Furthermore, Joyce's names for the three ages varied slightly from Vico's to underline his own special interpretation of them. As we have noted, Joyce's "Age of the Sons" and "Age of the People" stress psychological and social significance rather than historical theory. But for both Vico and Joyce, spiral succeeded spiral in the development of process, and for both the emphasis lay on the spiraling pattern itself rather than on a realm beyond it at the end of process.

In *Ulysses* the spiraling ages outlined above may be clearly seen in the structure of the book. In part three of this chapter I have suggested that the first three parts of *Ulysses*, often called the "Telemachia," may represent the completion of a cycle begun in the last chapter of *A Portrait of the Artist as a Young Man* where the "gods" (faculty) of the university become Stephen's new parents, after he has cast off his early life at home. The first episode in the "Telemachia" would represent, then, the Age of the Sons, the second—the "Nestor" episode—the Age of the People, and the third—"Proteus"—the *ricorso*. It would be logical to see *Ulysses* as continuing the story of Stephen at the point where it is broken off in A Portrait, following Stephen as he

continues on this second cycle of his life. The Age of the
Sons, the heroes, unfolds in his stay at the Martello Tower
with Buck Mulligan and Haines; the Age of the People
(men, women, and children), in his experiences at Mr.
Deasy's school; the *ricorso* in the circulation and recirculation represented symbolically in the swirling waters and,
metaphysically, in Stephen's swirling thoughts in the
"Proteus" episode (Proteus being a sea god of shifting
forms).

The middle section of *Ulysses* (episodes 4–15) replaces
Stephen as central character with the figure of Leopold
Bloom because, I believe, Joyce saw that Stephen himself
was incapable of relating to others, of ever assuming a real
role in the complex social milieu of the book. In this central
section of *Ulysses*, we find further evidence of the cyclical
and spiraling development of the novel. It is necessary, at
the beginning, to note Joyce's preoccupation with the consubstantiality of Father and Son, suggesting that the ages,
as I will outline them here, are actually not so neatly dis-
tinguishable as they will often appear to be.

Nevertheless, in the opening episode, "Calypso,"
Bloom is seen initially as husband and father, a kind of
mock *pater familias*, in his home at 7 Eccles Street, as he
feeds the cat and prepares Molly's breakfast. We see him
next in the "Lotus Eaters" episode, the Age of the Sons, as
Mr. Henry Flower, engaged in narcissistic and titillating
adolescent behavior in his secret correspondence with
Martha Clifford, and later in his scented bath as he views
his own navel. In "Hades," the Age of the People, we find
Bloom relating to the community, both to the *Umwelt* and
the *Mitwelt*, as he and his friends proceed through the
streets of Dublin in the funeral cortege of Paddy Dignam.
And finally in the *ricorso* to this first cycle, Bloom appears
in the newspaper offices where Aeolus (the printing press)
disperses, separates, and destroys lives and where circulation and recirculation run rampant. Although Vico's
cycles, as I have already maintained, were cycles of decline, the character of Joyce's cycles was more ambiguous.

Whereas Leopold Bloom may appear outwardly less heroic than his prototype, Ulysses, he has at the same time inner qualities of compassion, of understanding, and of forebearance that give him stature in a moral sense. Joyce continually mocks his hero, as in the newspaper office, where Bloom's only invitation is to kiss the editor's arse; but Bloom's self-restraint, his patience in the face of persistent frustrations he meets in every encounter during his day, raises him ethically above his archetype, the wily and brawny Ulysses. Joyce seems to say, therefore, that the cycles may spiral either upward or downward depending on one's perspective. Arbitration, understanding, concern for others, even one's enemies, characterize the modern hero, Leopold Bloom.

The next four episodes trace still another Viconian cycle. We find Bloom first, in the "Lestrygonians" episode, as provider, feeding the gulls, as in "Calypso" he had fed the cat and Molly, but the theme of this section centers around brutish father figures. The Lestrygonians were cannibals, and their descendants in Burton restaurant, where Bloom first goes for his luncheon, do not, like Bloom, feed others, but concentrate on "swilling, wolfing gobfuls of sloppy food, their eyes bulging." As he leaves, Bloom remarks: "Eat or be eaten."[41] Fleeing to Davy Byrne's pub, Bloom joins still other fathers, Nosey Flynn, Paddy Leonard, Bantam Lyons, and Tom Rocheford, in this Age of the Fathers. In the Age of the Sons that follows, we turn from Bloom to Stephen, as he holds forth in the library on another famous son, Hamlet. The Lestrygonians have been replaced by stone and whirlpool, Scylla and Charybdis, the latter a spiral within the larger spiral movement. Next in the Age of the People, the "Wandering Rocks," we follow persons and groups of persons, the populace of Dublin, as they circulate and recirculate through the streets.[42] And finally in the *ricorso* at the Ormond restaurant, the reader is besieged with clacks, taps, pops, crackling, and the breaking of wind, suggesting that the world of this second cycle is falling apart. One of the last images is that of the tram, a favorite Joycean device to suggest circularity, for the progress of the tram describes a circle, ending where it began. Often the tram was turned at the end of the line by a *round* table for its journey back along the streets.

A third group of episodes in this middle section of *Ulysses* opens with Cyclops, a cannibalistic giant, like the Lestrygonians in the Age of the Fathers in cycle two. It is clear that Cyclops and the Citizen are one, an ironic comment on the character of Dublin fathers in general. By contrast we see Bloom in this episode as he turns the other cheek to the Citizen's wrath and to the hostility of the group of barflies at Barney Kierrnan's tavern. "Nausicaa" describes a new Age of the Sons (or Daughters, in this episode), developing once again, as in the "Lotus Eaters," adolescent patterns (i.e., voyeurism and masturbation). Linking the two episodes is Bloom's letter to Martha Clifford, which he remembers as he watches Gerty. The Age of the People follows at the laying-in hospital, where we see that all men are connected by means of the umbilical cord to where we join, instead of Mina Purefoy, a party of medical students and their friends, "all off for a buster, armstrong, hollering down the street."[43] The grand *ricorso* is, of course, the "Circe" episode, a potpourri of all previous sections, concluding with its thunderclap, the shattering of the chandelier, and the celebration of a Black Mass. One great concussion here replaces the slighter but more numerous sound effects of the *ricorso* of the "Sirens" episode and that of "Aeolus." As the thunderclap of war had caused Hans to change his direction in *The Magic Mountain,* so in *Ulysses,* the thunderclap will cause Stephen and Bloom to seek new cycles of development.

One of these is begun in the *Nostos* portion of *Ulysses,* composed of the final three sections of the book. Here we start again with a new Age of the Fathers as we read about Bloom in "Eumaeus," as father to a new son, as protector and guide for Stephen. In keeping with Joyce's theme of consubstantiality, the next section, "Ithaca," portrays

father and son as equal and interchangeable, Blephen and
Stoom, predecessors of Shem and Shaun. Both are sons
and lovers of Molly, who in the final section, the Age of the
People, becomes the earth goddess, Gaea Tellus, where all
men meet. Bloom through his relation to Molly is seen in
this Age of the People in his relation to all men, as he
himself says in "Ithaca": "neither first nor last nor only nor
alone in a series originating in and repeated to infinity."[44]
"Riverrun" and Anna Livia derive from Molly, who circulates and recirculates, leading to the giant *ricorso* (*Finnegans
Wake*) that Joyce provides for the cycle begun in the *Nostos*
of *Ulysses*.

Let us examine briefly the different emphases placed on
cyclical return by Mann and by Joyce. With Joyce (despite
his concern with the historical theories of Vico), the stress
is ultimately on individual development, whereas Mann
stresses the collective experience. Mann himself often wor-
ried about the individuality of his characters, fearing that
they were more archetypes than persons.[45] In the same
way, Vico's philosophy of the recurrence of the three ages
suggested to Joyce (born in Catholic Ireland) a new social
resurrection, a view of history, reborn phoenix-like, from
the ashes of the past, a Lazarus risen, although it was used
to outline the individual development of his hero, Leopold
Bloom. The spiraling reality, the repetition of event, provided a rich source of imagery for Joyce. Thus Bloom's own
gentle fathering of others could be contrasted to advantage
with the cannibalism of the Cyclops and Lestrygonians,
with tyrants of earlier Ages of the Fathers. In the Age of
the Sons, Bloom's adolescent preoccupations seem relatively harmless when contrasted with the delusions and
stupor of Homer's lotus eaters. And Scylla and Charybdis
offer far more danger to life and limb than the perils experienced by Stephen, as he holds forth in the library "between the Saxon smile and Yankee yawp."[46] The earlier
Ages of the People, as symbolized by "Hades," the
"Wandering Rocks," and "Oxen of the Sun," are fraught
with physical danger by comparison with life in Dublin.

On another level we see the world of Leopold Bloom as a diminished and impoverished world when compared with the epic grandeur of the golden court of Menelaus, the splendid horses of Nestor, or the enchanted isle of Calypso. But the heroic age of the epic gives way finally in *Ulysses* to the Age of the People and yields honor at the end not to an ideal past but to an unassuming Leopold Bloom for his wisdom and ethical maturity. Bloom, rather then the wily Ulysses, is crowned compassionate father, as well as consubstantial, a compassionate Christ. Thus the emphasis turns inward from the outward glory of things past to the inner triumphs of Joyce's twentieth-century hero. As Hans Castorp sheds Settembrini and Naphta, the gods of his early stay at the sanatorium, so Bloom sheds the problems and preoccupations of the earlier part of his day as he reaches a calm resolution in "Ithaca." Both Joyce and Mann see, in other words, that development of civilization as well as that of individuals within it moves from focus on exterior reality to awareness of inner worlds. (As Berdyaev suggests, Renaissance man, having discovered that the earth was not at the center of the universe and that the universe extended apparently to infinity, that the earth was not even the center of its own planetary system, turned from scrutiny of impossible space to scrutiny of self.[47] In ancient Greece, Psyche was the last of the gods to be created.)

Joyce's use of Viconian cycles, then, is in the interest of depicting the psychological ("cycle-logical") maturity of his hero, Bloom. Rather than slaughtering the suitors to Penelope's hand, Bloom becomes reconciled at the end to the fact of mathematical sequence. Rather than hurling insults back at Cyclops (another cycle within a cycle), Bloom departs from the Citizen's wrath without retaliation as "ben Bloom Elijah," "having raiment as of the sun."[48] Finally, instead of encouraging Stephen to take the place of his lost son, Rudy, Bloom gives Stephen freedom.

The spiral development is given closure in *Ulysses* by the *ricorso,* whereby one cycle cracks, collapses, or explodes only to be reformed and recycled. We recall that it is in similar fashion through the thunderbolt, the title of Mann's final chapter in *The Magic Mountain*, that Hans Castorp is freed from his life-denying enchantment—the thunderbolt that is seen as a hellhound, "a huge explosive shell, a disgusting sugar-loaf from the infernal regions."[49] Neither Joyce nor Mann sees fulfillment in the still center. Death is the enemy come from the infernal region. Death is part of process, but not in itself fulfilling for the individual. Joyce and Mann may be seen, then, to complement one another (Joyce more Freudian, Mann more Jungian), to fulfill the same ultimate aim, essentially humanistic and Greek in character.

Furthermore all metafiction, from *Don Quixote* down to its numerous descendants, rests on a view of fiction that is basically concentric in character, incorporating books within books in an infinite regress. Cervantes himself employs a far more complex circular reality than Mann's relatively simple progression of cycles and Joyce's slightly more complicated one. It is a circular reality particularly well suited to mirroring the meshing of countless wheels that, in the view of Cervantes, characterizes life. Behind the appearance of linear progression, in this understanding of life, lies repetition; no line is straight except in the abstract, for there is always a perspctive to prove it curved.

It is an observation of a circular reality, made with the help of fiction and basic to many points of view, which, in my opinion, strengthens and substantiates the philosophical metaphors of time as *circular, spiral, cyclic,* or simply *round*, not unlike watches, clocks, sundials, and perhaps even space itself.

---

1. Richard Ellmann, *James Joyce*, pp. 429–30.
2. James Joyce, *Ulysses* (New York: Random House, 1961), p. 192.
3. James Joyce, *Finnegans Wake* (New York: Viking Press, 1955), p. 234.
4. Ibid., p. 482.

166

5. James Joyce, *A Shorter Finnegans Wake,* ed. Anthony Burgess (New York: Viking Press, 1967), p. xviii.

6. Ibid.

7. Robert Scholes and Richard M. Kain, eds., *The Workshop of Daedalus: James Joyce and the Raw Materials for "A Portrait of the Artist as a Young Man,"* pp. 247–48.

8. David Hayman, "Daedalian Imagery in A Portrait," in *Hereditas: Seven Essays on the Modern Experience of the Classical,* p. 33.

9. Hugh Kenner, *Flaubert, Joyce and Beckett: The Stoic Comedians.*

10. Richard Cross, *Flaubert and Joyce: The Rite of Fiction,* p. 105.

11. Anthony Thorlby, *Gustave Flaubert and the Art of Realism,* p. 39.

12. Ellmann, p. 78.

13. Giambattista Vico (1688–1744), Italian philosoher of law and cultural history, author of *Scienza nouva,* which appeared in 1725. An abridged translation is available: *The New Science of Giambattista Vico,* trans. Thomas Goddard Bergin and Max Harold Fisch (Garden City, N.Y.: Doubleday, 1961).

14. See J. T. Shaw "Literary Indebtedness and Comparative Literary Studies," in *Comparative Literature: Method and Perspective,"* ed. Newton P. Stallknecht and Horst Frenz, rev. ed. (Carbondale: Southern Illinois University Press, 1971), pp. 84–97

15. Jorge Luis Borges, "Kafka and His Precursors," in his *Labyrinths: Selected Stories and Other Writings,* p. 201.

16. Ibid., p. 44.

17. *Closing Time,* p. 25.

18. Margaret Church, *Time and Reality: Studies in Contemporary Fiction,* pp. 53–66.

19. Herbert Gorman, *James Joyce,* p. 150.

20. Ellmann, p. 351.

21. James Joyce, *Dubliners,* ed. Robert Scholes and A. Walton Litz (New York: Viking Press, 1959), pp. 13–14.

22. Ibid., p. 157.

23. Ellmann, p. 351.

24. A. Walton Litz, *The Art of James Joyce,* pp. 38–39.

25. "The Role of Structure in Joyce's *Portrait.*"

26. "Kinesis and Stasis: Structural Rhythm in Joyce's *Portrait of the Artist as a Young Man.*"

27. *Studies in Structure: The Stages of Spiritual Life in Four Modern Authors.*

28. "The Meditative Structure of Joyce's *Portrait.*"

29. Ellmann, pp. 306–9.

30. "A Slow and Dark Birth: A Study of the Organization of *A Portrait of the Artist as a Young Man.*"

31. William York Tindall, *The Literary Symbol,* pp. 78–86.

32. Lee T. Lemon, *"A Portrait of the Artist as a Young Man."*

33. *James Joyce: His Way of Interpreting the Modern World,* p. 65.

34. Ellmann, p. 361.

35. *A New Approach to Joyce: "A Portrait of the Artist" as a Guidebook.* Ryf sees *A Portrait* as a guidebook to Joyce's later work.

36. James Joyce, *A Portrait of the Artist as a Young Man* (New York: Viking Press, 1964), p. 13. Subsequent references to this volume will be cited in the text.

37. *Dublin's Joyce,* p. 121.

38. Maurice Beebe, whose book *Ivory Towers and Sacred Founts: The Artist as Hero in Fiction from Goethe to Joyce* I have in mind here, first suggested to me the possibility of Vico's influence on *A Portrait.*

39. *Letters of James Joyce,* p. 241.

40. Ellmann, p. 565.

41. James Joyce, *Ulysses* (New York: Random House, 1961), pp. 169–70.

42. The eighteen episodes in "Wandering Rocks" form a kind of *Ulysses* in miniature, redivided into Viconian cycles, like the subdivisions of "Aeolus," "Cyclops," and "Oxen of the Sun." Joyce amused himself by superimposing cycles upon cycles and inserting cycles within cycles.

43. *Ulysses,* p. 424.

44. Ibid., p. 731.

45. See Harry Slochower, *Thomas Mann's Joseph Story,* p. 13. Slochower discusses Mann's concern for balancing the individual and the typical in his novels.

46. *Ulysses,* p. 187.

47. Nicholas Berdyaev, *Dostoevsky,* pp. 44–50, 95–101.

48. *Ulysses,* p. 345.

49. Mann, *The Magic Mountain,* p. 715.

## Chapter Eight

# Joycean Structure in
*Jacob's Room* and *Mrs. Dalloway*

Like Thomas Mann, Virginia Woolf read *Don Quixote* with
mixed judgments and feelings. "With Cervantes," she
wrote, "everything's there; in solution if you like; but
deep, atmospheric, living people casting shadows solid,
tinted as in life."[1] In the same entry in her diary (5 August
1920), however, she speaks of much "of the tale-telling as
dull—not much," she decides on second thought, "only a
little at the end of the first volume" (2:55). Then shifting
ground once more, she adds: "I suspect the Fernando-
Cardino-Lucinda story was a courtly episode in the fashion
of the day, anyhow dull to me" (2:56). Five days later, on
10 August, she is still readng *Don Quixote*: "I confess rather
sinking in the sand—rather soft going—so long as the
stories aren't about him—but has the loose, far scattered
vitality of the great books, which keeps me going" (2:57).

In her own way, Virginia Woolf was as sensitive to
Cervantes' naturalness as both Flaubert and Mann had
been. She writes: "So far as I can judge, the beauty, &
thought come in unawares; Cervantes scarcely conscious
of serious meaning, & scarcely seeing D.Q. as we see him"
(2:55). And she goes on to wonder if "great characters have
it in them to change according to the generation that looks
at them" (2:55). "Yet how splendid it is," she continues,
"to unfurl one's sail & blow straight ahead in the gust of
the great story telling, as happens all through the first
part" (2:56). Like Mann she apparently prefers part one to
part two of the *Quixote*.

Virginia Woolf was reading *Don Quixote* at the same time
that she was working on *Jacob's Room* and shortly after her
first contacts with Joyce's *Ulysses*. In fact, a Quixotic image
creeps into her description of the process of writing *Jacob's*

*Room*: "every morning now, feeling each days work like a fence which I have to ride at, my heart in my mouth till its over, & I've cleared, or knocked the bar out" (2:56). A transposition of "fence" for "windmill" and of "ride at" for "tilt at" is easy to imagine, particularly because the sentence occurs in the same entry in which she first describes her reading of Cervantes.

Despite this clear evidence of Virginia Woolf's contact with *Don Quixote*, a case for the direct influence of the novel on her work is difficult to make. A concept of structure in the novel came to Virginia Woolf through other avenues, and her "individual talent" was served by the "tradition" rather than by her reading of Cervantes. Whereas Flaubert had been for Joyce a powerful catalyst informing Joyce's concept of the craft of fiction, it was ironically Joyce himself, perhaps, who acted as an early catalyst for Virginia Woolf's sense of form in the novel. (I say "ironically" because of her well-known ambivalence to Joyce's work—her strongly stated antipathies and at other times her intrinsic admiration for *Ulysses*.)

This chapter is not an attempt to enter into the controversy that has been waged for years on the matter of James Joyce's "influence" on Virginia Woolf. Jean Guiguet's *Virginia Woolf and Her Works* includes the most definitive treatment of this subject. Furthermore, James Hafley has rejected in no uncertain terms the possibility of direct "influence." Virginia Woolf's judgments of *Ulysses* in the diary and in the April 1918 letter to Lytton Strachey were generally strongly negative, although her essay "Modern Fiction" indicates a more positive relation to Joyce's work, for in this essay she associates it with her own theory of the novel and feels that Joyce was sincere, that he was concerned "with the flickerings of that inmost flame."[2]

Whether positive or negative, Virginia Woolf, it is clear, had at least read and reacted to Joyce. Although she again and again apparently found his work incompatible, although her own temperament was indeed different from his, although her interior monologue may be closer to

Proust's than to Joyce's, although the underlying purposes of their works differed, and although they saw life from different perspectives, in certain ways Joyce may have contributed to the insights and art of Mrs. Woolf. I find in *Jacob's Room* and *Mrs. Dalloway* such striking parallels to Joyce's structures (suggested even in the red morocco notebook on *Mrs. Dalloway*) that these parallels deserve mention with the goal of extending the meaning of these two novels.

Influence all depends on what one means by the word *influence*, a semantic problem. If we mean by *influence* a slavish dependence on source, the borrowing of all or many stylisic devices, the compatibility of temperaments and aims, then it is indeed difficult to see how Virginia Woolf could have been "influenced" by Joyce. My own view is that *influence* may be an intuitive or unconscious process, one that often permeates an area of an author's work without his being aware—a similarity, or simply a reaction, to mood, approach, tone, which, borrowing a phrase from Theodore Reik,[3] I feel the critic must often use a third ear to detect. I doubt that such influence can ever be proved or established by scientific method. For example, Chaucer's almost literal retelling of Petrarch's Latin translation of Boccaccio's Griselda tale is not in itself an example of influence. Something other than copying comprises influence. One can sense Virginia Woolf reacting to Joyce, rejecting some aspects and admiring others, and using them quite naturally, instinctively, and perhaps unconsciously as the occasion arose in the process of writing. Even a strong distaste could operate in the matter of influence by producing an opposite effect from that found in the source of influence. Quentin Bell in his recent biography of Mrs. Woolf writes of *Ulysses*, "It was a work which Virginia could neither dismiss nor accept," and later in discussing "Mr. Bennett and Mrs. Brown," he lists Joyce as among those whom Virginia Woolf saw as one of her "natural allies."[4]

A brief review of Virginia Woolf's early points of contact

with the works of Joyce will serve as a helpful preface to my remarks.[5] Although on 5 March 1919 Virginia Woolf noted in her diary, "But oh, dear, what a lot I've got to read!"[6] and listed the entire works of "Mr. James Joyce" as among those she must go through, ten months later, on 26 January 1920, she commented in the diary that it is "the damned egotistical self; which ruins Joyce to my mind" and which is, she feels, for Joyce both "narrowing and restricting" (2:14), suggesting at this time some knowledge of his work. Furthermore, two years earlier, in April 1918, a letter from her to Lytton Strachey indicated even then at least a cursory reading of *Ulysses*: ". . . We've been asked to print Mr. Joyce's new novel."[7] Twenty-three years later, in 1941, she recalled Harriett Weaver, "in wool gloves, bringing *Ulysses* in typescript to our teatable in Hogarth House."[8] And according to Ellmann in *James Joyce*, the Woolfs later told Miss Weaver that they were "interested in the first four episodes which they read" (p. 457). The letter to Strachey continued by commenting briefly on Joyce's method ("cutting out the explanations and putting in thoughts between dashes") and his subject matter ("First there's a dog that p's—then there's a man that forths").[9] As we know, *Ulysses* did not appear in Paris until 1922, but important fragments were published in the *Little Review* in 1919 and 1920;[10] it is clear, then, that Virginia Woolf had two possible sources of contact with the manuscirpt in the years 1918, 1919, and 1920.

Thus by 10 April 1920, when she wrote in her diary that she was "planning to begin *Jacob's Room* next week with luck" (2:28), the shadow of *Ulysses* was a reality. The kind of reading given *Ulysses*, as indicated above, would probably at least yield a sense of the general basis of his structures—especially of the hours of the day that govern the progression of his novel and the striking of clocks, in particular of Big Ben (to which there are at least nine references in *Ulysses*). There is also the frequently noted passage in her diary for 26 September 1920, in which she has come to a stop in the writing of *Jacob's Room* and reflects:

". . . What I'm doing is probably being better done by Mr. Joyce" (2:69). This statement cannot help but establish a connection, however tenuous, between *Jacob's Room* and *Ulysses*.

Although *Jacob's Room* is marked by a discontinuity, "an irregularity, complexity, fluidity," a "two-fold discontinuity and disconnectedness"[11] like that found in human beings, we can also see in it, I believe, the beginnings of an innate sense of structure that Virginia Woolf may have noted in the work of Joyce and that regulated her novels afer *Jacob's Room*, especially *Mrs. Dalloway*, in one way or another. Of her own novel, *Jacob's Room*, she wrote, ". . . all crepuscular but the heart, the passion, humor, everything as bright as fire in the mist."[12] It is perhaps this phrase "fire in the mist" that informs this early novel of Virginia Woolf, for, as Jean Guiguet shows,[13] there is a core of cohesive force in each character that gives direction to the scattered fragments of reality about him.

It is the desolate cry "Ja-cob! Ja-cob!";[14] the pale yellow ray of the lighthouse shot across the purple sea (p. 11); the sun blazing in their faces and gilding the great blackberries (p. 11); the light blazing out across the patch of grass (p. 13); the waves jerking the stars above the ships (p. 13) that set the pace, tone, and structure of *Jacob's Room*. All these images have the force of an epiphany, a showing forth, or of an explosion, of the burst of light destroying the old and establishing the new—"the seim anew" of the crab in the child's bucket "trying again and falling back, and trying again and again" (p. 14). Virginia Woolf, without doubt, began to explore the use of this method, a sudden and abrupt sound or sight, a shock administered to the senses—a ring, a shout, a clatter, a flash—in *Jacob's Room* to indicate structural divisions; in her next novel, *Mrs. Dalloway*, she brings the method to fulfillment.

All of the examples cited in the above paragraph occur in chapter one of *Jacob's Room*, laid in Cornwall. In fact, the chapter opens with an "accident"—mentioned in Betty Flanders's letter to Captain Barfoot. An accident marks a sudden turnabout of events, a reordering of reality such as Seabrook's death had necessitated for Betty Flanders, and her tears are a signature of this reordering. But by and large, the explosive imagery in the early chapters of *Jacob's Room* is part of the lyric effect rather than a methodical means of structuring the work. Thus in chapter two we hear the shouts of the boys at the Roman fortress, the call "Archer! Jacob!" echoed by Johnny, "Archer-Ja-cob!" (p. 19), or the military gait of Captain Barfoot on his way to visit Mrs. Flanders (p. 26). To recur later in the novel, however, is the "volley of pistol shots" (p. 23) made by the falling tree the night Jacob caught the moth. The moth is to be a central and significant image in the work of Virginia Woolf. It suggests, of course, the metamorphic and fleeting existence of human beings. Jacob's room is in a sense the cocoon of life, and Jacob's life, like that of the moth, is a brief one, set against a background of "pistol shots." At the end of chapter two, Mrs. Jarvis hears "distant concussions in the air" (p. 27), and the horsemen galloping are phantom, designating the gathering clouds of war. In chapter three Jacob's thoughts are to return to the "terrifying volley of pistol-shots" as he sits in King's College Chapel. The noises at Cambridge echo those in Scarborough at Cornwall: there is now and then a thud, Mr. Hawkins throws up his window and shouts, "Jo-seph! Joseph!"; the waltz crashes like waves, and the clock striking (as in Joyce) reminds Jacob of all the past and then of tomorrow. At the end of the chapter, after Jacob has said goodnight, his footsteps "ring out" (p. 46) as he returns to his room.

All these sounds, the shouts, shots, concussions, crashes, rings, remind one of Joyce, particularly of the "Sirens" episode in *Ulysses*. But they are not used by Mrs. Woolf in any systematic way, nor do they appear in the same profusion as in Joyce. However, they are often used with the same basic intent—to suggest the end of an old order and the beginning of a new, the emergence of the moth from the chrysalis. Only a few mark endings or beginnings in the structure of *Jacob's Room*—for example, the mention of the Guy Fawkes gunpowder plot at the beginning of Jacob's stay in London (p. 75) or the clock striking twelve at the end of chapter eleven as he leaves France for Italy and then Greece. At twelve o'clock, the hour of *ricorso* for Joyce, Jacob returns, then, to the cradle of Western civilization, to Italy and Athens, where its white skeleton is still to be found—prefigured perhaps in the huge white skull Jacob had discovered on the Cornish beach. Mrs. Woolf uses many of the same images to describe Athens that she had used to describe the beach at Cornwall—crashes, the dazzling glare of light, the rock "cleft with shadows" (p. 148). Furthermore, the pistol shots made by the falling tree in chapter two become the guns firing at Piraeus like "nocturnal women beating great carpets" (p. 175). "Greece was over; the Parthenon in ruins; yet there he was" (p. 150), signifying eternal renewal, the birth and death and death and birth of the moth. The Acropolis is a "jagged mound" (p. 159); the Parthenon has been the center of another "gunpowder plot"; guns on a battleship train a target that "flames into splinters" (p. 155) and sends a dozen young men into the depths of the sea—strokes that "oar the world forward, they say" (p. 156).

It is through the imagery of explosion that the ending of *Jacob's Room* becomes clear. The procession of life that has been used from time to time in the novel (as at the end of chaper five: "life is but a procession of shadows") becomes a central image in the concluding pages when a procession stops—omnibuses, vans, motorcars—like the vehicles representing circulation and recirculation in *Ulysses*; then suddenly the five strokes of Big Ben intone (as later they are to intone in *Mrs. Dalloway*). At the same time, another procession blocks Long Acre—carriages, intercepted cabs and motorcars. Clara in the blazing windows of one car suddenly sees Jacob (p. 174). The third interruption of process occurs in the final section, chapter fourteen, when the omnibuses become locked together at Mudie's Corner, and Bonamy, sensing Jacob's presence, cries: "Jacob! Jacob!" and the leaves suddenly seem to raise themselves. Each one of these three scenes of blocked process symbolizes, of course, Jacob's death. Yet each one ends with the shattering stroke of the Joycean *ricorso*—with the sounds of Big Ben, with a blazing vision of Jacob, and with Bonamy's cry of "Jacob! Jacob!" The meaning of the ending is thus clear, the explosive vision, accompanied by the raising of leaves, has given birth to a new cycle. Somebody would wear Jacob's shoes, and from the chrysalis of Jacob's room would emerge yet another moth. In the refrain "Jacob! Jacob!," which we have heard in the first chapter and in the last, lies inherent the recurring nature of human experience that Joyce celebrated again and again in the writing of *Ulysses*.

The structure of *Mrs. Dalloway* reflects *Ulysses* far more definitely than did *Jacob's Room*. To begin with, there is no question that Virginia Woolf was reading *Ulysses* as she was starting with *Mrs. Dalloway* in the summer of 1922. This fact alone would make an effect, whether conscious or unconscious, a matter of some likelihood. On 16 August 1922 she writes in her diary: "I have read 200 pages so far—not a third; and have been amused, stimulated, charmed, interested . . . and then puzzled, bored, irritated and disillusioned by a queasy undergraduate scratching his pimples" (2:188–89). In the next paragraph of the same entry, Mrs. Woolf discusses her own work on *Mrs. Dalloway*. Furthermore, T. S. Eliot had given her his opinion that *Ulysses* was on a par with *War and Peace*. A letter in the *James Joyce Quarterly* makes the point that Mrs. Woolf's "personal and professional jealousy" cannot be overlooked and that the fact that "Tom, great Tom" praised *Ulysses* could have provoked her negative remarks about the book. "The anguish that this sort of implied comparison caused her is made explicit in an earlier entry, September 26, 1920," an entry previously quoted in this chapter: ". . . What I'm doing is probably being better done by Mr. Joyce."[15] The possibility of direct influence, then, becomes at least a reasonable guess.

However, the read morocco notebook containing her
plans for *Mrs. Dalloway* makes her interest in Joyce's structure less a matter of conjecture. She writes:

> FURTHER PLAN.
>
> Hours: 10. 11. 12. 1. 2. 3. 4. 5. 6. 7. 8. 9. 10. 11. 12. 1. 2.
> Eleven o'clock strikes
>     This is the aeroplane hour which covers both Septimus and
> Rezia in Regent's Park and Clarissa [*sic*] reflections. Which last
> to 12 o'clock:
> interview with specialist. (P. 3)[16]

In 1923 and 1924 we see from the diary that she called her
book, temporarily, *The Hours.*
    In the red morocco notebook, she continues:

> But how is the transition to come from one to the other (p. 4)
> Why not have an observer in the street at each critical point
> who acts the part of Chorus—some nameless person? (p. 6)
>     also, could the scenes be divided like acts of a play into five,
> say, or six? (P. 7)

All these questions about structure are ultimately an-
swered in *Mrs. Dalloway* through the adoption of techniques reminiscent of Joyce. The eight divisions of the
novel are indicated simply by breaks in the text as in
*Ulysses,* and in both novels the street functions often as the
medium of transition between scenes, serving as Floris
Delattre has pointed out, "to establish a profound tie between the small incoherent universe of one man and the
immense unity of the great city representing the mysterious whole."[17]
    The first part of *Mrs. Dalloway*[18] serves as an overture in
which Clarissa is introduced as well as some of the central
motifs of the book. Many of these are Joycean in tone; for
example: ". . . Big Ben strikes. There! Out it boomed. . . .
The leaden circles dissolved in the air" (p. 5) suggests a
sense of circular reality common to Joyce's Dance of the
Hours. "The morning and noon hours waltz in their
places, turning, advancing to each other, shaping their

curves, bowing vis à vis."[19] Furthermore, references to Big Ben are found in both the "Sirens" and "Circe" episodes, episodes based on Joyce's concept of *ricorso*. Street scenes are also, of course, common to both novels: Clarissa "stiffened a little on the kerb, waiting for Durtnall's van to pass" (p. 4), reminding one of descriptions of Bloom as he walks streets of Dublin. The day of Clarissa is a day like Joyce's, in "the middle of June" (p. 5). But the decisive Joycean touch is the ending of this first part with "a pistol shot in the street outside!" (p. 19), reminiscent of "A shout in the street," in the "Nestor" episode (the phrase A. M. Klein used as the title of his article discussing Vico's influence on Joyce's novel).[20] This pistol shot was heard earlier in *Jacob's Room* whereas the Joycean "shout in the street" will be repeated in the sixty-two puffs of air or of gas in the "Aeolus" episode, in the explosive noises permeating the "Sirens" episode, and in the cracking of the chandelier in the "Circe" episode. (These episodes are the fourth, eighth, and twelfth episodes of the central section of *Ulysses*, strategically located if seen in the context of Vico's *ricorso*.) The "pistol shot" at the end of the first part of *Mrs. Dalloway*, as with some of the Joycean "thunderclaps," brings this section of the novel to a conclusion and at the same time serves as a transitional device into part two, which opens with the "violent explosion," the same motorcar, and circulation of rumors of *the* mysterious car on Bond Street. Likewise Bloom's "thunderclap" concludes the Sirens episode and is followed by the various inflated styles of the Cyclops episode and the circulation of drink. The motorcar, and later the aeroplane, is a unifying device, like Hely's sandwich men or the Viceregal procession of any of the other wandering and circulating people or things in *Ulysses*. As for Joyce, the street is for Virginia Woolf in *Mrs. Dalloway* an umbilical cord. It is shortly after the aeroplane appears that the bells strike eleven times (p. 30) "up there among the gulls" (sounding another Joycean note) "and the car went in at the gates and nobody looked at it." The eleven bells thus accompany the disappearance of the car and the appearance of the aeroplane, thereby provoking a minor revolution, from street to air, in this section. Part two ends with the aeroplane flying out over Ludgate Circus—*Circus* again with the suggestion of cyclical recurrence. Carl Woodring notes the importance of the circle to this novel as a means of putting death in its place.[21] For Joyce, too, of course, the circle was of utmost significance. One has only to consult Hanley's *Word Index* to find how often *circle* and its derivatives are used in *Ulysses* as well as words with the prefix *circum*.[22] Doubtless he delighted in the happy chance that placed the "Circe" episode at the end of the central section of *Ulysses*, for the spelling of *Circe* reminds one of *circle*, and Bella Cohen as Circe clearly represents a vehicle of circulation.

In part three of *Mrs. Dalloway* (pp. 42–72), we find Clarissa at home, but the circular character of the section is informed by the return in her fantasies of Sally Seton and in reality of Peter Walsh. At the end of this part of the book, Big Ben once again strikes and all the clocks are striking—11:30—as Clarissa calls to Peter, "Remember my party tonight," and Peter Walsh "shut the door" (p. 72). Parties, as in Joyce, are another means of circulation; and the striking of Big Ben serves both as a transition between the two sections and also as a link between this passage and the opening of the book in the repetition of "The leaden circles dissolved in the air" (p. 72), suggesting another opening as we begin to follow Peter as he proceeds through London. Big Ben is in *Mrs. Dalloway* both an explosive signal of change and a unifying device, the same functions assigned the clock in Joyce's work.[23]

Section four (pp. 72–85), beginning with the continuing sound of Big Ben, traces Peter as he circulates in the streets of London "speaking to himself rhythmically, in time with the flow of the sound" (p. 72) until "the last tremors of the great booming voice shook the air round him" (p. 73). We become involved with the flow of Peter's thoughts and with the refrain "Remember my party" (p. 81). Motorcars continue to circulate and stop and then to recirculate. As

Peter approaches Regent's Park, "the thought of childhood keeps coming back" to him (p. 83). And finally seated on a bench in the park amid "moving branches . . . the shuffle of feet, and the people passing, and humming traffic, rising and falling traffic" (pp. 84–85), Peter sinks into sleep "and was muffled over" (p. 85), another ending reminiscent of Joyce in the "Ithaca" episode as Bloom falls asleep: "He rests. He has travelled" with "Sinbad the Sailor and Tinbad the Tailor and Jinbad the Jailer" (p. 737).

It is no surprise, then, to one versed in Joyce to find that the next section of Mrs. Dalloway, the fifth (pp. 85–88), deals with a dream Peter has of "the solitary traveller, haunter of lanes, disturber of fens" (p. 85). These visions of himself "murmur in his [Peter's] ear like sirens lolloping away on the green sea waves" (p. 86), the sirens who enticed Ulysses. The solitary traveler, like both Ulysses and Peter, is welcomed home by an elderly woman "who seems to seek, over a desert, a lost son; to search for a rider destroyed" (p. 87)—the theme of the lost son central to the Nostos of Ulysses. And section five concludes with an unanswered question, "But to whom does the solitary traveller make reply? (p. 88) as does the "Ithaca" episode with "Where?"—both endings suggesting the conclusion of a cycle through the sleep of the protagonists.

The sixth section of Mrs. Dalloway (pp. 88–97) opens with Peter's awakening but closes with another conclusion of a cycle: "'Clarissa!' he cried 'Clarissa!' But she never came back. It was over. He went away that night. He never saw her again" (p. 97). The general theme of this section concerns the breakup of Clarissa as Peter remembers it. Glancing at the overall structure of Mrs. Dalloway, we find that the first four sections tend to employ the unifying factors of the Joycean method—the various umbilical cords of circulation and circles of sound as viewed in the purlieus of the London street and in Clarissa's home, where she and Peter are re-united. Starting with the fifth section, however, telling of the dream of the solitary traveler, with the shutting of the cupboard door and the unanswered question at its conclusion, we find instead a sense of breakup, of old structures being reshuffled and of new combinations being formed—the same sense that permeates the three episodes in *Ulysses* that stress the end of the old and the beginning of new cycles of experience. Thus the "Aeolus" episode, which concludes the morning of Bloom's day, is filled with more or less discrete incidents punctuated by cryptic newspaper headlines—a fragmentation and cracking up of the flow of experience in preparation for the reformulation of the afternoon. The "Sirens" episode, with its well-known crepitations, crackings, clackings, and cloppings, comes at the conclusion of Bloom's afternoon, and his evening outing is brought to an end with the shattering of the chandelier in the "Circe" episode.

In keeping with this whole pattern, many characters and episodes fragment the seventh section of *Mrs. Dalloway* (pp. 97–250), following the breakup of Peter and Clarissa as it is remembered by Peter in the sixth section. In the seventh division of the book, we are provided, moreover, with a double for Mrs. Dalloway in Septimus Smith— suggesting the kind of splitting of emphasis Joyce likes to make in handling character—as with two fathers, Simon Dedalus and Leopold Bloom; two sons, Stephen and Rudy; or two father-sons, Stoom and Blephen or Shem and Shaun. By far the longest of *Mrs. Dalloway*, the seventh section begins at 11:45 A.M. as "the quarter struck" (p. 106) and includes ten separate episodes—moving from Septimus Smith to Peter Walsh to Sir William Bradshaw to Lady Bruton's lunch to Elizabeth and Miss Kilman to Septimus's suicide. "Shredding and slicing, dividing and subdividing, the clocks of Harley Street nibbled at the June day" (p. 154)—"it was half-past one" (p. 155). And the reference to Greenwich time in the passage cannot help but remind us of Joyce's ballast office clock worked by electric wire from Dunsink.[24] As Lady Bruton sleeps after lunch, the striking bells once again sound, and Hugh Whitbread and Richard Dalloway make their way through London traffic (as both Clarissa and Peter have done earlier) while a newspaper placard swoops up in the air (reminiscent of the placards and gulls in *Ulysses*), yellow awnings tremble in the wind, and "single carts rattled carelessly down half-empty streets" (p. 171)—sounding echoes from Leopold Bloom's day in June 1904. At 3 P.M. as Richard enters Dean's Yard, Big Ben once again strikes, serving to link him with Clarissa, for the sound also floods the room where she sits and where he will soon arrive. To continue to enumerate passages reminiscent of Joyce in this section can only become tedious. Big Ben persistently punctuates the structure, calls out the hours; the voice of clocks "beaten up, broken up by the assault of carriages, the brutality of vans, the eager advance of myriads of angular men, of flaunting women" (p. 194). Omnibuses circle—"this van; this life; this procession" (p. 210). In the fantasies of Septimus, even the image of Icarus, son of Daedalus, may be implicit ("falling down, down into the flames" [p. 213]; "loneliness, falling through the sea, down, down into flames"[p. 216]). In the red morocco notebook, Virginia Woolf had written: "There must be a reality which is not in human beings at all. What about death for instance? Sense of falling through into discoveries like a trap door opening" (pp. 11–12). At 6 P.M. as the clocks strike the hour denoting the end of day, Septimus Smith falls violently down "on to Mrs. Filmer's area railings" (p. 226), concluding another cycle of existence with final and shattering force.

The last section of *Mrs. Dalloway*, the eighth, concerns a party—a function that Clarissa has defined as "an offering; to combine and to create" (p. 185). Basically Joyce and Virginia Woolf view the party in the same light. Joyce had concluded *Dubliners* with a party the function of which had also been to "combine and to create"; a party for Joyce was often the setting for this theory of cyclical recurrence, of "the same renew."[25] Through its explosive character, its release of feeling, it both destroys and re-creates. The gatherings at the newspaper office, at the Ormond bar, and at Bella Cohen's brothel all serve both separating and

unifying functions. In her *Worlds in Consciousness*, Jean O.
Love writes of the party in *Mrs. Dalloway*: "The party rein-
stitutes and unites all the earlier events of the novel and
expresses separateness . . . followed by reunion."[26] And
she could have added "reunion followed by separateness." The party is ultimately the symbol of the crash (on
another level the crash of Septimus's suicide) or the explosion, suggested also throughout *Ulysses* and *Mrs. Dalloway*
in the striking (note its literal meaning) of the hour. And so
it is appropriate that at the end of the party Big Ben should
once more strike "the hour, one, two, three" (p. 283). It is
at this moment that Clarissa identifies with Septimus in an
epiphany like those found in the works of Joyce. For characters who experience an epiphany, portions of their past
lives are shattered and new cycles begun as "the leaden
circles dissolved in the air" (pp. 283–84). Thus the shattering of the chandelier in the "Circe" episode with ensuing
darkness and "falling masonry" leads to the appearance of
Rudy (diamond and ruby buttons on his suit) in Bloom's
fantasy and to Bloom's return home with Stephen in the
*Nostos*. The showing forth of Clarissa (whose name, of
course, means "light") in the final sentence, "For there she
was," at the end of her party, has similar epiphanous
overtones.

I must conclude then that Joyce's concept of the hours
(underlying the structures of both *Jacob's Room* and *Mrs.
Dalloway*) was significant for Virginia Woolf, although employed by her in different contexts and with different tone
and emphasis. Comparing her work with Joyce's gives us
better insight into what she was attempting to do in these
two novels. Moments of vision, of epiphany, of explosion,
of breakup, of *ricorso*; the flash of light or the boom of
sound, the striking of Big Ben—all represent the attempt to
make something permanent of the moment, to arrest the
mysterious and continual flux seen in the ambience of the
great city. Through such an effort comes the only hope of
structuring and molding the small and incoherent universe
of one man to a purpose.

1. *The Diary of Virginia Woolf, 1920–24*, 2:56. Subsequent references to this volume will be cited in the text.

2. Virginia Woolf, *The Common Reader*, p. 190.

3. See Theodor Reik, *Listening with the Third Ear* (Garden City, N.Y.: Garden City Books, 1938).

4. Quentin Bell, *Virginia Woolf: A Biography*, 2:54, 185.

5. The review done by Jean Guiget in *Virginia Woolf and Her Works*, pp. 214–27, contains a somewhat different emphasis.

6. *The Diary of Virginia Woolf, 1915–1919*, 1:247.

7. Virginia Woolf and Lytton Strachey, *Letters*, pp. 98–99.

8. Virginia Woolf, *A Writer's Diary*, p. 349.

9. Woolf and Strachey, p. 98.

10. Floris Delattre, *Le Roman psychologique de Virginia Woolf*, p. 160.

11. Guiguet, p. 222.

12. *A Writer's Diary*, p. 22.

13. Guiguet, p. 222.

14. Virginia Woolf, *"Jacob's Room" and "The Waves"* (New York: Harcourt, Brace, and Company, 1959), p. 8. Subsequent references to this volume will be cited in the text.

15. Pp. 75–76.

16. Quotations from: Virginia Woolf. [*Mrs. Dalloway*]. Holograph notes, unsigned, dated Nov. 9, 1922–Aug. 2, 1923. Henry W. and Albert A. Berg Collection, The New York Public Library, Astor, Lenox, and Tilden Foundations.

17. DeLattre, p. 160.

18. Virginia Woolf, *Mrs. Dalloway* (New York: Harcourt, Brace, and Company, 1925), pp. 3–19. Subsequent references to this volume will be cited in the text.

19. Joyce, *Ulysses* p. 576.

20. *New Directions* 13 (1951): 327.

21. Carl A. Woodring, *Virginia Woolf*, p. 23. Woodring cites the "leaden circles," Peter's vision of the traveler, the car of state, the aeroplane, Peter's opening and shutting of his knife, and Peter's return to London.

22. Miles L. Hanley, ed., *Word Index to James Joyce's "Ulysses"* Madison: University of Wisconsin Press, 1951.

23. Although James Hafley questions David Daiches's opinion that clocks serve as transitional devices in this novel (*The Glass Roof: Virginia Woolf as Novelist*, p. 65), Jean O. Love feels, on the contrary, that Big Ben provides "pattern, order, and unity" for the book (*Worlds in Consciousness: Mythopoetic Thought in the Novels of Virginia Woolf*). She continues in less convincing fashion to assign masculine and feminine roles to Big Ben and the clock of St. Margaret's (pp. 145–60).

24. Joyce, *Ulysses*, p. 165.

25. Joyce, *Finnegans Wake*, pp. 215, 226.

26. P. 159.

# The More or Less Inward Turn of Post-Renaissance Fiction

None of the structures discussed in the eight chapters of this book are entirely exterior to the context, to character or to action, to which they give shape. But some are more inward than others. The inner world of Don Quixote is mirrored in the structures Cervantes gives his novel. Werther's absorption in nature is mirrored in the seasonal structures of his book; and the philosophical, religious, and psychological tensions of characters give order and form to Dostoevsky's long works. In the novels of James Joyce, we find a psychological patterning, based on the Viconian system, exterior to the works but molded and redesigned by Joyce so that it becomes an interior pattern of the development of his protagonists, beginning with the age when parents dominate, moving to adolescence and its adjustments, then to maturity and a role in society, until lightning strikes and one must phoenix-like rise from ashes to begin anew, "a commodius vicus of recircula-tion."[1]

It is more difficult to assert, however, that the structures used in *Joseph Andrews*, for example, mirror character in the same way or that Madame Bovary's inner world may be interpreted through Flaubert's tripartite structure of that novel. In fact, Flaubert's subtitle, *Patterns of Provincial Life*, clearly indicates that Flaubert's emphasis will be not on psychological but on sociological insight. Nor does Thomas Mann's use of circular and spiral forms relate to the inner consciousness of Hans Castorp so much as to the theory that Mann is developing about the nature of reality, an equation in which Hans reckons as an integer. The movement of the needle of the gramophone, the circle de-

185

scribed by the round table at the séance, or that described by Hans as he circles in the snowstorm, tend to serve in the development of a *Weltanschauung*, rather than in the development of Hans Castorp himself, who at the end is dismissed, whether to live or to die, with poor prospects. "We even confess," writes Mann, "that it is without great concern that we leave the question open" (p. 716).

There is perhaps then in the history of post-Renaissance fiction an alternating emphasis, from inner turn to outer, then back to inner turn, even though in general, as Erich Kahler points out, "formulaic mythic elements that governed narrative from outside no longer rule"[2] since *Don Quixote*. Fielding claims to imitate *Don Quixote* in *Joseph Andrews*, but his imitation is characterized by an eighteenth-century stamp. The sallies and withdrawals of Joseph and Parson Adams are not related to alternating euphoria and melancholia of the heroes but governed by practical and exterior concerns, such as Adams setting forth at the beginning to sell his sermons. Events in *Joseph Andrews* do not extend symbolically to throw light on the hero's psychology as Don Quixote's tilting at windmills extends to reveal his inner world. These differences have been discussed above at some length in Chapter One, Part Two, as well as elsewhere in that chapter.

All the symbolism in *Don Quixote* is directed toward revealing Quixote's manic devotion to chivalry. Fanny exists in her own right in Joseph's affections, but Don Quixote views his ideal woman through a farm girl, a catalyst for Dulcinea. Joseph and Adams battle the squire's dogs, but Don Quixote in attacking sheep attacks an army. Thus the reader is always in *Don Quixote* involved in at least two, sometimes three, levels of perception, whereas in *Joseph Andrews* the surface level prevails. I would suggest that Fielding's structures and techniques are less integrated with the characters because his focus is society, not the individual, a comedy of manners, not of mind. In Fielding's work society is exterior to the character, as the structure is exterior to the theme; in the psychological novel, character development and structure go hand in hand.

Realism as interpreted by Flaubert also did not reveal the inner world of the main characer in its form. The basic earth elements used to forge the pattern of *Madame Bovary* relate more to a person like Catherine Leroux than to Emma herself. In fact, Flaubert may have emphasized animal, vegetable, and liquid elements in his structuring, in earthy contrast to his flighty heroine, whose fantasies led her from disaster to worse disaster, and also in contrast to the hypocrisy and superficiality of the bourgeois temperament that he despised. Although as Erich Kahler writes of *A Simple Heart*: "The attentive reader will notice how Flaubert, this master of 'realism,' has employed all the devices of sober factuality to produce a pattern whose every detail is shot with symbolism,"[3] the integration of this symbolism in *Madame Bovary*—for example, nature symbolism—with Emma's inner world is not close at all. Emma's concept of nature is entirely different from that nature which surrounds her in the Norman countryside. Vegetable, animal, and water form settings, exterior objects, creature life that Emma merely observes, whereas Werther's conflict, although much the same as Emma's, is embodied in the structures and the symbolism of the book. Thus, although Flaubert's work is, as Kahler points out, "shot with symbolism," it is a symbolism directed toward a social, not a psychological, purpose and, like the structures in *Joseph Andrews*, less closely integrated with character. The social structure of a July monarchy and the structure of nature are for Flaubert worlds apart and can serve only as foils for one another, not as complements.

Turning to Thomas Mann, we find that his structures, too, direct the reader more to the outer world of Hans Castorp than to the inner. Mann would create a philosophy or a world view by means of circles and spirals, so that it becomes clear that he is eventually describing process, rather than the individual interior development of his hero. Thus whereas the christening basin in *The Magic Mountain* describes a closed circle symbolizing the deadening "ewige Wiederkehr" of family tradition, Hans Castorp's train on his way up to the Berghof wound in ascending curves. But neither of these symbols reflects what is going on in the mind of Castorp; they are exterior to him because Mann in the novel sees Hans as *ingénu*, a blackboard upon which words must be inscribed. It is the reader, not the hero, who perceives that the spiraling ascent up the mountain provides an escape from the deadening circularity of the flatlands. Mann uses Hans in almost naturalistic fashion as the subject of his experiments. Imposing certain experiences and conditions upon his hero, he watches carefully the results and draws his ultimate theory of the interdependency of love and death in life from Hans Castorp's trial run.

It will be noted then that the structure of the novel since *Don Quixote* turns more inward when the emphasis is on the individual hero and his psychological development, more outward when the emphasis lies on exterior concerns like manners, society, or a philosophy. The eighteenth century turned its attention outward to ridicule of the social animal; romanticism turned inward to explore the feelings and emotions of that animal; realism adapted itself to both inner and outer modes, depending on the intention, purpose, and the interests of the author—in other words, on his definition of what is "real"; impressionism (Virginia Woolf) and expressionism (Kafka) always take the "inward turn," closely integrating the psychology of the subject with the form. Thus the so-called psychological novel employs structure in a way different from that of the social or philosophical novel. Ortega y Gasset points out: "I understand, then, by literary genres, certain basic themes, mutually exclusive, true esthetic categories."[4] But one may go a step further to state that literary techniques, like structure, can also be characterized as thematic, "wide vistas seen from the main sides of human nature."[5] The architecture of the novel, like that of a building, is informed by the total environment; technique is a part of subject matter, not imposed upon subject matter. Proust, a great impressionistic architect himself, wrote of the structuring of the novel that one must "build it like a church";[6]

thus the Gothic arch, which points to heaven, informs the structuring of *Remembrance of Things Past*, one pier representing the individual, the other society, both mutually supported by, and supporting, the keystone that is art. The structure of Proust's novel is thus in itself thematic.

Another way of looking at the inward turn of fiction is through the physical environment of the novel, another structure that supports and informs it. How is this environment reflected in the work? In *Don Quixote* the flat, dry prairie land of La Mancha, the torrid Spanish summers, windmills, and clusters of white houses with red-orange roofs (impressions gained by the traveler to this part of Spain) are rarely seen in Cervantes' novel except through the perception of the hero. It is Don Quixote, not Cervantes, who interprets his physical surroundings in the novel, and they thus become part of *his* world, not a world exterior to him and shared by all. Even Sancho is frequently surprised at his master's interpretation of reality: inns become castles and fulling mills become giants. On the other hand, despite Parson Adams's own dream world (based on Christianity and the tenets of the classical moralists), the English countryside, the inns, the endless roads, and the country houses exist in their own right, apart from Adams's perceptions of them and apart from his dreams of perfection.

In Goethe's *Werther*, however, nature is interpreted and idealized by the letter-writer, seen through his eyes alone, so that storms become part of his own interior raging, "every tree, every hedge . . . a nosegay,"[7] and turbulent and dangerous floods a rapture and a delight.[8] On the other hand, as we have already noted in this conclusion, the Norman countryside is merely a setting for the emotional life of Emma Bovary, completely exterior to her, though sometimes a source of her distaste. Unlike Quixote, she does not impose her daydreams of an ideal world upon the objects that surround her; and, unlike Werther, she does not interiorize nature. It exists in its own right, and her fantasies of ideal nature (storms experienced through operatic music or turtledoves in "Gothic bird cages")[9] are merely vanities, the vapors of a sentimental mind.

In *Crime and Punishment*, on the contrary, one is struck by the way in which the streets, bridges, and squares of Saint Petersburg scarcely have an existence except as part of Raskolnikov's tortured wanderings and searchings for himself. In the entire novel, there is only one short description of the Haymarket (Sennaya Ploshchad), "three or four lines to give an impression of the square emptying at evening";[10] and, although maps can be drawn indicating the various points the hero visits and the streets he traveled, the places in the novel that are real are those places where "concentrations of spiritual energy took place. . . . They were real only because it was in these places that the mind of Raskolnikov erupted with startling violence."[11]

Still another use of settings is found in Mann's *The Magic Mountain*. Davos, the Schatzalp, or the Strela become for Mann symbols in a philosophical system he expounds. The setting, splendid in its own right, is always exterior to the mind of Hans Castorp and observed by him objectively, as Emma Bovary observed the Norman scene. But ascent and descent come to have philosophical content; snowfields become an objective correlative for a timeless present; and the thin air of the mountain heights becomes "a rarified atmosphere," a symbol of Germany's withdrawal to the enchanted peaks of theory and ideality.

Dublin, on the other hand, is internalized by Leopold Bloom and London by Virginia Woolf and Mrs. Dalloway. As with *Crime and Punishment*, one can draw a map designating Bloom's wanderings in Dublin on 16 June. One can even walk these streets and byways, following Bloom's path throughout his entire day. But rarely in *Ulysses* do we find an objective description of setting. Places are mentioned, but they are interpreted by Bloom or Stephen and exist through their eyes. Thus, for example, the Ormand bar is characterized by its crepitations, the rebound of a garter, the tympanum; the Martello Tower is an omphalos;

or Burton restraurant at 1 P.M. a place of swilling, wolfing, or cannibalism and hot fresh blood, hating and being hated. When Joyce does externalize settings in *Ulysses*, it is for purposes of contrast, for example, the stage directions in the "Circe" episode or the "old narrative style" in "Eumaeus." Such anomalies tend to intensify the much stronger inward focus of the novel.

In the psychological novel, then, setting and character are interpenetrative and sail the centuries together. As Marcel Proust wrote of Combray, "It was the steeple of Saint-Hilaire which shaped and crowned and consecrated every occupation, every hour of the day, every point of view in the town."[12] In novels with a focus other than psychological, we tend to see setting and environment as elements apart from, and exterior to, character. In each instance the emphasis is man, his everyday concerns, "a cry in the street"; but there are various avenues of approach to this subject matter, and the word *inward* is interpreted in the light of the particular approach employed by an author.

1. Joyce, *Finnegans Wake*, p. 3.
2. *The Inward Turn of Narrative*, p. 15.
3. Ibid., p. 65.
4. *Meditations on Quixote*, p.113.
5. Ibid.
6. Marcel Proust, "To the Reader," trans. Richard Macksey, in *Proust*, ed. René Girard (Englewood Cliffs, N.J.: Prentice-Hall, 1962), p. 179.
7. *The Sorrows of Young Werther*, p. 4.
8. Ibid., p. 102.
9. Flaubert, *Madame Bovary*, p. 43.
10. Robert Payne, *Dostoyevsky, A Human Portrait*, p. 203.
11. Ibid.
12. Marcel Proust, *Swann's Way*, trans. C. K. Scott Moncrieff (New York: Modern Library, 1928), p. 79.

# Bibliography

The purpose of the bibliography is to arrange criticism, letters, diaries, and interviews cited in this volume, in addition to other works not cited, according to authors and novels treated in the text, so that sources on structure for each book are readily available to the reader. The bibliography is by no means exhaustive, but it does list works that I have found especially useful in the study of structures in the fiction discussed in my book.

Miguel de Cervantes Saavedra (1547–1616)
*The Adventures of Don Quixote*

Auden, W. H. *The Dyer's Hand.* New York: Random House, 1956. Pp. 135–38.

Borges, Jorge Luis. "Pierre Menard, Author of the *Quixote.*" In *Labyrinths: Selected Stories and Other Writings.* Ed. Donald A. Yates and James E. Irby. New York: New Directions, 1964.

Casalduero, Joaquin. "The Composition of *Don Quixote.*" In *Cervantes across the Centuries.* Ed. Angel Flores and M.J. Benardete. New York: Gordian Press, 1969.

———. *Sentido y forma del Quijote.* Madrid: Ediciones Insula, 1949.

Church, Margaret. *Don Quixote: The Knight of La Mancha.* New York: New York University Press, 1971.

Gerhardt, Mia. *Don Quixote, la vie et les livres.* Amsterdam: Noord-Hollandsche Uitg. Mij., 1955.

Gottfried, Leon. "The Odysseyan Form: An Exploratory Essay." In *Essays on European Literature.* St. Louis, Mo.: Washington University Press, 1972.

Grossvogel, David I. "Cervantes: *Don Quixote.*" In *Limits of the Novel.* Ithaca, N.Y.: Cornell University Press, 1968.

Immerwahr, Raymond. "Structural Symmetry in the Episodic Narratives of *Don Quixote,* Part One." *Comparative Literature* 10 (1958): 121–35.

Kahler, Erich. *The Inward Turn of Narrative.* Trans. Richard and Clara Winston. Princeton, N.J.: Princeton University Press, 1973.

Meyer, Herman. *The Poetics of Quotation in the European Novel.* Trans. Theodore and Yetta Ziolkowski. Princeton, N.J.: Princeton University Press, 1968.

Ortega y Gasset, José. *Meditations on Quixote.* Trans. Evelyn Rugg and Diego Marín. New York: W. W. Norton and Company, 1961.

Riley, E. C. *Cervantes' Theory of the Novel.* Oxford: Clarendon Press, 1962.

Togeby, Knud. *La Composition du roman "Don Quijote."* Supp. 1 of *Orbis Litterarum.* Copenhagen: n.p., 1957.

Willis, Raymond S., Jr. *The Phantom Chapters of the Quijote.* New York: Hispanic Institute of the United States, 1953.

——. "Sancho Panza: Prototype for the Modern Novel." *Hispanic Review* 37 (1969): 207–27.

Henry Fielding (1707–1754)
*The History and Adventures of Joseph Andrews
and of His Friend Mr. Abraham Adams*

Battestin, Martin. *"Joseph Andrews"* and *"Shamela."* London: Methuen, 1965.

Cauthen, I. B., Jr. "Fielding's Digressions in *Joseph Andrews.*" *College English* 17 (1956): 379–82.

Digeon, Aurélien. *Les Romans de Fielding.* Paris: Hatchette, 1923.

Ehrenpreis, Irvin. "Fielding's Use of Fiction: The Autonomy of Joseph Andrews." In *Twelve Original Essays on Great English Novels.* Ed. Charles Shapiro. Detroit, Mich.: Wayne State University Press, 1960.

Fielding, Henry. In *Covent Garden Journal.* Vol. I. Ed. G. E. Jensen. New Haven, Conn.: Yale University Press, 1915. P. 281.

Goldberg, Homer. *The Art of "Joseph Andrews."* Chicago: University of Chicago Press, 1969.

Johnson, Maurice. *Fielding's Art of Fiction.* Philadelphia: University of Pennsylvania Press, 1961.

Karl, Frederick. *The Adversary Literature.* New York: Farrar, Strauss, Giroux, 1974.

Macallister, Hamilton. *Fielding.* London: Evans Brothers, 1967.

Parker, Alexander A. "Fielding and the Structure of *Don Quixote.*" *Bulletin of Hispanic Studies* 33 (1956): 1–16.

Wright, Andrew. *Henry Fielding: Mask and Feast.* London: Chatto and Windus, 1965.

Johann Wolfgang von Goethe (1749–1832)
*The Sorrows of Young Werther*

Bergel, Lienhard. "Cervantes in Germany." In *Cervantes across the Centuries.* Ed. Angel Flores and M. J. Benardete. New York: Gordian Press, 1969.

Clark, Robert T., Jr. "The Psychological Framework of Goethe's *Werther.*" *Journal of English and Germanic Philology* 46 (1947): 273–78.

Dieckmann, Liselotte. "Repeated Mirror Reflections: The Technique of Goethe's Novels." *Studies in Romanticism* 1 (Spring 1963): 154–59.

Dvoretzky, Edward. "Goethe's *Werther* and Lessing's *Emilia Galotti.*" *German Life and Letters* 16 (October 1962): 23–26.

Foster, Leonard. "Werther's Reading of *Emilia Galotti.*" *Publications of the English Goethe Society* 27 (1958): 33–45.

Ittner, Robert. "Werther and 'Emilia Galotti.'" *Journal of English and Germanic Philology* 41 (1942): 418–26.

Lange, Victor. "Die Sprache als Erzählform in Goethe's *Werther.*" In *Formenwandel: Festschrift zum 65 Geburtstag von Paul Bockmann.* Hamburg: Hoffmann und Campe Verlag, 1964.

Lukács, Georg. *Goethe und seine Zeit.* Bern: A. Francke Ag. Verlag, 1947.

Reiss, Hans. *Goethe's Novels.* Coral Gables, Fla.: University of Miami Press, 1969.

Storz, Gerhard. *Goethe-Vigilien.* Stuttgart: E. Klett, 1953.

Trunz, Erich. "Altersstil." In *Goethe-Handbuch.* Ed. A. Zastran. Stuttgart: J. B. Metzlar, 1955.

Wilkinson, Elizabeth M., and L. A. Willoughby. "The Blind Man and the Poet: An Early State in Goethe's Quest for Form." In *German Studies Presented to Walter Horace Bruford.* London: George G. Harrap and Co., 1962.

——. *Goethe, Poet and Thinker.* London: Edward Arnold, 1962.

Gustave Flaubert (1821–1880)
*Madame Bovary, Patterns of Provincial Life*

Bart, Benjamin F. *Flaubert.* Syracuse, N.Y.: Syracuse University Press, 1967

Bonwit, Marianne. "Gustave Flaubert et le principe d'impassibilité." *University of California Publications in Modern Philosophy.* Vol. 33, No. 4, pp. 286–301.

Bopp, Léon. *Commentaire sur "Madame Bovary."* Neuchâtel: A. la Baconnière, 1951.

Brombert, Victor. *The Novels of Flaubert.* Princeton, N. J.: Princeton University Press, 1966.

Demorest, D.-L. *L'Expression figurée et symbolique dans l'oeuvre de Gustave Flaubert.* Geneva: Slatkine Reprints, 1967.

Dumesnil, René. *Flaubert: Son hérédité, son milieu, sa méthode.* Geneva: Slatkine Reprints, 1977.

Flaubert, Gustave. *Correspondance 1850–1859.* Vol. 13. Paris: Club de l'Honnête Homme, 1974.

Gothot-Mersch, Claudine. *La Genèse de "Madame Bovary."* Paris: J. Corti, 1966.

Levin, Harry. *The Gates of Horn: A Study of Five French Realists.* New York: Oxford University Press,, 1963. Chapter 5.

Steegmuller, Francis. *Flaubert and "Madame Bovary."* New York: Viking Press, 1939.

Thorlby, Anthony. *Gustave Flaubert and the Art of Realism.* New Haven, Conn.: Yale University Press, 1957.

Fyodor Dostoevsky (1821–1881)
*Crime and Punishment*
*The Brothers Karamazov*

Amend, Victor E. "Theme and Form in *The Brothers Karamazov.*" *Modern Fiction Studies* 4 (Autumn 1958): 240–52.

196

Bakhtin, Mikhail. *Problems of Dostoevsky's Poetics*. N.p.: Ardis, 1973.

Chaitin, Gilbert. "Religion as Defense: The Structure of *The Brothers Karamazov*." *Literature and Psychology* 22 (1972): 69–87.

Dauner, Louise. "Raskolnikov in Search of a Soul." *Modern Fiction Studies* 4 (Autumn 1958): 199–210.

Dostoevsky, Fyodor. *The Notebooks for "The Brothers Karamazov."* Ed. and trans. Edward Wasiolek. Chicago: University of Chicago Press, 1971.

————. *The Notebooks for "Crime and Punishment."* Ed. and trans. Edward Wasiolek. Chicago: University of Chicago Press, 1967.

Feldman, A. Bronson. "Dostoevsky and Father-Love Exemplified by *Crime and Punishment*." *Psychoanalysis and the Psychoanalytical Review* 45 (Winter 1958–59): 84–98.

Florance, Edna C. "The Neurosis of Raskolnikov." In *"Crime and Punishment" and the Critics*. Ed. Edward Wasiolek. San Francisco: Wadsworth Publishing Company, 1961.

Holquist, Michael. *Dostoevsky and the Novel*. Princeton, N.J.: Princeton University Press, 1977.

Jackson, Robert Louis. *Dostoevsky's Quest for Form*. New Haven, Conn.: Yale University Press, 1966.

Lord, Robert. *Dostoevsky*. Berkeley: University of California Press, 1970.

Payne, Robert. *Dostoyevsky, A Human Portrait*. New York: Alfred A. Knopf, 1961.

Rahv, Philip. *The Myth and the Powerhouse*. New York: Farrar, Strauss, and Giroux, 1965.

Simmons, Ernest J. *Dostoevsky: The Making of a Novelist*. New York: Vintage Books, 1940.

Turkevich, Ludmilla B. "Cervantes in Russia." In *Cervantes across the Centuries*. Ed. Angel Flores and M. J. Benardete. New York: Gordian Press, 1969.

Franz Kafka (1883–1924)
*The Trial*

Borges, Jorge Luis. "Kafka and His Precursors." In *Labyrinths: Selected Stories and Other Writings*. Ed. Donald A. Yates and James E. Irby. New York: New Directions, 1964.

Brod, Max. *Franz Kafka: A Biography*. Trans. G. Humphreys and Richard Winston. New York: Schocken Books, 1960.

————. *Franz Kafka Today*. Ed. Angel Flores and Homer Swander. Madison: University of Wisconsin Press, 1958.

Church, Margaret. "Time and Reality in the Work of Franz Kafka." In *Time and Reality: Studies in Contemporary Fiction*. Chapel Hill: University of North Carolina Press, 1963.

Emrich, Wilhelm. *Franz Kafka*. Bonn: Athenäum Verlag, 1957.

Fraiberg, Selma. "Kafka and the Dream.' In *Art and Psychoanalysis*. Ed. William Phillips. New York: Criterion Books, 1957.

Gray, Ronald. *Franz Kafka*. Cambridge, England: At the University Press, 1973.

Heselhaus, Clemens."Kafkas Erzählformen." *Deutsche Vierteljahrsschriften für Literaturwissenschaft und Geistesgeschichte* 26 (1952): 353–76.

Hoffman, Frederick J. "Kafka and Mann." In *Freudianism and the Literary Mind*. Baton Rouge: Louisiana State University Press, 1957.

Janouch, Gustav. *Conversations with Kafka: Notes and Reminiscences*. Trans. Goronwy Rees. New York: F. A. Praeger, 1953.

Kafka, Franz. *The Diaries of Franz Kafka, 1910–1913*. Ed. Max Brod. Trans. Joseph Kresh. New York: Schocken Books. 1965.

———. *The Diaries of Franz Kafka, 1914–1923*. Ed. Max Brod. Trans. Martin Greenberg and Hannah Arendt. New York: Schocken Books. 1965.

———. *I Am a Memory Come Alive*. Ed. Nahum Glatzer. New York: Schocken Books, 1974.

Kahler, Erich. "Untergang und Übergang der epischen Kunstform." *Neue Rundschau* 64 (1953): 1–44.

Lesser, Simon. "The Source of Guilt and the Sense of Guilt—Kafka's *The Trial*." *Modern Fiction Studies* 8 (Spring 1962): 44–60.

Spilka, Mark. *Dickens and Kafka*. Bloomington: Indiana University Press, 1963.

Uyttersprott, Hermann. "Zur Struktur von Kafkas *Der Prozess*." *Revue des Langues Vivantes*, 1953, pp. 332–76.

Thomas Mann (1875–1955)

*The Magic Mountain*

Church, Margaret. "Thomas Mann: The Circle of Time." In *Time and Reality: Studies in Contemporary Fiction*. Chapel Hill: University of North Carolina Press, 1963.

Heller, Erich. *The Ironic German*. Boston: Little, Brown, and Company, 1958.

Hoffman, Frederick. "Kafka and Mann." In *Freudianism and the Literary Mind*. Baton Rouge: Louisiana State University Press, 1957.

Mann, Thomas. *Essays of Three Decades*. Trans. H. T. Lowe-Porter. New York: Alfred A. Knopf, 1947.

———. "The Making of *The Magic Mountain*." In *The Magic Mountain*. Trans. H. T. Lowe-Porter. New York: Alfred A. Knopf, 1960.

———. *A Sketch of My Life*. Trans. H. T. Lowe-Porter. Paris: Harrison, 1930.

Mayer, Hans. *Thomas Mann: Werk und Entwicklung*. Berlin: Volk und Welt, 1950.

Sandt, Lotti. *Mythos und Symbolik im "Zauberberg" von Thomas Mann*. Bern: Verlag Paul Haupt, 1979.

Slochower, Harry. *Thomas Mann's Joseph Story*. New York: Alfred A. Knopf, 1938.

———. *Three Ways of Modern Man*. New York: International Publishers, 1937.

Spitzer, Leo. "Thomas Mann y la muerta de Don Quijote." *Revista de Filologia Hispanica* 2 (1940): 46–48.

Thomas, R. Hinton. *Thomas Mann: The Mediation of Art.* Oxford: Oxford University Press, 1956.

Weigand, Herman J. "The Magic Moment." In *The Stature of Thomas Mann.* Ed. Charles Neider. New York: New Directions, 1947.

———. *The Magic Mountain: A Study of Thomas Mann's Novel, "Der Zauberberg."* Chapel Hill: University of North Carolina Press, 1964.

James Joyce (1882–1941)
*Dubliners*
*A Portrait of the Artist as a Young Man*
*Ulysses*

Andreach, Robert. *Studies in Structure: The Stages of Spiritual Life in Four Modern Authors.* New York: Fordham University Press, 1964.

Beebe, Maurice. *Ivory Towers and Sacred Founts: The Artist as Hero in Fiction from Goethe to Joyce.* New York: New York University Press, 1964.

Breech, Christine St. Peter. "Letter to Editor." *James Joyce Quarterly* 2 (Fall 1979): 75–76.

Brown, Norman O. *Closing Time.* New York: Random House, 1973.

Church, Margaret. "James Joyce: Time and Time Again." In *Time and Reality: Studies in Contemporary Fiction.* Chapel Hill: University of North Carolina Press, 1963.

Connolly, Thomas E. "Kinesis and Stasis: Structural Rhythm in Joyce's *Portrait of the Artist as a Young Man.*" *University Review* 3 (1966): 21–30.

Cope, Jackson I. *Joyce's Cities: Archaeologies of the Soul.* Baltimore, Md.: Johns Hopkins University Press, 1981.

Cross, Richard. *Flaubert and Joyce: The Rite of Fiction.* Princeton, N.J.: Princeton University Press, 1971.

Ellmann, Richard. *James Joyce.* New York: Oxford University Press, 1959.

Feshbach, Sidney. "A Slow and Dark Birth: A Study of the Organization of *A Portrait of the Artist as a Young Man.*" *James Joyce Quarterly* 4 (Summer 1967): 289–300.

Gorman, Herbert. *James Joyce.* New York: Farrar and Rinehart, 1939.

Hampshire, Stuart. "Joyce and Vico: The Middle Way." *New York Review of Books,* 18 October 1973, pp. 8–21.

Hayman, David. "Daedalian Imagery in A Portrait." In *Hereditas: Seven Essays on the Modern Experience of the Classical.* Ed. Frederick Will. Austin: University of Texas Press, 1964.

Joyce, James. *Letters.* Ed. Stuart Gilbert. New York: Viking Press, 1957.

Kenner, Hugh. *Dublin's Joyce.* London: Chatto and Windus, 1955.

———. *Flaubert, Joyce and Beckett: The Stoic Comedians.* Boston: Beacon Press, 1962.

———. *Ulysses.* London: Allen and Unwin, 1980.

Klein, A. M. "A Shout in the Street." *New Directions* 13 (1951): 327–45.

Lemon, Lee T. *"A Portrait of the Artist as a Young Man." Modern Fiction Studies* 12 (Winter 1966–67): 441–52.

Litz, A. Walton. *The Art of James Joyce.* New York: Oxford University Press, 1964.

———. "Vico and Joyce." In *Giambattista Vico: An International Symposium.* Ed. Giorgio Tagliacozzo and Hayden V. White. Baltimore, Md.: Johns Hopkins University Press, 1969.

Redford, Grant. *"The Role of Structure in Joyce's Portrait." Modern Fiction Studies* 4 (Spring 1958): 21–30.

Robinson, K. E. *"The Stream of Consciousness Technique and the Structure of Joyce's Portrait." James Joyce Quarterly* 9 (1971): 63–84.

Ryf, Robert. *A New Approach to Joyce: "A Portrait of the Artist" as a Guidebook.* Berkeley: University of California Press, 1962.

Scholes, Robert, and Richard M. Kain, eds. *The Workshop of Daedalus: James Joyce and the Raw Materials for "A Portrait of the Artist as a Young Man."* Evanston, Ill.: Northwestern University Press, 1965.

Steinberg, Erwin. *The Stream of Consciousness and Beyond in "Ulysses."* Pittsburgh, Pa.: University of Pittsburgh Press, 1973.

Tindall, William York. *James Joyce: His Way of Interpreting the Modern World.* New York: Scribner's, 1950.

———. *The Literary Symbol.* New York: Columbia University Press, 1955.

Van Laan, Thomas. *"The Meditative Structure of Joyce's Portrait." James Joyce Quarterly* 1 (Spring 1964): 3–13.

Vico, Giambattista. *The New Science of Giambattista Vico.* Trans. Thomas Goddard Bergin and Max Harold Fisch. Garden City, N.Y.: Doubleday, 1961.

Virginia Woolf (1882–1941)

*Jacob's Room*

*Mrs. Dalloway*

Alexander, Jean. *The Venture of Form in the Novels of Virginia Woolf.* Port Washington, N.Y.: Kennikat Press, 1974.

Bell, Quentin. *Virginia Woolf: A biography.* New York: Harcourt Brace Jovanovich, 1972.

Church, Margaret. "The Moment and Virginia Woolf." In *Time and Reality: Studies in Contemporary Fiction.* Chapel Hill: University of North Carolina Press, 1963.

Delattre, Floris. *Le Roman psychologique de Virginia Woolf.* Paris: J. Vrin, 1932.

Fishman, Solomon. "Virginia Woolf on the Novel." *Sewanee Review* 51 (1943): 321–40.

Freedman, Ralph. *"The Form of Fact and Fiction: Jacob's Room* as Paradigm." In *Virginia Woolf: Revaluation and Continuity.* Ed. Ralph Freedman. Berkeley: University of California Press, 1980.

Guiguet, Jean. *Virginia Woolf and Her Works.* Trans. Jean Stewart. London: Hogarth Press, 1965.

Hafley, James. *The Glass Roof: Virginia Woolf as Novelist.* Berkeley: University of California English Studies, 1954.

Love, Jean O. *Worlds in Consciousness: Mythopoetic Thought in the Novels of Virginia Woolf.* Berkeley: University of California Press, 1970.

Mayoux, Jean-Jacques. "Le Roman de l'espace et du temps Virginia Woolf." *Revue Anglo-Américaine* 7 (1930): 312–26.

Roberts, John Hawley. "Vision and Design in Virginia Woolf." *PMLA* 61 (1946): 835–47.

Tindall, William York. "Many-Leveled Fiction: Virginia Woolf to Ross Lockridge." *College English* 10 (1948): 65–71.

Woodring, Carl R. *Virginia Woolf.* New York: Columbia Essays on Modern Writers, 1966.

Woolf, Virginia. *The Common Reader.* 1st Ser. London: Hogarth Press, 1925.

———. *The Diary of Virginia Woolf, 1915–1919.* Ed. Anne Olivier Bell. Vol. 1. New York: Harcourt Brace Jovanovich, 1977.

———. *The Diary of Virginia Woolf, 1920–1924.* Ed. Anne Olivier Bell. Vol. 2. New York: Harcourt Brace Jovanovich, 1978.

———. *A Writer's Diary.* Ed. Leonard Woolf. New York: Harcourt, Brace, and Company, 1953.

Woolf, Virginia, and Lytton Strachey. *Letters.* Ed. Leonard Woolf and James Strachey. New York: Harcourt, Brace, and Company, 1956.

Wright, Nathalia. "*Mrs. Dalloway*: A Study in Composition." *College English* 5 (1944): 351–58.

# Index

Absurd, the, 118–19; in modern novel, 119
Aeschylus, 20, 30
"After the Race" (Joyce), 142
*Amelia* (Fielding), 36
Amend, Victor E., 81
Andreach, Robert, 147
"Araby" (Joyce), 141, 146, 156
Arnold, Matthew, 81
*As You Like It*, 26
Auden, W. H., 27

Baktin, Mikhail, 89
Bart, Benjamin, 63
Battestin, Martin, 36 n. 4
Beebe, Maurice, 167
Bell, Quentin, 171
Berdyaev, Nikolai, 164
"Boarding House, The" (Joyce), 142, 146
Boccaccio, 171
Borach, Georges, 135
Borges, Jorge Luis, 34, 137
*Bovarism*, 64
Brentano, Clemens, 129
Brod, Max, 105, 112, 116
*Brothers Karamazov, The*, 81–100, 103, 119 n. 14, 130; analysis of, 81–100; contrapuntal dialogue in, 89; contrapuntal structure in, 103; Grand Inquisitor in, 89–90, 98; grotesque humor in, 93–94; musical structure in, 81; objective correlative in, 82, 83, 93, 99; polar opposition in, 82–100 passim; sphere in, 83–100 passim; symbolism in, 91–92; triad in, 83, 85, 86, 89–90, 94, 95, 99
Brown, Norman O., 137
Bruntière, Ferdinand, 63, 74
Burgess, Anthony, 135

Céline, Louis-Ferdinand, 137
Cervantes (Saavedra), Miguel de, 5, 9, 10, 11, 14, 15, 16, 17, 18, 26, 27, 29, 30, 31, 32, 33, 34, 35, 42, 43, 49, 61, 62, 81, 93, 121–22, 135, 136, 165, 169–70, 185, 189; Dostoevsky's attitude toward, 81; Joyce's attitude toward, 135; techniques contrasted with Fielding's, 35; Woolf's attitude toward, 169–70. *See also Don Quixote, The Adventures of*
Chaucer, 171
Circular patterns: circle and spiral, in *The Magic Mountain*, 122–26, 127, 128–29, 130–32, 185–86, 187–88; concentricity, in *The Brothers Karamazov*, 83, 85, 86, 90–91, 92 93, 95, 98, 99; cyclical return (in Mann, 12, 126, 131; in *Madame Bovary*, 72; in Mann and Joyce, 163–64, 165)
Clark, Robert T., Jr., 39
Classical form, 30
"Clay" (Joyce), 143, 146
Colet, Louise, 61
Collective unconscious, 159
Comic romance, 16
Connolly, Thomas E., 147
"Counterparts" (Joyce), 143
*Covent Garden Journal* (Fielding), 11
*Crime and Punishment*, 82, 91, 93, 103, 104, 105, 106–19, 136, 190; absurdity in, 118–19; analysis of, 106–19; confrontation with authority in, 106, 107, 108, 109, 113, 114, 115, 118; contrapuntal structure in, 103, 104, 119; the double in, 114–15; father figures in, 103, 104, 107; Kafka's attitude toward, 105; mother figures in,

*Crime and Punishment (continued)*
103, 104, 107; motif of mother/
son in, 106, 108, 109, 111, 114,
115, 116, 118; parallels to *The
Trial*, 104, 106, 107–19; projection
in, 107; psychological approaches to, 106; redemptive pattern in,
116–17 revolt against bureaucracy in, 118–19; state as father
figure in, 118
Croce, Benedetto, 138
Cross, Richard, 136
Cuzzi, Paolo, 138, 147, 151
*Cymbeline*, 47

Daiches, David, 184 n. 23
Dante, 125, 126, 135
Dauner, Louise, 120 n. 15
"Dead, The" (Joyce), 138, 145, 146–
47, 152
Delattre, Floris, 177
Demorest, D.-L., 63, 64, 75, 79
Dialectic. *See* Polar opposition
*Diaries, The* (Kafka), 105
*Diary of Virginia Woolf, The*, 169,
172, 173, 176, 177
Dichotomy. *See* Polar opposition
*Dichtung und Wahrheit* (Goethe),
39, 50
Dieckmann, Liselotte, 47
Digeon, Aurélien, 36 n. 4
Digressions. *See* Plot interruptions
*Don Quixote, The Adventures of*, 4–
10, 11–36 passim, 40, 41, 42, 43,
49, 50, 61, 79, 81, 121–22, 135,
136, 137, 165, 169–70, 186, 189;
actors in, 26; analysis of, 4–10;
Cervantes as narrator in, 27;
chivalric formula in, 30; Cide
Hamete as narrator in, 27, 32, 33,
34, 43; compared to *Joseph Andrews*, 34–35; digressions in, 5–7,
9, 14, 23, 24, 45; Don Quixote as
author of, 50; Don Quixote compared to Parson Adams, 27, 28–
29, 31; Don Quixote and Werther, 42–43, 50; Dostoevsky's attitude toward, 81; Dulcinea contrasted to Fanny and Lotte, 40–
41; Flaubert's attitude toward,

61; Goethe's attitude toward, 41;
ideal/real dichotomy in, 31, 35,
42; influence of, on *Joseph
Andrews*, 36 n. 4; letters in, 49;
life/books dichotomy in, 26;
Mann's attitude toward, 121–22;
as metafiction, 4, 165; mirroring
in, 8, 9, 17, 26; mock epic devices
in, 35; paired episodes in, 8; as
picaresque novel, 13–14; Pierre
Menard as author of, 34, 137;
poet/player dichotomy in, 26–27;
readers in, 27; reality/illusion in,
28; sally/withdrawal pattern in,
6, 7–8, 9, 10, 14–15, 17; Sancho
Panza compared to Joseph
Andrews, 28–29, 31; schizophrenia in, 9–10, 65; textual quotation in, 33; unity in, 17, 20,
Woolf's attitude toward, 169–70
*Don Quixote in England* (Fielding),
11
Donne, John, 9
Dostoevsky, Fyodor, 81, 82, 83, 84,
85, 88, 93, 95, 98, 103, 104, 105,
106, 109, 110, 112, 115, 185; atti-
tude of, toward *Don Quixote*, 81.
*See also Brothers Karamazov, The;
Crime and Punishment*
Double, the, 114–15
*Double, The* (Dostoevsky), 105
*Dubliners*, 138–47, 148, 150, 151,
153, 158, 182; analysis of, 138–47;
*Mrs. Dalloway* in relation to, 182;
Oedipus and Electra complexes
in, 143; quest motif in, 140, 141,
143, 145; Viconian patterns in,
138–45
Dvoretzky, Edward, 55

Ehrenpreis, Irvin, 37 n. 4
*Einschränkung, Die*, 39, 42, 47, 53,
57
Electra complex, 143
Eliot, T. S., 176
Ellmann, Richard, 136, 138, 147,
148, 159, 172
*Emilia Galotti* (Lessing), 55–57
"Encounter, An" (Joyce), 140–41,
146

Epictetus, 26
Epiphany: in *Dubliners*, 155, 158; in *Jacob's Room*, 173; in *Portrait of the Artist as a Young Man*, 152, 156–58; related to Vico's *ricorso*, 155
Epistolary form: in *Don Quixote*, 49; in *Joseph Andrews*, 49; in *Pamela*, 49; in *Sorrows of Young Werther*, 49–51, 53, 54
"Eveline" (Joyce), 142, 143
*Die ewige Wiederkehr*, 123, 129
Expressionism, 188

Faguet, Emile, 36
Fairy tale motif, 113
*Faust* (Goethe), 135
Felman, A. Bronson, 106
Feshback, Sidney, 147
Fielding, Henry, 12–36 passim, 186, 187; attitude of, toward *Don Quixote*, 35; attitude of, toward structure, 24; technique of, contrasted with Cervantes's, 35; understanding of realism, 187; use of narrator by, 33. *See also Joseph Andrews, The History and Adventures of*
*Finnegans Wake* (Joyce), 135, 137, 138, 148, 150, 153, 155; John MacDougal as Don Quixote, 135; Shem and Shaun as Don Quixote and Sancho Panza, 135
Flaubert, Gustave, 4, 5, 61, 62, 63, 64, 65, 66, 68, 69, 70, 71, 72, 74, 75, 122, 136, 169, 170, 185; attitude of, toward *Don Quixote*, 61; attitude of, toward imagery, 63. *See also Madame Bovary*
Florance, Edna C., 106
Formalist criticism, 3
Forster, Leonard, 56
Fraiberg, Selma, 106
Freud, Sigmund, 133, 147, 151, 155

Gerhardt, Mia, 25, 27, 32
*Gil Blas* (Le Sage), 34
Goethe, Johann Wolfgang von, 39–57 passim, 131, 189; attitude of, toward *Don Quixote*, 41; on morphology in nature, 57–58;

Quixotic features in *Der Triumph der Empfindsankeit*, 41; understanding of form, 57; use of letters by, 50. *See also Sorrows of Young Werther, The*
Goldberg, Homer, 34
Gorman, Herbert, 166
Gothot-Mersch, Claudine, 63, 64
Gottfried, Leon, 13, 33
"Grace" (Joyce), 144–45, 151
Gray, Ronald, 105
Grotesque humor, 93–94
Guiguet, Jean, 170, 173

Hafley, James, 170
*Hamlet*, 118, 135
Hanley, Miles L., 179
"Harmotton," 24, 31, 36 n. 4
Harold, Brent, 3, 4
Hayman, David, 136
Heller, Erich, 123, 127
Herder, Johann Gottfried von, 39, 57
Hoffman, E. T. A., 121
Hoffman, Frederick J., 124
Homer, 31, 55

*Idiot, The* (Dostoevsky), 85
*Iliad, The*, 10, 54
*Imitatio Christi* (à Kempis), 137
Impressionism, 188
Internal monologue, 170–71
Irony, 51–52
Ittner, Robert, 56
"Ivy Day in the Committee Room" (Joyce), 144–45, 150

Jackson, Robert Louis, 82
*Jacob's Room*, 169–70, 171, 172–76, 178; analysis of, 172–76; epiphany in, 173; hours and clocks as structuring device in, 172, 175, 176; imagery in, 173–76; *ricorso* in, 175–76
James, Henry, 81
Janouch, Gustav, 105
Johnson, Maurice, 12, 25
*Joseph Andrews, The History and Adventures of*, 4, 9, 11, 12, 13–36, 37, 40, 45, 49, 137, 186, 187;

*Joseph Andrews (continued)*
analysis of, 13–36; chapter openings in, 15–17; chastity as theme in, 12, 15, 17; city/country motif in, 12, 17; Fanny and Dulcinea, 40; "Harmotton" in, 24, 31; human folly as theme in, 22; influence of *Don Quixote* on, 36 n. 4; influence of French classical drama on, 36 n. 4; Joseph Andrews and Sancho Panza, 14, 15, 28, 31; lack of paragraphing as technique in, 22–23; letters in, 49; life/books dichotomy in, 24, 25, 26; mentions of *Don Quixote* in, 35; narrator in, 32–34; parallels to *Don Quixote* in, 34–35; Parson Adams and Don Quixote, 14, 27, 28–29, 31, 34; as picaresque novel, 13–14; plot interruptions in, 14, 22–25, 37 n. 45; reader in, 27; reality/illusion in, 28; sally-withdrawal pattern in, 13, 14–15, 186; social ladder as topic in, 24; spirit/body dichotomy in, 24; structure in, 11, 12; use of quotation in, 33
Joyce, James, 31, 57, 62, 135–65 passim; attitude of, toward Cervantes, 135; cyclical recurrence in, 148, 150; indebtedness of, to Flaubert, 136; influence of, on Woolf, 170–73, 174, 176–77; *Madame Bovary*'s influence on, 136, 137; on the Odyssey motif, 135; quest motif in, 140, 141, 143, 145, 149; related to Freud, 147, 151, 155, 165; Vico's influence on, 136, 138, 139, 145–47, 148–49, 152–60 passim. *See also Dubliners; Portrait of the Artist as a Young Man; Ulysses*

Kafka, Franz, 104, 105, 106, 109, 112, 115, 119n, 188; attitude toward Dostoevsky, 105; attitude toward Mann, 106; influences on, 105. *See also Trial, The*
Kahler, Eric, 5, 186, 187
Karl, Frederick, 37 n. 4

Kenner, Hugh, 136, 148, 153
Kestner, Joseph A., 55
Klein, A. M., 178

Lange, Victor, 40
*Laws* (Plato), 26
Leitmotif, 37, 127–28
Leskov, Nikolai S., 84
Lessing, Gotthold Ephraim, 55, 57
Literary influence, 171
"Little Cloud, A" (Joyce), 146
*Little Review*, 172
Litz, A. Walton, 147
Lord, Robert, 83
Love, Jean O., 183
Lukács, Georg, 39, 55

Macallister, Hamilton, 36 n. 4
Mack, Maynard, 12
*Madame Bovary, Patterns of Provincial Life*, 4, 61, 62–79, 136, 137, 185, 187; analysis of, 62–79; animal imagery in, 62, 64–68 passim, 69–74, 75–79 passim; Charles and Sancho Panza, 65; counterpart in, 62, 63, 64, 72; Emma and Don Quixote, 61, 65, 189; ideal/real dichotomy in, 64–65; liquid imagery in, 64–71 passim, 73–79; mineral imagery in, 62–63; nature imagery in, 63, 65, 66, 67, 70, 72, 74, 75, 76, 77, 78; as parodic fiction, 136; Phaedra-Hippolytus myth in, 74–75; related to *Ulysses*, 136; spatial form in, 136; symbolism in, 187; triadic structure in, 62, 63–64, 65; vegetable imagery in, 62, 64, 65–69, 70, 71, 73, 76, 77, 78, 79
*Magic Mountain, The*, 4, 122–33, 158, 159, 162, 165, 187, 188, 190; analysis of, 122–33; compared to *Ulysses*, 158–59, 162, 165; Eros and Thanatos in, 133; Hans Castorp and Don Quixote, 9; myth in, 126; objective correlative in, 122, 124, 125–26, 130–31; as philosopical novel, 122; philosophy of love in, 130, 133; setting in, 190; the spiral in, 123–24,

129, 131, 132; symbolism in, 187–88; use of music in, 131–33

Mann, Thomas, 23, 27, 106, 121, 122, 126, 136, 158, 163, 164, 165, 169, 185, 187, 190; attitude of, toward Cervantes, 121–22; Joseph books, 122, 126; Kafka's attitude toward, 106; philosophy of process, 122; understanding of myth, 126; "Voyage with Don Quixote," 121

Mayer, Hans, 125

Maynial, Edouard, 63

*Meditations on Quixote* (Ortega y Gasset), 61

Metafiction, 4, 33, 165

*Metamorphosis, The* (Kafka), 105

Metrical romance, 29

Meyer, Herman, 23, 33

Mock epic devices, 35

"Modern Fiction" (Woolf), 170

"Mother, A" (Joyce), 144, 145, 146

"Mr. Bennett and Mrs. Brown" (Woolf), 171

*Mrs. Dalloway*, 171, 173, 176–83; analysis of, 176–83; epiphany in, 183; Joycean imagery in, 178–82; Joycean structure in, 176–77; the party in, 182–83; red morocco notebook entries about, 171, 177, 182

Myth, 74–75, 124–25, 126

Narrator: in *Don Quixote*, 27, 32, 33, 34; in *Joseph Andrews*, 20, 32–34

Neoclassical form, 30

Nietzsche, Friedrich, 3, 123

*1984* (Orwell), 120 n. 16

Objective correlative, 82, 83, 92, 99, 122, 124, 125–26, 130–31, 190

*Odyssey, The*, 31, 54–55, 56

Oedipal situation, 106, 118, 119, 143; in modern novel, 118–19

*Oedipus Rex* (Sophocles), 106, 118

Ortega y Gasset, José, 3, 10, 61, 62, 188

*Ossian* (Macpherson), 42, 45, 48, 55

"Painful Case, A" (Joyce), 143

*Pamela* (Richardson), 49

Parker, Alexander A., 15

Pearce, Richard, 157

Petrarch, 171

Picaresque novel, 13–14, 36 n. 4

Play-within-a-play, the, 21

Plot interruptions: in *Don Quixote*, 5–7, 18–19, 21, 23, 24, 45; in *Joseph Andrews*, 18–22, 23–24, 37 n. 4; in *Sorrows of Young Werther*, 45

Polar opposition: between idea and reality (in romantic period, 40; in *Sorrows of Young Werther*, 54); between ideal and real (in *Don Quixote*, 31, 42; in *Madame Bovary*, 64–65; in medieval times, 31; in the Renaissance, 36, 40); between life and books (in *Don Quixote*, 25, 28, 35; in *Joseph Andrews*, 25–26, 35); between life and death in *Brothers Karamazov*, 82–100 passim; between madman and realist (in *Don Quixote*, 30; in the Renaissance, 36); between poet and player (in *Don Quixote*, 26–27, 31; in *Joseph Andrews*, 20, 26, 31); between reality and illusion (in *Don Quixote*, 8; in *Madame Bovary*, 61–62; in the Renaissance and 18th century, 28); between reason and feeling (in 18th century, 40; in *Sorrows of Young Werther*, 54); between soul and body (in classical epic, 31; in *Don Quixote*, 25, 35; in *Joseph Andrews*, 25, 35; in medieval theology, 31); between spirit and nature (in classical literature 31; in *Don Quixote*, 28; in *Joseph Andrews*, 28)

*Portrait of the Artist as a Young Man, A*, 138, 147–58, 159; analysis of, 147–58; *ricorso* in, 156–58; Stephen Dedalus and Don Quixote, 151; structuring devices in, 147; Viconian structure in, 148–55

206

Proust, Marcel, 136, 171, 188, 191; Woolf's interior monologue as related to, 171 Psychological novel, 188, 191; interpenetration of setting and character in, 191

Quest motif: in *Dubliners*, 140, 141, 143, 145; in *Portrait of the Artist as a Young Man*, 149

Rabelais, François, 33
Raskin, Marina Bergelson, 83, 84
Realism, 188
Redford, Grant, 147
Reik, Theodore, 171
Reiss, Hans, 39, 49, 54
*Remembrance of Things Past* (Proust), 189
Richardson, Samuel, 49
*Ricorso*: in *Dubliners*, 138, 145, 146, 152, 155; in *Finnegans Wake*, 153; in *Portrait of the Artist as a Young Man*, 152, 153, 156–58; related to Joycean epiphany, in *Ulysses*, 160, 161, 162, 163, 164
*Roman comique, Le* (Scarron), 34
Romantic form, 40
Rublev, Andrei, 84
Ryf, Robert, 148

Sally-withdrawal pattern: in *Don Quixote*, 6, 7–8, 9, 10, 14–15, 17; in *Joseph Andrews*, 13, 14–15; 186
Scholes, Robert, 136
*Scienza Nuova* (Vico), 57, 136, 137
Shaw, J. T., 166
Simmons, Ernest J., 87
*Simple Heart, A* (Flaubert), 187
"Sisters, The" (Joyce), 139–40, 141
Slochower, Harry, 133 n. 10, 167 n. 45
Smith, Marcus, 120 n. 16
*Sorrows of Young Werther, The*, 39, 40, 41, 42–58, 189; analysis of, 42–58; composition of, 39; digressions in, 45; the Editor as author in, 50–51, 52, 53; *"die Einschränkung"* in, 39, 42, 47, 53, 57; environment in, 189; epistolary form in, 42, 44, 49–51, 53,

54; idea/reality dichotomy in, 42; irony in, 51–52; language as form in, 40; Lotte and Dulcinea, 40–51, 52; parallel situations in, 44–45; Quixotic features in, 41–42; 1787 revision of, 45; society vs. individual in, 39–40, 42, 49, 53; structure as related to hero's sensibilities in, 43–44; *Sturm und Drang* in, 40; symbolism as structuring device in, 45–49; thought/feeling dichotomy in, 54; use of *Emilia Galotti* as contrast in, 55–57; use of *Odyssey* as contrast in, 54–55; Werther as author in, 50; Werther and Don Quixote, 42–43; "Wertherism" in, 57
Source study, 136–37
Spilka, Mark, 105
Spiral process: in *Magic Mountain*, 123–24, 129, 132, 158–59; in *Ulysses*, 158–64; in Vico and Joyce, 159
Spitzer, Leo, 121
*Steigerung*, 127, 131, 132
Sterne, Richard, 23, 33
Strachey, Lytton, 170, 172
Structure: as articulating theme in *Joseph Andrews*, 12; as circular in *Magic Mountain*, 123–32; as contrapuntal in *Brothers Karamazov* and *Crime and Punishment*, 103; as effected by hours and clocks in Woolf, 172, 175, 176, 177–83; as epic in *Joseph Andrews*, 15; as exterior to protagonist's consciousness (outward), 4, 186, 187, 188, 189, 190, 191; as interpenetrative with theme, 4, 188, 189; as musical in *Brothers Karamazov*, 81; as related to physical environment, 189; as related to protagonist's inner world (inward), 4, 5, 9, 185–86, 188, 189, 190, 191; as tripartite (in *Brothers Karamazov*, 83, 85, 86, 89–90, 94, 95, 99; in *Don Quixote*, 5–8; in *Madame Bovary*, 62, 63–64, 65; in *Sorrows of Young Werther*, 43–44)

*Sturm und Drang*, 40
Symbolism: in *Brothers Karamazov*,
  91–92; in *Crime and Punishment*,
  190; in *Don Quixote*, 5, 9, 186; as
  exterior to character, 187–88,
  190; as interior to character, 189,
  190; in *Madame Bovary*, 62, 63, 64,
  65–79, 187, 189; in *Magic Mountain*, 122, 124, 187–88, 190; in
  *Portrait of the Artist as a Young
  Man*, 150–51, 152; in *Sorrows of
  Young Werther*, 187, 189

*Theatrum mundi*, 26
Thomas, R. Hinton, 129
Time: as circular in *Magic Mountain*, 123; as of the mind in *Joseph
  Andrews*, 16, 18
Tindall, William York, 148
*Tom Jones* (Fielding), 15, 16, 24
"Tonio Kröger" (Mann), 106
*Trial, The*, 104, 105, 106–19, 136;
  absurdity in, 118; analysis of,
  106–19; confrontation with authority in, 106, 107, 108, 109,
  113, 114, 115, 118; the double in,
  114–15; homosexuality in, 111,
  115, motif of mother/son in, 106,
  107, 108, 109, 111, 116, 118;
  Oedipal situation in, 106; ordering of chapters in, 112–13, 116;
  parallels to *Crime and Punishment*, 104, 105, 106, 107–19; projection in, 107, 111, 114; revolt
  against bureaucracy in, 119; state
  as father figure in, 118
*Tristram Shandy* (Sterne), 137
*Triumph der Empfindsamkeit, Der*
  (Goethe), 41
Trunz, Erich, 39
Turkevich, Ludmilla B., 81

*Ulysses*, 31, 62, 135, 148, 150, 153,
  154, 155, 157, 158–65, 169, 170,
  171 172, 174, 175, 176, 177–83,
  190–91; analysis of, 158–65; circle
  in, 179; compared to *Magic
  Mountain*, 158–59; George Moore
  and Edward Martyn as Don

Quixote and Sancho Panza, 135;
  *Mrs. Dalloway* related to, 177–83;
  Nostos in, 162–63, 180, 183; setting in, 190–91; spiral development in, 158–65; Vico's influence
  on, 158–64
Uyttersprot, Hermann, 112, 116

Van Laan, Thomas, 147
Vico, Giambattista, 50, 136, 137,
  138, 139, 144, 145, 147, 148, 149,
  152, 153, 154, 155, 156, 157, 158,
  159, 160, 163, 178
Viconian cycles: in *Dubliners*, 138–
  47; in *Portrait of the Artist as a
  Young Man*, 148–55; in *Ulysses*,
  159–64, 167 n. 42
*Vie de Marianne, La* (Marivaux), 34
"Voyage with Don Quixote"
  (Mann), 121, 126

*War and Peace* (Tolstoy), 176
Warren, Austin, 3
Wassiolek, Edward, 82, 85, 95
Weaver, Harriet, 159, 172
Wellek, René, 3
*Weltanschauung*, 186
Wilkinson, Elizabeth M., 54, 55
Willis, Raymond, 31
Willoughby, L. A., 54, 55
Woodring, Carl, 179
Woolf, Virginia, 5, 137, 169, 170–78
  passim, 182, 183; attitude of, to-
  ward Cervantes, 169; attitude of,
  toward Joyce, 170; attitude of,
  toward *Ulysses*, 172–73, 176;
  *Diaries* quoted from, 169, 172,
  173, 176, 177; epiphany as used
  by, 173, 183; imagery as used by,
  173–76; Joycean structure as
  used by, 176–80; Joyce's influence on, 170–73, 174, 176–83;
  Proustian interior monologue as
  used by, 170, red morocco notebook quoted from, 171, 177, 182.
  *See also Jacob's Room; Mrs. Dallo-
  way*
Wright, Andrew, 12